Culture and Customs of Vietnam

**Recent Titles in
Culture and Customs of Asia**

Culture and Customs of Taiwan
Gary Marvin Davison and Barbara E. Reed

Culture and Customs of Japan
Norika Kamachi

Culture and Customs of Korea
Donald N. Clark

Culture and Customs of Vietnam

Mark W. McLeod
and Nguyen Thi Dieu

Culture and Customs of Asia
Hanchao Lu, Series Editor

GREENWOOD PRESS
Westport, Connecticut • London

Library of Congress Cataloging-in-Publication Data

McLeod, Mark W.
    Culture and customs of Vietnam / Mark W. McLeod and Nguyen Thi Dieu.
      p.   cm.—(Culture and customs of Asia, ISSN 1097–0738)
    Includes bibliographical references and index.
    ISBN 0–313–30485–8 (alk. paper)
    1. Vietnam—Civilization. 2. Vietnam—Social life and customs. 3. Vietnam—History. I.
Nguyen, Thi Dieu. II. Title. III. Series.
DS556.42.M43   2001
959.7—dc21   00–052120

British Library Cataloguing in Publication Data is available.

Library of Congress Catalog Card Number: 00–052120
ISBN: 0–313–30485–8
ISSN: 1097–0738

First published in 2001

Greenwood Press, 88 Post Road West, Westport, CT 06881
An imprint of Greenwood Publishing Group, Inc.
www.greenwood.com

Printed in the United States of America

The paper used in this book complies with the
Permanent Paper Standard issued by the National
Information Standards Organization (Z39.48–1984).

10 9 8 7 6 5 4 3 2 1

Contents

Illustrations

Series Foreword

GEOGRAPHICALLY, Asia encompasses the vast area from Suez, the Bosporus, and the Ural Mountains eastward to the Bering Sea and from this line southward to the Indonesian archipelago, an expanse that covers about 30 percent of our earth. Conventionally, and especially insofar as culture and customs are concerned, Asia refers primarily to the region east of Iran and south of Russia. This area can be divided in turn into subregions commonly known as South, Southeast, and East Asia, which are the main focus of this series.

The United States has vast interests in this region. In the twentieth century the United States fought three major wars in Asia (namely, the Pacific War of 1941–45, the Korean War of 1950–53, and the Vietnam War of 1965–75), and each had profound impact on life and politics in America. Today, America's major trading partners are in Asia, and in the foreseeable future the weight of Asia in American life will inevitably increase, for in Asia lie our great allies as well as our toughest competitors in virtually all arenas of global interest. Domestically, the role of Asian immigrants is more visible than at any other time in our history. In spite of these connections with Asia, however, our knowledge about this crucial region is far from adequate. For various reasons, Asia remains for most of us a relatively unfamiliar, if not stereotypical or even mysterious, "Oriental" land.

There are compelling reasons for Americans to obtain some level of concrete knowledge about Asia. It is one of the world's richest reservoirs of culture and an ever-evolving museum of human heritage. Rhoads Murphey, a prominent Asianist, once pointed out that in the part of Asia east of Afghanistan and south of Russia alone lies half the world, "half of its people and far more than half of its historical experience, for these are the oldest living civilized traditions." Prior to the modern era, with limited interaction and mutual influence between the East and the West, Asian civilizations developed largely independent from the West. In modern times, however, Asia and the West have come not only into close contact but also into frequent conflict: The result has been one of the most solemn and stirring dramas in world history. Today, integration and compromise are the trend in coping with cultural differences. The West—with some notable exceptions—has started to see Asian traditions not as something to fear but as something to be understood, appreciated, and even cherished. After all, Asian traditions are an indispensable part of the human legacy, a matter of global "common wealth" that few of us can afford to ignore.

As a result of Asia's enormous economic development since World War II, we can no longer neglect the study of this vibrant region. Japan's "economic miracle" of postwar development is no longer unique, but in various degrees has been matched by the booming economy of many other Asian countries and regions. The rise of the four "mini dragons" (South Korea, Taiwan, Hong Kong, and Singapore) suggests that there may be a common Asian pattern of development. At the same time, each economy in Asia has followed its own particular trajectory. Clearly, China is the next giant on the scene. Sweeping changes in China in the last two decades have already dramatically altered the world's economic map. Furthermore, growth has also been dramatic in much of Southeast Asia. Today war-devastated Vietnam shows great enthusiasm for joining the "club" of nations engaged in the world economy. And in South Asia, India, the world's largest democracy, is rediscovering its role as a champion of market capitalism. The economic development of Asia presents a challenge to Americans but also provides them with unprecedented opportunities. It is largely against this background that more and more people in the United States, in particular among the younger generation, have started to pursue careers dealing with Asia.

This series is designed to meet the need for knowledge of Asia among students and the general public. Each book is written in an accessible and lively style by an expert (or experts) in the field of Asian studies. Each book focuses on the culture and customs of a country or region. However, readers should be aware that culture is fluid, not always respecting national boundaries. While every nation seeks its own path to success and struggles to maintain its own identity, in the cultural domain mutual influence and integration among Asian nations are ubiquitous.

Each volume starts with an introduction to the land and people of a nation or region and includes a brief history and an overview of the economy. This is followed by chapters dealing with a variety of topics that piece together a cultural panorama, such as thought, religion, ethics, literature and art, architecture and housing, cuisine, traditional dress, gender, courtship and marriage, festivals and leisure activities, music and dance, and social customs and lifestyle. In this series, we have chosen not to elaborate on elite life, ideology, or detailed questions of political structure and struggle, but instead to explore the world of common people, their sorrow and joy, their pattern of thinking, and their way of life. It is the culture and customs of the majority of the people (rather than just the rich and powerful elite) that we seek to understand. Without such understanding, it will be difficult for all of us to live peacefully and fruitfully with each other in this increasingly interdependent world.

As the world shrinks, modern technologies have made all nations on earth "virtual" neighbors. The expression "global village" not only reveals the nature and the scope of the world in which we live but also, more importantly, highlights the serious need for mutual understanding of all peoples on our planet. If this series serves to help the reader obtain a better understanding of the "half of the world" that is Asia, the authors and I will be well rewarded.

Hanchao Lu
Georgia Institute of Technology

Introduction

CULTURE AND CUSTOMS OF VIETNAM is an exploration of Vietnamese culture as it developed from pre-colonial times until the present. Our motivation stems from the fact that the general reader, high school student, or undergraduate who wants an introduction to Vietnamese culture must choose between a plethora of works by nonspecialists that are often factually erroneous and works by Vietnam specialists that are narrowly focused, extremely detailed, and mainly concerned with theoretical issues of interest only to other scholars.

We have tried to write a survey of the basic features of Vietnamese culture that is factually accurate but clear in its presentation and limited to information that is likely to be useful for the general reader. We thus emphasize patterns common to the Vietnamese as a whole during the periods under consideration and do not always distinguish between regional variations or account for subtle changes over time. The view of Vietnamese culture that informs this work is that of the hybrid model. No distinction is made between "primordial" or "truly Vietnamese" cultural patterns and those that have been assimilated from Southeast Asians, Indians, Chinese, Mongols, Chams, French, or Americans. Just as a hybrid plant can no longer cast off its "foreign" elements, a Vietnamese culture stripped of its "foreign" borrowings would be unrecognizable as Vietnamese. Although it is worthwhile to explore the sources of particular beliefs or practices, one must remember that their foreign origins do not make them any less Vietnamese at present.

The work is based on original research using French and Vietnamese primary sources, the scholarly and popular literature in English, French, and

Vietnamese, and on our experiences of living and working in Vietnam during the past three decades. Readers wishing to pursue the topic further may consult the selected bibliography, which cites accessible English language works (or translations into English) by the leading scholars of Vietnamese history, culture, and society. We have also included some general introductions to Vietnamese culture. It is customary in works of synthesis to spare the reader the often tedious footnoting found in specialized studies, but our intellectual debts to those scholars whose works are listed in the bibliography, and to many whose works are not, will be obvious to them.

All illustrations, excepting the map, are our photographs taken during 1987–2000. We are grateful to Angela Hoseth and Tara Webber of the University of Delaware's History Department Media Center for creating the original map featured in the front of this work.

Nguyen Thi Dieu would like to thank Temple University for its generous financial support over the years, which facilitated the researching and writing of this work.

We would also like to express our gratitude to our series editor, Hanchao Lu, and our Greenwood editors, particularly Wendi Schnaufer, for their patience, support, and advice.

Chronology

?–C. 10,000 B.C.E.	Paleolithic Era
C. 9000–7000 B.C.E.	Hoa Binh Culture
C. 7000–3000 B.C.E.	Bac Son Culture
C. 2500–1500 B.C.E.	Phung Nguyen Culture
C. 2879–258 B.C.E.	Hung Dynasty
C. 900–200 B.C.E.	Dong Son Culture
257–208 B.C.E.	Thuc Dynasty
207–111 B.C.E.	Nam Viet Kingdom
111 B.C.E.	Nam Viet is conquered by Chinese Han Dynasty.
40–43 C.E.	Revolt of the Trung sisters.
43	Beginning of direct Chinese rule.
544–602	Early Ly Dynasty
938	Ngo Quyen defeats Chinese forces at Bach-dang.
939–965	Ngo Dynasty
968–980	Dinh Dynasty
980–1009	Early Le Dynasty
1009–1225	Later Ly Dynasty

1225–1400	Tran Dynasty
1400–1407	Ho Dynasty
1407–1427	Ming Chinese occupation
1428–1788	Later Le Dynasty
1611	Annexation of Champa
1627–1672	Conflict between Trinh and Nguyen lords
1627	Alexandre de Rhodes arrives in Ha-noi.
1672	Seizure of Sai-gon (then Gia-dinh) by Nguyen forces.
1771	Beginning of Tay-son Rebellion
1788	Nguyen Hue declares himself Emperor Quang Trung.
1788–1802	Tay-son Dynasty
1802	Nguyen Anh defeats Tay-son forces, founds Nguyen Dynasty.
1802–1945	Nguyen Dynasty
1858	French forces land at Da-nang.
1859–1861	French defeat Nguyen forces in southern Vietnam.
1862	Treaty of Sai-gon establishes colonial regime in South.
1863	French protectorate over Cambodia initiated.
1874	Treaty of Ha-noi confirms expanded French rule in southern Vietnam and opens Red River to French trade.
1883–1884	Treaty of Protectorate and Treaty of Hue establish French protectorate over central and northern Vietnam.
1885–1896	*Can Vuong* anti-French resistance movement
1887	Establishment of Indochinese Union.
1893	French protectorate over Laos is established.

1897–1902	Administration of Governor-General Paul Doumer.
1904	Phan Boi Chau founds Modernization Society.
1911	Ho Chi Minh leaves Vietnam for Europe.
1912	Phan Boi Chau founds Vietnam Restoration Society.
1925	Formation of Vietnamese Revolutionary Youth League
1927	Nguyen Thai Hoc founds Vietnam Nationalist Party.
1930	Founding of Indochinese Communist Party (ICP)
1939	World War II begins in Europe.
1940	Franco-Japanese Treaty is signed, setting modalities of French collaboration in Indochina.
1941	ICP founds Viet Minh Front.
1944–1945	Famine in northern and central Vietnam causes circa two million deaths.
1945	Japan surrenders; Viet Minh seizes power in August Revolution, founds Democratic Republic of Vietnam (D.R.V.).
1946–1954	First Indochina War
1949	Founding of People's Republic of China; France creates Associated State of Vietnam with Bao Dai as head of state.
1951	Vietnam Workers' Party (*Dang Lao Dong*) is founded, superseding ICP.
1954	French defeat at Dien Bien Phu; Geneva Accords create provisional military regroupment zones to North and South of Seventeenth Parallel; Bao Dai appoints Ngo Dinh Diem as prime minister.
1955	United States begins direct aid to Diem's regime; Republic of Vietnam (R.V.N.) is established in South with Diem as president.

1960	National Front for the Liberation of Southern Vietnam (NLF) is founded.
1963	Assassination of Ngo Dinh Diem
1964	Gulf of Tonkin incident and resolution authorizing presidential use of force by American forces in Vietnam.
1965	United States begins bombing D.R.V.; first U.S. ground combat troops land at Da-nang.
1968	Tet Offensive by People's Army of Vietnam (PAVN) and NLF.
1970	United States and R.V.N. forces invade Cambodia.
1972	PAVN Spring Offensive; Richard Nixon launches "Christmas Bombing."
1973	Paris Accords are signed; U.S. forces withdraw.
1975	PAVN/NLF general offensive; fall of R.V.N.
1976	Proclamation of the Socialist Republic of Vietnam (S.R.V.); Vietnam Workers' Party is renamed Vietnam Communist Party (*Dang Cong San Viet Nam*).
1977	S.R.V. is admitted to the United Nations.
1978	China terminates economic aid to Vietnam; Vietnam signs Treaty of Friendship and Cooperation with USSR; PAVN occupies Cambodia in response to Khmer Rouge attacks.
1979	China invades northern Vietnam.
1980	S.R.V. promulgates new Constitution stressing Marxism-Leninism and calling for rapid advance to socialism.
1982	Fifth National Party Congress moderates policy, calls for slower, more cautious advance.
1986	Sixth National Party Congress; Nguyen Van Linh becomes general secretary; launching of *Doi Moi*, or Renovation.

1991   Paris Agreement ends Vietnamese occupation of
                Cambodia; Nguyen Van Linh retires.

1992   Revised Constitution promulgated; stress on
                Marxism-Leninism attenuated; leading role of
                Communist Party affirmed.

1994   American-led embargo on Vietnam is terminated.

1995   Diplomatic relations between United States and
                S.R.V. are established; Vietnam joins Association
                of Southeast Asian Nations.

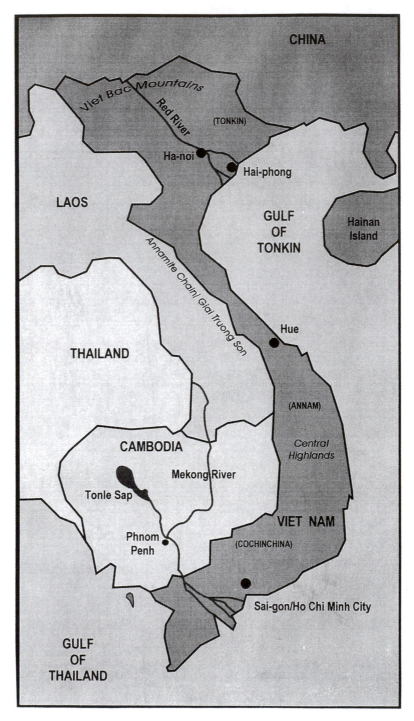

CHINA

Viet Bac Mountains

Red River

(TONKIN)

Ha-noi

Hai-phong

LAOS

GULF
OF
TONKIN

Hainan
Island

Annamite Chain/ Gioi Truong Son

THAILAND

Hue

(ANNAM)

Central
Highlands

CAMBODIA

Mekong River

Tonle Sap

VIET NAM

Phnom
Penh

(COCHINCHINA)

GULF
OF
THAILAND

Sai-gon/Ho Chi Minh City

Map of Vietnam

1

Land, People, and Language

GEOGRAPHY

VIETNAMESE DESCRIBE VIETNAM as resembling a shoulder pole with a rice basket at each end. The image is useful, for the heavily populated, grain-producing areas of modern Vietnam are in the extreme North (in the Red River Delta, also called the Tonkin Delta) and South (the Mekong Delta), with a thin, less productive, and less densely inhabited coastal region linking them. Modern Vietnam is bordered by China to the North, by Laos and Cambodia to the West, and by the South China Sea (Vietnamese call it *Bien Dong*, or "Eastern Sea") to the South and East. The distance from the Sino-Vietnamese border to Vietnam's southernmost point—the Ca-mau peninsula—is about 1,000 miles. It is about 300 miles from the northern Vietnamese port of Hai-phong to the Sino-Laotian-Vietnamese border.

The triangle-shaped Red River Delta is enclosed to the North and West by hills and mountains jutting southward from the Yunnan Plateau and called the *Viet Bac*, some of which are more than 9,000 feet in elevation. The northern highlands are rich in minerals, including iron ore, coal, and lead. The Red River (*Song Hong*), originating in China's Yunnan Province, is about 750 miles long. The Red River and its major tributaries, the Clear (*Song Lo*) and Black Rivers (*Song Da*), are vital for irrigation, transportation, and hydroelectric power but are subject to violent and unpredictable flooding. Flood control has always been crucial to the Delta's habitation and exploitation, and a vast system of dikes and canals contains the Red River and irrigates the Delta's flatlands. Despite their dangers, the rivers deposit rich silt on the

Women transplanting rice seedlings, near Hue City, central Vietnam

lowlands, and the Tonkin Delta has been intensively cultivated since the origins of Viet settlement. This remains true today, with irrigated or "wet" rice the principal crop.

South of the Tonkin Delta, a narrow gateway of flatlands allows access to central Vietnam, an extremely thin region, only about thirty miles from the South China Sea to Laos at its narrowest. To the West, along the Vietnamese-Laotian border, run mountains known in Vietnamese as the *Giai Truong Son*, or "Long Mountains," still usually known in English as the Annamite Chain. The central Vietnamese lowlands are narrow coastal strips, sometimes wide enough to support only a single village and its fields between the sea and the mountains. Given their proximity to the South China Sea and its teeming marine life, most of these coastal villages combine farming with fishing, and some are devoted almost exclusively to marine pursuits, with pisciculture increasingly important as catches of fish and crustaceans decline due to pollution and over-fishing. Central Vietnam is intersected by the Seventeenth Parallel, which was a contested political boundary from 1954 to 1975.

About 100 miles below the Seventeenth Parallel, Vietnam widens again, becoming almost 100 miles from West to East on the average. Heavily forested mountains and high plateaus, called the *Tay Nguyen*, or Central Highlands, dominate most of the southern part of central Vietnam. The sparsely populated Highlands, parts of which are more than 6,000 feet above sea level, yield valuable harvests of rubber and coffee as well as wood and other forest products. In recent years, Vietnam has become a major coffee-exporting country, largely thanks to crops produced in the Central Highlands and its foothills.

About fifty miles north of *Thanh Pho Ho Chi Minh*, or Ho Chi Minh City (the former Sai-gon), the Central Highlands yield to southern Vietnam's alluvial plains. The South's major river is the Mekong, known in Sino-Vietnamese as *Song Cuu Long*, or "Nine Dragons' River," given its many branches that open on the South China Sea. One of the world's great rivers, the Mekong is more than 2,700 miles long from its recently discovered source in Tibet to its mouths on the South China Sea. The Mekong River's annual floods, usually calmer and more predictable than the Red River's due to the flatter local terrain and the stabilizing influence of Cambodia's Tonle Sap Lake, deposit rich silt throughout the Mekong Delta, making it one of the world's most fertile regions. The Mekong Delta is modern Vietnam's second great agricultural and population center, although the Viet did not begin significant settlement there until the 1600s. In addition to rice, still the main crop, sugarcane, bananas, and coconuts are produced abundantly.

GEOGRAPHICAL TERMINOLOGY

Geographical terminology is a problem for students of Vietnamese culture. Given the country's tumultuous history, there have been many changes in regime and in place names; to complicate matters, the former names are sometimes still used along with the newer ones, and speakers indicate political preference by choosing one over another.

Vietnamese from the nineteenth century until today have generally known their country as *Viet Nam*—two words, each with a distinct meaning. *Viet* refers to the ethnolinguistic group composed of people of mainly Mongoloid and Indonesian racial stock who speak Vietnamese as their native tongue. *Nam* means "South" and is understood in relation to China, the northern neighbor. *Viet Nam* thus means "southern land of the Viet people." *Nam*, alone or in combination, is also often used independently of *Viet* to refer to things Vietnamese in juxtaposition to those pertaining to China. Thus, *Nuoc Nam* (literally "southern land") is another name for Vietnam, the inhabitants of which are also called *Nguoi Nam* ("southerners"). *Thuoc Nam* ("southern medicine") refers to Vietnamese traditional medicine as opposed to *thuoc Bac* ("northern medicine"), or Chinese traditional medicine, both of which are widely used among Vietnamese today instead of or in complement to modern, or Western, medicine.

However, Vietnamese lands have not always been called Viet Nam. For example, *An-nam* was used by officials of the Chinese Tang Dynasty, which colonized Vietnam from the seventh century until the tenth. For the Chinese, it meant "pacified South," a conquered land that accepted and presumably benefited from Chinese civilization. This was abandoned when independence from Chinese rule came in 938 C.E. Independent states in the Vietnamese-speaking lands were henceforth alternately called *Dai Viet* or *Dai Co Viet* ("Greater Vietnam"), *Dai Nam* ("Great South"), *Viet Nam*, or *Nam Viet*. In the nineteenth century, French colonizers resurrected *An-nam*, using it until 1945 and beyond, calling its possession *Annam* and the people *Annamites* or *Annamese*. So used, *Annam* and *Annamites* were considered insulting by many Viet because they invoked a formerly dependent status vis-à-vis China. Vietnamese today never refer seriously to their country as *Annam* or to themselves as *Annamese*; some use them jokingly, satirizing French pretensions. French people nostalgic for the "good old days" of colonial rule still use the terms *Annam* and *Annamites*, but this is increasingly rare.

The names for Vietnam's regions also changed during colonial times. The French attached their Vietnamese holdings to a larger empire in mainland Southeast Asia called *l'Indochine française*, French Indochina—the lands between India and China that were under French control. French Indochina comprised the territories of the modern nation-states of Laos, Cambodia, and Vietnam. For political and administrative reasons, the French also divided Vietnam into three units called *pays* ("lands"): Tonkin, Annam, and Cochinchine (Cochin China in English). *Tonkin* referred to the northern part of the country and comes from the Sino-Vietnamese *Dong Kinh*, meaning "eastern capital." The Sino-Vietnamese *Annam* referred to central Vietnam and means "pacified South." This creates potential confusion, because the French used *Annam* to indicate all of Vietnam as well as its central region alone. If a modern writer uses it, it probably means just the central area; if a colonial-era writer uses it, it may mean either. *Cochinchine* referred to the South and comes from *Giao Chi*, an ancient Sino-Vietnamese administrative term for part of today's northern Vietnam. When Europeans began trading in Asian waters in the fifteenth and sixteenth centuries, they pronounced it "Cochin," adding "China" to distinguish it from what was for them the better-known

Cochin, in India. The French pronounced it "Cochinchine" and applied it to the Vietnamese lands as a whole and to the southern region alone. Today it would probably mean the latter, although it is no longer commonly used. To describe these entities created and named by the French, the Vietnamese began using *Bac-ky, Trung-ky,* and *Nam-ky,* the northern, central, and southern "zones" (*ky*), respectively.

A final complication derives from the Second Indochina War (i.e., the Vietnam War), 1960–1975. The northern territories above the Seventeenth Parallel, controlled by the Communist-led Democratic Republic of Vietnam (D.R.V.), were designated by the Western media as North Vietnam, even though no state by this name had ever existed. The southern lands under the control of the U.S.-supported Republic of Vietnam (R.V.N.), were termed South Vietnam, although there had never been a state bearing this name. Today, well-informed English speakers refer to modern Vietnam's three regions as northern, central, and southern Vietnam (or as the North, Center, and South). This corresponds to contemporary Vietnamese usage, which is to call the three regions *Bac Bo* ("northern part"), *Trung Bo* ("central part"), and *Nam Bo* ("southern part") in recognition of Vietnam's overall unity.

CLIMATE

Vietnam lies between roughly eight and twenty-three degrees north latitude, which places it within the tropical monsoon belt. Due to differences in latitude and uneven topography, Vietnam's climatic conditions are far from uniform. The differences in average annual high temperatures may be illustrated by looking at the major cities of each of the three regions. In northern Vietnam, Ha-noi has an average annual temperature of seventy-four degrees Fahrenheit. In central Vietnam, Hue's mean annual temperature is seventy-seven degrees. In southern Vietnam, Ho Chi Minh City has an annual average of eighty-one degrees. It is cooler in mountainous areas: Da-lat, for example, located in the southern Central Highlands, has an average annual temperature of seventy degrees. During colonial times, it was a favorite vacation spot for French officials and Vietnamese royalty seeking relief from the steaming lowlands.

Vietnam's weather is controlled by seasonal monsoons called *gio mua.* The relatively cold and dry winter monsoon comes out of the northeast between October and March, affecting mainly central and northern Vietnam. From April to October, the warm and wet summer monsoon blows out of the southwest, depositing moisture from the Indian Ocean and Gulf of Thailand on southern and southern-central Vietnam. Vietnam's average annual rainfall

Boats docked on the banks of the Perfume River, Hue City, central Vietnam

is generally high (about fifty-nine inches) but varies from place to place. Hue is probably the "wettest" major lowlands city, receiving more than 110 inches of precipitation per year. Overall, about 90 percent of Vietnam's total rainfall occurs during the southwesterly summer monsoon season. Rainfall in the North and Center is erratic, and destructive typhoons often strike there between July and November; 1999 was one of the worst years of flooding in modern times.

ETHNOLINGUISTIC GROUPS

Although the precise physical origins of the modern Vietnamese people remain in dispute, most scholars agree that they derive from a combination of aboriginal Australoid peoples with Indonesian and Mongoloid peoples from outside the region. Since historical times, the Viet have been a sedentary, rice-growing, village-dwelling people. They have clustered in the deltas at the northern and, beginning in the seventeenth century, southern extremities of the country—the Red and Mekong Deltas—as well as, to a lesser extent, in the coastal deltas of central Vietnam. Today there are more than 80,000,000 Vietnamese citizens, most of whom are ethnic Viet and live packed together on about 20 percent of Vietnam's territory, an area that roughly corresponds to the percentage of the national territory that is on level ground. Indeed, the Vietnamese deltas are among the most heavily populated and intensively cultivated areas in Asia. The rest of Vietnam—the remaining 80 percent, which has a more uneven topography—is for the most part left to non-Viet peoples. These areas are mountainous and covered by jungle and brush; they are less suitable for the irrigated rice cultivation and residence in compact villages that have been the historical prerequisites of Vietnamese civilization.

The mountains are also more dangerous to the Viet, because the anopheles mosquito, carrier of the plasmodium parasites that cause malaria, breeds more readily in the mountains than in the deltas and low-lying plains, although it is found in both areas. The non-Viet peoples seem to be more resistant to malaria than are the Viet. Before modern times, the Viet, observing that people sickened and died shortly after going to the mountains, concluded that the water was poisonous (*nuoc doc*) and the regions inhabited by vengeful ghosts (*ma qui*). Taking advantage of the situation, the Viet emperors exiled rebels and criminals to such regions, knowing that they would fall ill and die. Hence, the Viet have long been content to leave the mountains and high plains to the non-Viet peoples. In the post–World War II era, however, independent Viet states—including the D.R.V., the R.V.N., and today's Socialist Republic of Vietnam (S.R.V.)—have encouraged Viet migration into these regions to relieve overcrowding in the deltas and to facilitate the economic development and political control of the highlands; this phenomenon has been especially noticeable since reunification in 1975.

Vietnam's mountains and high plains are thus inhabited by a variety of non-Viet ethnic groups, many of them similar to the peoples who live in Laos and Thailand. There are at least sixty different peoples in this category; collectively they total more than 4,000,000 people. They mostly live in the mountainous provinces surrounding the Red River Delta and in the Central Highlands. The French called them *montagnards*, or "mountaineers." In English they have been called the "hill peoples," "tribal minorities," or, more recently, "highlanders." Under the S.R.V., they are designated *nguoi thuong*, or "highlands peoples," as opposed to the *nguoi Kinh*, or "ethnic Vietnamese" (literally, "people of the capital"). Official euphemisms aside, *Kinh* still privately often refer to *Thuong* by pejorative terms such as *moi*, "savage," reflecting the long-standing tensions between the two groups. These tensions were militarily significant during the post–World War II conflicts in Vietnam, for many strategic regions were inhabited mainly by highlanders. Any policy applied by Western forces or Vietnamese antagonists had to take the highlanders into account, something that the revolutionary forces usually did more skillfully than their opponents.

Several non-Vietnamese ethnolinguistic groups also inhabit the lowlands of today's Vietnam. In southern Vietnam, there remains a group (approximately 300,000 at the end of the Vietnam War) of Khmers Krom. The Khmers are the lowland people that constitute the majority population of the present nation-state of Cambodia. *Krom* means "South" in Khmer, and the Khmers Krom are the remnants of the time when the Khmer Empire controlled the Mekong Delta. Since the Vietnamese and Khmers developed different cultures and rival polities and coveted the same territories, their interactions have often been violent. When the Viet seized the Mekong Delta from the declining Khmer Empire in the eighteenth century, some Khmers remained in what has since been Viet territory. The Khmers Krom are mostly Theravada Buddhists, in contrast to the Viet preference for Mahayana schools, and live in communities that are distinct from Viet settlements. Modern Khmers and Vietnamese still bear the weight of these historical hatreds, which continue to influence their views of each other.

The Chams are another non-Viet lowland people, the human vestiges of an ancient empire called Champa that was conquered and absorbed by the Viet in the fifteenth century. The ruins of their beautiful Hindu-influenced temples still dot the central coastline and are currently being restored by the Vietnamese government in light of their historical interest and attractiveness to international tourists. Today about 50,000 Chams live in the central Vietnamese plains.

There is also a large Chinese population in Vietnam, totaling almost 1,000,000. Many are descendants of Chinese who came to Vietnam shortly after China's Ming Dynasty was replaced by the Qing in 1644. They are called *Minh Huong*, those who burn incense (*huong*) in honor of the defunct Ming (*Minh* in Vietnamese) Dynasty. Other Chinese, whose ancestors arrived during the eighteenth, nineteenth, and twentieth centuries, are called *nguoi hoa*, or "ethnic Chinese." Many Chinese from both groups have intermarried with Viet and are presently almost indistinguishable from them. Others have retained their Chinese identities by living in distinct communities, teaching their children the Chinese language and culture, and maintaining clan organizations.

Vietnam's Chinese community has historically been successful in the landowning and commercial sectors of the economy, particularly milling and export of rice as well as moneylending. The Chinese quarter of Ho Chi Minh City is still called *Cho-lon*, "big market" in Vietnamese, in reference to the commercial aptitudes of its Chinese residents. Some Chinese became wealthy, especially in colonial times. This was in part due to the prejudices of the French, who did not trust the Viet and gave the Chinese opportunities denied to "natives." Some Viet still resent Chinese successes, a situation typical of relations between majority peoples and Chinese minorities throughout Southeast Asia. One of the pejorative Vietnamese terms for Vietnam's Chinese, for instance, is *khach*, or "guest," which implies the speaker's hope that they will soon leave.

THE VIETNAMESE LANGUAGE

Scholars do not agree on the best way to classify the Vietnamese language, which seems to share structures with and borrow words from many of the languages spoken in East and Southeast Asia. Vietnamese is tonal, suggesting an affinity with the Sino-Tibetan family, which includes the Chinese and Tai languages. It also has structural similarities to languages in the Mon-Khmer group (e.g., Khmer, or "Cambodian") of the Austro-Asiatic family, which are not tonal. Some linguists have argued that Vietnamese should be classified as a member of the Tai group and placed in the Sino-Tibetan family, whereas others consider it part of the Mon-Khmer group and place it in the Austro-Asiatic family. Still other scholars view Vietnamese as a unique language that virtually constitutes a family unto itself, albeit one that has borrowed extensively from other families.

Throughout their history, the Viet have used a variety of writing systems: *chu Han*, or "Chinese characters," also called *chu nho*, or "scholars' characters"; *chu nom*, "southern characters"; and *chu quoc ngu*, or "national language characters."

Like many other Asian peoples, the Viet began their experience with writing by borrowing the "ready-made" system of Chinese characters (*chu Han*) and used it for representing the spoken Chinese language. Long after direct Chinese political domination ended in 938 C.E., the Chinese language and characters continued to be used in the independent Viet dynastic states for official business as well as in education, literature, and correspondence, cementing its position as the prestige language. Elite Viet could carry on "writing-brush conversations" with classically educated Chinese, Koreans, and Japanese, even though they did not always speak the Chinese language in mutually comprehensible ways. Chinese may thus be considered the functional equivalent of Latin for Sinitic Asia, including Vietnam.

From at least the thirteenth century onward, Viet scholars developed a second system, an indigenous character-based vernacular (*chu nom*) that adopted and adapted some of the symbols of Chinese characters to express Vietnamese-language sounds. Nguyen Thuyen, who lived during the reign of Tran Nhan-tong (1279–1293), is often credited with inventing or at least vulgarizing *nom* characters. According to legend, he composed a short *nom* poem entitled *Van te ca sau* ("Crocodile Oration") and recited it to the Red River's crocodiles. It boasts of the Viet people's fishing and fighting skills and orders the crocodiles to return to the South Sea "where you belong." Upon hearing it, the reptiles left the river and returned to the sea. Despite the questionable veracity of this account, the *Van te ca sau* is one of the oldest surviving *nom* poems. Vietnamese vernacular characters look superficially like Chinese ones but are mostly indecipherable to people literate only in the latter. Although *nom* succeeded in representing native Vietnamese sounds as well as the many Chinese terms that had entered elite Vietnamese speech, it did not enter widespread usage alongside Chinese until the early fifteenth century. Even then, however, *nom* was used mainly in popular literature and unofficial documents and lacked the prestige of the officially sanctioned *chu Han*.

Each of these systems requires years of study to master tens of thousands of characters, and neither is widely used in modern Vietnam. A third system, *chu quoc ngu*, which remains in usage today, was invented by Catholic missionaries in the sixteenth and seventeenth centuries. Needing to learn Vietnamese but wanting to avoid the years of study required to master character-based systems, the missionaries, with the assistance of their Vietnamese speaking acolytes, developed an alphabetical system based on a smaller number of Latin letters, which in combination express the sounds of spoken Vietnamese, including Chinese loan words. Two sets of diacritical marks indicate the pronunciation of vowels and identify the tonal quality or pitch with which each syllable must be said (or "sung"). The Jesuit missionary Alexandre de Rhodes is usually credited in the West with inventing *quoc ngu*, but it is more accurate to consider *quoc ngu* a collective achievement that was first presented to Western readers in a systematic form by Father Rhodes, who published a Latin-Portuguese-Vietnamese dictionary in 1651.

This romanized Vietnamese was for several centuries the exclusive property of the Catholic missionaries, indigenous priests, and Vietnamese faithful. It began to enter wider usage in the nineteenth century due to efforts of the French colonial regime, which had it taught in schools as a means of giving basic instruction on Western subjects while also alienating France's Viet "subjects" from their Sino-Vietnamese cultural heritage and reducing their exposure to potentially subversive ideas carried by Chinese-language materials. In the twentieth century, Viet nationalists, including communists, seized upon *quoc ngu* as a means of raising literacy and generating popular support for their programs. Given its limited number of letters and diacritical symbols and nearly perfect "one-sound, one-syllable" correspondence, modern *quoc ngu* is quickly learned by Vietnamese speakers and well suited to mass literacy programs. After the end of colonialism in 1954, *quoc ngu* became the official writing system for government business and public education on both sides of the Seventeenth Parallel, and it remains so today in the S.R.V. Almost 92 percent of Vietnam's population is currently classified as literate, which means literate in *quoc ngu*. Only a few traditionalists and scholars still learn the character-based systems.

There are three main regional variations in Vietnamese pronunciation. They correspond to the three regions in which they are spoken—northern, central, and southern Vietnam—and are known as the Ha-noi, Hue, and Sai-gon "languages" (*tieng*). Many Vietnamese consider the Ha-noi "language" to be the "official" or "correct" one. It is also the version most learned by foreigners. Despite some differences in pronunciation and vocabulary, these variations do not prevent the Vietnamese from understanding each other, regardless of their region of origin. Regional stereotyping, some of which is the result of France's colonial division of Vietnam into three *pays*, is perhaps a greater barrier to interregional understanding than are the relatively minor linguistic differences. Southerners see themselves as friendly, honest, and easygoing; they see northerners as cold, cunning, and ambitious; they see centrists as conservative, stingy, and strict. Northerners and centrists, for their part, consider southerners lazy, simple, frontier people lacking in culture. Whatever their veracity may be, such feelings of regional distinctiveness contribute to tensions when Vietnamese from different regions interact. When the people are faced with external threats, however, a common Vietnamese identity tends to assert itself, leading to the solidarity of "we Vietnamese" against the outsider.

From the phonological point of view, Vietnamese is a monosyllabic and tonal language. Its monosyllabism is manifested in the articulation of syllables in connected speech, but many of its words are disyllabic and even polysyllabic. For English speakers, the tonal quality of Vietnamese is one of its most interesting aspects. Each word is formed with at least one vowel that is voiced with either level or changing pitch. Depending on regional variations, there may be four to six of these pitches or tones. Unlike the intonations that English speakers use to express shades of meaning or emphasis, these changes in tone or musical pitch affect the lexical meaning of Vietnamese words. A word's tonal quality is indicated in *quoc ngu* by diacritical marks over or under the main vowel (or by their absence). Although we do not generally indicate the tonal quality of Vietnamese words throughout this text, it may be useful to consider the following example. In northern Vietnamese pronunciation, for example, the six tones (*thanh*) are as follows: the level tone (*thanh khong dau*), such as *ma* ("ghost"); the high-rising tone (*thanh sac*), such as *má* ("cheek"); the low-falling tone (*thanh huyen*), such as *mà* ("but" or "then"); the falling-rising tone (*thanh hoi*), such as *mả* ("tomb"); the high-rising tone with glottal stop (*thanh nga*), such as *mã* ("horse"); and the low-falling tone with glottal stop (*thanh nang*), such as *mạ* ("rice seedling"). If the tone is mispronounced or omitted, it may produce a meaningless syllable or a word completely different from the intended one, with confusing or embarrassing consequences.

Vietnamese is an isolating language: words do not change their forms, and grammatical categories cannot be expressed by prefixes or suffixes. Although syntax and context are usually relied on to indicate grammatical meaning, function words may be added for clarification. However, Vietnamese words remain invariable, be they singular or plural, masculine or feminine, subject or object. For example, the word *toi* (literally, "servant" or "slave"), may serve as subject ("I") or object ("me"), depending on its placement in a sentence. Vietnamese verbs do not change their form to express contrasts between past, present, and future actions; the same word is used for past, present, and future actions as well as for first, second, or third person. For example, the verb *di* ("to go") may be used alone to indicate action taking place in the past, present, or future, although the function words *da*, *dang*, or *se* may be added to clarify the past, present progressive, or future locus of the actions.

Vietnamese has also appropriated words from foreign languages, particularly Chinese and, more recently, French and English. Vietnamese speakers usually change the original pronunciation of a borrowed word to fit the Vietnamese system. For example, the Chinese term for "China," *Chong guo* (literally, "Central Kingdom"), becomes *Trung Quoc* in Vietnamese. Polysyllabic French words may be shortened as well as broken up into manageable combinations: for example, "cinema" has become *ci-ne*. The most commonly learned foreign languages in twentieth-century Vietnam have been French and English. Today the educated or elite Vietnamese of the older generation often know French, whereas the younger generation of students is more likely to know English, which is avidly studied in public and private schools and is seen as the business language of the future.

FORMS OF ADDRESS

Given the emphasis on social status and familial hierarchy that pervaded Viet society in the pre-colonial period, the modern Vietnamese language is permeated with indicators of status and of the relationships between speaker and interlocutor.

Within the family, hierarchy was based on a person's relationship to other family members in terms of age, sex, generation, paternal or maternal lineage, and marriage. Older siblings are addressed as *anh* ("older brother") or *chi* ("older sister"). Younger siblings are addressed generally as *em* and may be referred to as *em trai* ("younger brother") or *em gai* ("younger sister"). The father's older siblings are called *bac*; the mother's siblings are called *cau* (for males) and *di* (for females); younger siblings of the father are called *chu* (for males) and *thim* (for females). Grandmothers and grandfathers are called *ba* and *ong*, respectively, with a further distinction made between paternal (*ong ba noi*, the "inside" grandparents) and maternal (*ong ba ngoai*, the "outside" grandparents). Although the basic equivalent to the English "I" is *toi*, it is usually replaced with a word more specific to the relationship between speaker and interlocutor. For example, one's older sister would be addressed as *chi* ("elder sister"), while the speaker would refer to him- or herself as *em*, or "younger sibling."

Many of the terms deriving from these familiar relationships are applied by extension to social address to express differences between speaker and interlocutor in regard to gender, social status, age, and profession. Three commonly employed forms of social address, mentioned above in the context of familial address, are *ong*, *ba*, and *co*. *Ong*, the basic meaning of which is "grandfather," is used to address men, in particular those older and of higher status than the speaker, but also men of any age who may be only casual acquaintances or business associates of the speaker. *Ba*, which means "grandmother," is applied to married women or to single women older than the speaker. *Co*, or "aunt," is used for unmarried women who are younger than the speaker.

English speakers put the given name first, followed by a middle name and completed by the family, or "last," name. For Vietnamese speakers, family name comes first, followed by the middle and then the given name. Nguyen Ngoc Tho, who was vice-president of the R.V.N. in the early 1960s, may serve as an example. The family name is Nguyen which—along with Ho, Le, Phan, Pham, Tran, Ngo, Dinh, and Trinh—is one of the most common. Vietnamese middle names usually have meanings. In Nguyen Ngoc Tho's case, the middle name Ngoc means "precious stone," and may be applied to men or women. Other common middle names are gender-specific. Van, meaning "literature," is a male's middle name, while Thi indicates that the bearer is female. Given names also usually have meanings that may or may not be gender-specific. Names such as Hong ("rose"), Lan ("orchid"), and Huong ("fragrance") are used exclusively for females; names such as Hung ("heroic") and Tien ("progress") are reserved for males; names such as Loc ("prosperity") and Phuc ("happiness") may be applied to members of either sex. In Nguyen Ngoc Tho's case, the given name Tho means "poetry" and is usually reserved for males. It is customary to address people by given names rather than by family names. Nguyen Ngoc Tho would have been addressed as *Ong* Tho, or "Mr. Tho" (literally, "grandfather" Tho)—never as *Ong* Nguyen, or "Mr. Nguyen." There are exceptions: Ho Chi Minh (a pseudonym), the D.R.V.'s late president, was publicly referred to by the family name Ho combined with an indicator of respect such as *bac* ("uncle") or *cu* ("venerable"). The use of the last name as form of address is reserved to well-known historical or literary figures, however.

A special convention is followed for naming imperial rulers. Before the Nguyen era, upon assuming the throne, a monarch's personal name became taboo, and he took instead a reign name, or *nien hieu*, to evoke the prosperity of his reign. These names were sometimes changed in the course of a reign in order to commemorate a fortuitous turn of events or to attempt to alter a difficult situation. Rulers also received a posthumous dynastic title, or *mieu hieu*, by which they would henceforth be known. Le Loi, for example, who founded the Later Le Dynasty in 1428, is known to posterity by his dynastic title, Le Thai-to. The Nguyen Dynasty's rulers, however, generally adopted but a single reign name and were known by it during their reigns as well as after death. The Nguyen founder, for example, whose personal name was Nguyen Phuoc Anh, assumed the *nien hieu* of Gia-long, by which he was known to contemporaries and is known to history. The practice was followed by the other Nguyen rulers. Like their predecessors, the monarchs of former dynasties, the Nguyen rulers attempted to choose reign titles with felicitous meanings, although in some cases historical events later gave them ironic connotations. Nguyen Vinh Thuy, whose reign as the Bao-dai Emperor coincided with World War II, the Japanese occupation of Indochina, and the termination of the Nguyen Dynasty in the August Revolution of 1945, is a case in point: the reign title Bao-dai means "Protector of Greatness."

2

History and Institutions

ORIGINS AND EARLY HISTORY

THE ANCESTORS of the modern Vietnamese appeared in the second millennium B.C.E. as part of a group of peoples spread throughout the lands stretching from the Yangzi Basin in today's People's Republic of China to the Red River Valley in modern Vietnam. These peoples were known to the Chinese as Yueh ("Viet"), and most would be assimilated during the Han expansion of the early Common Era. The southernmost Yueh, who inhabited the Red River Valley and were called Lac, however, constructed a distinct, non-Han identity that would endure repeated attempts at conquest and assimilation.

During the middle of the second millennium B.C.E., the Lac founded an organized society characterized by aristocratic predominance under a loosely structured monarchy based in the Red River Delta and called Van Lang. In addition to their political precociousness, the Lac were among the first peoples in Asia to employ irrigation systems and practice wet-rice agriculture; they were also among the area's earliest masters of bronze casting.

THE ERA OF CHINESE DOMINATION

Like other Yueh peoples, the Lac would confront the expanding Han Chinese of the Qin and Han Dynasties during the last centuries B.C.E. The Han empire initially dominated the Lac peoples indirectly by working through the indigenous aristocracy, but rebellions led by the latter in 39–43 C.E. brought a more direct rule and greater efforts at Sinification by the victorious Han. The territories of the Lac states were annexed and ruled directly, along with other former Yueh territories to the North, as provinces of the Han empire. With only periodic interruptions caused by Chinese dynastic interregnums or regional rebellions, the Chinese bureaucrats and their indigenous collaborators would implant much of Chinese high culture, including Legalist bureaucratic techniques and Confucian ethics, art, litera-ture, and language. Some Viet welcomed the chance to assimilate to what they considered to be a superior culture. These literati studied Confucianism avidly, some even passing the Han Dynasty's civil service examinations and taking bureaucratic positions locally or in China itself. Remarkably, however, and in contrast to the northern Yueh, the Southern Yueh retained historical memory of ancient Van Lang's independence and preserved aspects of Lac cultural patterns beneath multiple layers of Chinese culture. These conti-nuities contributed to the repeated rebellions against Chinese domination, the most famous being that of the Trung sisters in 39–43 C.E. Finally, taking advantage of the disunity that signaled the end of the Chinese Tang Dynasty (618–907), insurgents led by Ngo Quyen defeated the resident Chinese forces in 938 C.E. and initiated the era of independent monarchies in 939.

INDEPENDENT MONARCHIES

The early independent states would usually be called *Dai Co Viet* or *Dai Viet*, but, for the sake of convenience, we often call their majority people by their modern name of Vietnamese. The Vietnamese dynasties guarded their independence zealously but did not abandon Chinese culture. The pattern was set by the Later Ly Dynasty (1009–1225), which seized the Viet throne in the wake of civil wars following the death (in 944) of Ngo Quyen and the collapse of the Ngo Dynasty (in 965). The Ly founders applied the lessons of the Chinese occupation regimes and began the process of bureaucratic centralization, implementing civil service examinations on Chinese texts about Taoism, Buddhism, and Confucianism. They also yielded to Chinese demands to send tributary missions to the northern court; submission was perfunctory and preferable to invasion.

These trends continued under the Ly's successor, the Tran Dynasty (1225–1400). Under the Tran, the Viet faced threats by the Mongols, who had obliterated the Chinese Song Dynasty in 1279 and founded their Yuan Dynasty (1279–1368). When, in 1285, the Tran refused the Mongols' de-mands to traverse Viet territory in order to attack their southern neighbor, Champa, the Mongols attacked Dai Viet instead. Although the Mongol on-slaughts were devastating to Dai Viet, the Mongols were repeatedly defeated and finally expelled by Tran Hung Dao, who mobilized resistance and applied guerrilla tactics against the invaders.

The last sustained Chinese effort at conquest and assimilation of the Viet came when Ho Quy Ly, regent for an immature Tran emperor, seized Dai Viet's throne in 1400 and attempted an administrative reorganization. Profiting from the resulting confusion and uncertainty, the Chinese Ming Dynasty overpowered Viet defenders and annexed the rebellious province (as the Chinese saw it) in 1407. The Ming occupation attempted to undo 500 years of Viet independence by returning the region to the status of a Chinese province and applying Sinification with a vengeance—even destroying works of literature in the Vietnamese vernacular.

The experiment was to be short-lived. In 1418, Le Loi, a commoner landlord and ex-official from Thanh Hoa province, proclaimed himself to be a "pacification king" and gathered partisans to wage guerrilla warfare against the occupation. With the help of powerful military leaders including Nguyen Trai, Le Loi expelled Ming forces and returned Dai Viet to independence under his (Later) Le Dynasty (1428–1788).

DIVISION AND WESTERN PENETRATION UNDER THE LATER LE DYNASTY

Having repulsed the Chinese, the Le founders adopted Chinese-style government and Confucianism. Legalist concepts guided bureaucratic reorganization to help the emperor control and tax his people. Confucianism justified imperial authority by linking it to a Heavenly Mandate. While the concept of a Chinese-style emperor retained its potency, real power eluded the Le monarchs, who soon became the pawns of military leaders. The Nguyen and Trinh families came to the forefront in the 1500s. Each took the title *chua* ("lord") and claimed to serve the Le while denouncing the other as usurper of the Le's mandate. Le emperors remained enthroned in Thang-long, but the militarists wielded power. The Trinh held the North, dominating the Le court, and, in 1558, forced the Nguyen into exile at the country's southernmost extreme. A de facto partition resulted, with the Trinh to the North and Nguyen to the South of the Eighteenth Parallel. From the mid-1500s to the late 1700s, the Le nominally reigned while the Nguyen and Trinh fought, each claiming to be the Le's servant. Meanwhile, important developments occurred: the *Nam tien*, or Southward Movement, which expanded Vietnamese territory southward; and Catholic proselytization.

With Trinh expansion blocked, the Nguyen advanced southward. Nguyen *chua* encouraged migration to increase production and tax revenues. Viet settlers moved to the southern extremes of Viet-occupied areas and founded villages. The *chua* provided arms, tools, and tax exemptions to encourage settlement. Conflicts arose between the settlers and the Chams, whose state covered much of present-day central Vietnam; and between the settlers and the Khmers, whose state extended from what is now Cambodia through the Mekong Delta in today's Vietnam. Localized conflicts were handled by settlers, but Nguyen forces intervened when states were involved. During the sixteenth and seventeenth centuries, Nguyen forces took Cham lands and drove the Khmers from the Delta. Vietnam's central coastline is littered with Cham temples to the Hindu deity Shiva; and Cham and Khmer minorities still live in central and southern Vietnam, respectively. Other non-Viet peoples were also assimilated or expelled.

The first Catholic missions in Viet lands were founded in Cochin China in 1615 and Tonkin in 1626. A remarkable early missionary was the Jesuit Alexandre de Rhodes (1591–1660), who believed missionaries should learn indigenous languages and began studying Vietnamese upon his arrival in northern Vietnam in 1627. To facilitate his confreres' progress, he developed a system that came to be called *quoc ngu*, or "national language." A limited number of symbols were used to express Vietnamese sounds, and learning to read and write was simplified. He also published a Portuguese-Latin-"Annamese" dictionary, an "Annamese" grammar, and a *quoc ngu* catechism. Rhodes also helped to found an institute to train missionaries. After winning approval by Pope Innocent X and King Louis XIV, he founded the Société des Missions-Etrangères in 1665 in Paris. French missionaries had not been very active in Viet lands; henceforth, French priests from the Society would always be present.

To understand Viet reactions, one must remember the elite's attitudes as well as the wartime context. Viet Confucians viewed religion in terms of a dichotomy between orthodox and heterodox doctrines. Confucianism was orthodox: it taught reverence for parents and the emperor. It was considered the only correct moral system, and political stability required its unaminous acceptance. Confronted with Catholicism, Viet authorities—the Le, Trinh, and Nguyen—banned it because it placed God above the emperor. Due to the wartime context, however, the Trinh and Nguyen rarely enforced such edicts. Each wanted contacts with Western states, sources of weapons and supplies. The missionaries, hoping to avoid expulsion, served as commercial agents and interpreters.

The era of civil war was not a happy one for most Viet: both *chua* enforced high demands for taxes, soldiers, and laborers. Neither practiced Confucian government or enjoyed popular support. In 1771, the situation was transformed by a movement led by three brothers from Tay-son village in

Binh-dinh province. They rallied the people against such excessive demands and never-ending wars. By 1788, the Tay-son had defeated the Nguyen and Trinh and then did what neither had dared: abolished the Le Dynasty, founding their Tay-son Dynasty (1788–1802). Having tasted power, the brothers grew alienated from their supporters and from each other. They divided Viet lands among themselves and competed for supremacy. Their regimes resembled military dictatorships rather than benevolent monarchies. The Tay-son lost their supporters, leaving themselves vulnerable in turn.

REUNIFICATION UNDER THE NGUYEN DYNASTY

Finally, a survivor of the Nguyen family mobilized this discontent. The Tay-son had tried to exterminate the Nguyen in 1777, but Prince Nguyen Anh had escaped, fled to Siam, and gathered partisans. Assuming that popular pro–Tay-son sentiment would fade, Nguyen Anh invaded the Mekong delta region in 1788 and began to reestablish Nguyen power there. Acknowledging that his ancestors' exploitative rule had caused their loss of the South, he took care to portray his perspective as Confucian-inspired and benevolent.

The new Nguyen regime took advantage of the fertility of the under-exploited southern lands. Nguyen Anh settled supporters on uncultivated land, which helped southerners meet their needs and generated supplies for the reconquest. The successful program allowed him to tax lightly while marshaling resources to support the war effort. Produce was traded to Western merchants for war materials. Nguyen Anh organized an administration and military machine that was effective relative to the Tay-son's disunity and corruption. Nguyen forces began advancing northward, supplying themselves from the South. By 1802, they had destroyed the Tay-son and executed their hard-core supporters. For the first time in 200 years, Viet lands were united under one ruler, including areas added during the *Nam tien*. Nguyen Anh took the title of Gia-long (1802–1820) and built a capital at Hue. After obtaining the approval of the Qing authorities in China, Gia-long officially announced that the name of his kingdom would be Viet Nam. In 1813, however, he changed the name to Dai Viet. His successor, Minh-mang, forbade the use of Dai Viet, replacing it with Dai Nam. For convenience, we often refer to the lands controlled by the Nguyen emperors as Vietnam.

France played a role in the reunification due to the actions of Bishop Pigneau de Behaine (1744–1798). In Siam, Behaine convinced Nguyen Anh to offer France concessions in return for aid and to use him, Behaine, as intermediary. When Nguyen Anh agreed, Behaine went to France in 1787 to negotiate with Louis XVI (1754–1793), producing the Treaty of Versailles, according to which France would effectively aid Nguyen Anh, who would grant France commercial contracts, territory, and toleration for Catholics. Behaine left for French India, where French forces were to assemble; but Louis reconsidered, declaring the treaty void. When the news reached India, Behaine assembled a fleet by combining Nguyen Anh's funds, his own resources, and contributions from local French traders, who hoped to gain preferential treatment. Behaine also recruited European mercenaries. The Europeans joined Nguyen Anh in July 1789 and contributed to his efforts by forging cannon and training Nguyen forces in Western tactics. Missionaries helped to purchase supplies and weapons. French aid was significant to the Nguyen victory but not decisive. The main causes of victory were the Tay-son's factionalism and failure to maintain popular support; Nguyen Anh capitalized by establishing a regime in the South with a solid economic and fiscal base. Having done so, he was able to win popular support by playing the role of the benevolent monarch. With popular support in the South and that region's resources at his disposal, he advanced northward to victory in 1802. France would later insist that the Nguyen Dynasty owed it the concessions promised in the 1787 treaty, arguing that Behaine had fulfilled its obligations. Nguyen Anh refused since the treaty said that France would help him but said nothing of individuals.

After 1802, Franco-Vietnamese contacts were interrupted by the Napoleonic Wars, but French missionaries would remain in Vietnam. Gia-long tolerated them lest he appear ungrateful, but he began a Confucian revival that would increase tensions between Catholic and non-Catholic Vietnamese. Gia-long and his heirs followed Le precedent in adopting Chinese models of bureaucratic government and political thought. The Nguyen state established six boards (for taxation, works, rituals, war, public office, and justice) and otherwise resembled China's government in many respects. Vietnam was divided into provinces, to which centrally appointed officials were sent to collect taxes and enforce laws. Confucian studies were linked to bureaucratic appointment. After Gia-long's death in 1820, these trends would provoke conflict, giving France an excuse to attack in 1858.

PRE-COLONIAL INSTITUTIONS

Social Classes

On the eve of the colonial conquest, Vietnam's elite accepted Confucian conceptions of society as comprising four ranked classes: scholars (si), peasants (*nong*), artisans (*cong*), and merchants (*thuong*). In theory, rank reflected each's contribution to society. Scholars ranked highest as they provided ethical leadership and held office in the monarch's service. Peasants came second since their labor provided necessary resources. Artisans ranked third as they made useful or beautiful objects. Merchants were lowest because they were considered parasitic elements who profited from exchanging goods produced by others. However, this schema represented the Confucian scholars' worldview and did not correspond to Vietnamese realities.

Early Nguyen-era society actually functioned as follows. At its pinnacle were the emperors and their relatives, who held positions by hereditary right or marriage. Next came the central-level officials, who worked in Hue, and local-level officials, who staffed the provincial- and district-level offices. These officials, who generally won their positions by passing examinations on the Confucian canon, history, and administration, exercised authority on the emperor's behalf and shared his prestige.

Below officialdom was a diverse class whom Western scholars term the "gentry." Strictly speaking, Vietnam's gentry comprised scholars who held examination degrees but had not entered or had retired from civil service; it included by extension scholars studying for the examinations and locally powerful landowners. Gentry members, by virtue of their association with Confucian studies and nearness to the bureaucracy, enjoyed a level of prestige just below that of officeholders.

Similar to the gentry were religious specialists such as Buddhist monks, Taoist masters, and geomancers. Local practitioners were supported by followers or clients, with income dependent on their local reputations. All participated in the prestige that scholars enjoyed, in that their positions derived from ancient learning, with pride of place going to the Confucian scholar-officials.

The peasantry, officially ranked second, was the most numerous and least prestigious sector. Eighty percent of Viet lived in rural society, and cultivating rice in the fields surrounding the villages was the main economic activity. Until colonial times, most farming families owned some land and, barring natural disaster, banditry, or warfare, produced enough to support themselves and pay taxes. Although powerful landowners or officials sometimes dispossessed peasants, familial ownership remained generalized before the colonial era. This was in part due to the Nguyen Dynasty's efforts to prevent the rise of powerful landed interests. Also important were opportunities provided by migration to the southern frontiers. Most production was for consumption rather than the market. Money was not widely used: taxes and rent were usually paid in rice; farmers traded rice for other foods or goods. Most people practiced subsidiary activities such as fishing, raising ducks, and weaving.

The third-ranking class, the artisan class, was in fact almost nonexistent in late traditional Vietnam, if we mean a distinct and significant sector of society practicing a specialized trade. Most farming families practiced a non-agricultural trade some of the time: fishing in rivers or lakes, or weaving hats for sale at local markets. Some villages focused more exclusively on a trade to the virtual exclusion of farming. Some northern villages, for example, followed a single trade such as pottery making, teaching its skills to the boys of each generation. Villagers sometimes forbade daughters from marrying outside the village to prevent rival villages from learning trade secrets. Likewise, some coastal villages relied almost entirely on ocean fishing, but these were exceptions to the pattern of reliance on agriculture. In cities, some Vietnamese artisans practiced trades like silversmithing, but generally markets were dominated by articles made by Chinese artisans in China or Vietnam. Moreover, Vietnam's imperial state hindered the development of an independent Viet artisan class by ruinous taxation and the impressment of gifted artisans into royal service. Thus, a true artisan class did not exist in precolonial Vietnam, the artisan's relatively privileged place in the four-class hierarchy notwithstanding.

Finally, only part of the merchant class was as lowly as its ranking. Petty retail commerce in urban and rural markets was and remains the prerogative of Vietnamese women. Some operated permanent shops in towns and cities, but most opened stalls or displayed wares on the ground in periodic village markets. Large-scale trade, including interregional and international trade in items such as precious metals or sacred texts, was controlled by Chinese merchants, whose wealth and influence were vastly greater than that of Vietnamese retailers.

The Village

The village was the basic administrative and social unit of rural life. Each village (*lang* or *xa*) was divided into clusters of settlements called hamlets (*ap*). Northern villages were surrounded by bamboo walls, making it hard for outsiders to enter. The typical village had between 500 and 1,000 residents who lived in from five to ten hamlets of about 100 people each and farmed in nearby fields.

Each village had a meeting house, or *dinh*, which was its administrative and spiritual center. Administration was the prerogative of a council of notables (*hoi lang*), twelve men chosen by co-option. When a council needed a new member, members consulted lists of resident males ranked by age, wealth, and learning. Voting was secret and unanimity was required. Council membership was ardently desired, for it brought honor as well as local power; the notables ran village affairs since the state rarely interfered. Families were not directly taxed; the state kept records of how many lived in each village and presented the notables with demands. The notables assigned obligations to each family and collected the proceeds on the state's behalf; the state intervened only if villages failed to meet obligations. The council also administered communal lands (*cong dien*), inalienable lands owned by the village as a corporate body. Under its supervision, *cong dien* were let to individuals or families, the proceeds allowing the council to meet its expenses, sponsor festivals, and support widows and orphans.

Villagers' solidarity was reinforced by the worship of a patron deity, or *thanh hoang*. The deity, often the spirit of the village's founder or local beast, was responsible for protecting villagers and was worshiped in the *dinh*. Organizing festivals in its honor was one of the notables' most important responsibilities, and their participation was a manifestation of their local status. Villages were not democratic or socialist, as some scholars have maintained, but they did enjoy limited self-government and aid some of their less fortunate members.

The Imperial State

Founding the dynasty in 1802, the Nguyen emperors based their policy on their admiration and fear of China: they admired Chinese culture and statecraft but feared Chinese domination. Their solution was to adopt China's political theories and institutions to make Vietnam capable of resisting its domination. The Nguyen tried to remake Vietnam in accordance with the Chinese model, emphasizing Confucian ideology and Legalist statecraft. In many ways the Nguyen state was a miniature model of the Qing: a centralized system with the emperor at the top; a Grand Secretariat and a Privy Council to help formulate policy; *Luc Bo*, or Six Ministries, each with a specialized function (war, taxation, public office, justice, public works, rites); and officials working for these ministries assigned to govern the provinces and districts. Impressed by Nguyen Vietnam's borrowing, some scholars have dubbed it a "Smaller Dragon" or "Little China." Such terms exaggerate the emperors' success, however. Sinicization was never so complete as they wished, even among the elite, and popular culture remained the religious focus for most villagers, despite Confucian influences that trickled down.

Cities

The Nguyen Dynasty's centralization stimulated the development of administrative centers, with 31 provincial seats and 250 district-level capitals. Three cities may be contrasted in terms of their differing roles and subsequent development.

The preeminent administrative city was Hue. Under the name of Phu-xuan, it had been the locus of the Nguyen lords' power since the 1600s. When the Nguyen Dynasty was founded, Hue became its imperial capital, the hub of administration and home of the court and its highest officials. Hue became a scaled-down model of the Chinese capital, Beijing. It was laid out in accordance with geomancy, which placed structures in relation to the environment and each other. Buildings and gates associated with the emperor opened to the South, as the Sage faced southward to impart wisdom. When completed, Hue was three cities in one. At its center was the walled "forbidden city" called *Dai Noi*, or "Great Within," where the royal palaces and halls were housed. Surrounding this was another walled city called the *Hoang Thanh*, or "Imperial Citadel," which housed ceremonial halls such as the *Thai Hoa Dien*, or "Hall of Supreme Harmony." Both of these were surrounded by a larger, capital city called the *Kinh Thanh*, in which were housed the Six Ministries and other offices. High-ranking officials worked in the outermost or capital city. Other structures associated with the court were beyond the city proper, including the Esplanade of Heaven and Earth, site of royal *Nam Giao* rituals; court-sponsored monasteries such as the *Chua Thien Mu*, or "Heavenly Lady Pagoda"; and the imperial tombs. The Nguyen tombs were major works. For Tu-duc's necropolis, 3,000 laborers worked for three years on pavilions, gardens, and lakes covering thirty acres.

Hue was not a major commercial center in Nguyen times; its population numbered but 60,000 in the 1820s. With colonial rule, France's administrative and commercial interests focused on Ha-noi and Sai-gon, to Hue's detriment. With the Nguyen monarchs reduced to figureheads, Hue's policy-making role was eliminated. Even this reduced role was ended by the 1945 August Revolution. Many of Hue's buildings and artifacts were destroyed in the Indochina Wars. Hue and its monuments are now considered part of the World's Cultural Patrimony by the United Nations and benefit from funding for restoration. Postwar Hue has developed small-scale industry, particularly weaving, but with a population of a quarter million, it has not experienced the growth that has characterized postwar Ha-noi and Ho Chi Minh City.

Under the names Thang-long and Dong Kinh, Ha-noi (the latter, used since 1831, means "Between the Rivers") had been the capital of Viet

The *Ngo Mon*, or Noontime Gate, entrance to the *Hoang Thanh*, or Imperial City, Hue City, central Vietnam

dynasties from the eleventh century until the nineteenth. Thus, it had long been the political and cultural model for the states it served, housing the Temple of Literature (*Van Mieu*), examination fields, and an eleventh-century temple, *Chua Mot Cot* ("One-Pillar Pagoda"). More of a political, administrative, and cultural center than a commercial or industrial one, Ha-noi was still tiny (several tens of thousands of people) when seized by the Nguyen. Nguyen Anh demoted Ha-noi to "auxiliary capital," believing Hue's location more suitable for uniting Vietnam. However, Ha-noi, though damaged during France's conquest, found an enhanced importance under colonial rule. Given its proximity to China, it became French Indochina's capital in 1902. A major center of French finance, commerce, and society, Ha-noi's population grew to 150,000 by the period between the World Wars, mainly due to the Viet and other Asians who came seeking employment. Held by the French throughout most of World War II and the First Indochina War, Ha-noi has been the capital of the D.R.V. from 1954 to 1976 and of the S.R.V. from 1976 to today. Ha-noi suffered from bombing during the Second Indochina War, but many monuments (or restored versions) can still be seen, including the One-Pillar Pagoda and Temple of Literature.

Other cities were prominent for commercial reasons. Sai-gon had been (as

Prei Kor) a Khmer outpost until the late 1500s, when the region came under Viet control. Although it became an administrative center for Nguyen lords and Nguyen monarchs, its characteristics as a Southeast Asian market town were never effaced. Western observers in the 1820s noted the bustling atmosphere of its commercial quarters, where Chinese, Viet, and other merchants exchanged silks, paper, and teas. Sai-gon was captured by the French in 1859 and ceded to them in 1862. As French Cochin China's capital, it became a major port through which the Mekong Delta's production passed en route to international markets. By World War II, Sai-gon (including Cho-lon) housed a quarter million people. Sai-gon continued to be administered by the French during most of World War II and the First Indochina War. During the Second Indochina War, it was the capital of the R.V.N. and the headquarters of U.S. military operations. By the 1960s, swelled by refugees, its population grew to 2,000,000. After reunification, Sai-gon lost its position as national capital to Ha-noi, but as Ho Chi Minh City it has led by example in the post-1987 reforms. Its prosperity—based on its port facilities, role in the export of agricultural production, and position as an international commercial center—currently supports more than 3,000,000 people. Despite the official change of name, most of its inhabitants still refer to it as "Sai-gon" rather than as "Ho Chi Minh City."

THE FRENCH CONQUEST

Vietnam's Nguyen-era institutions and the beliefs that underpinned them came under attack during colonial rule, beginning in 1858.

The Nguyen emperors viewed Catholicism as heterodox and resented the missionaries' activities. The emperors knew that missionaries had ties with foreign powers and supported rebellions against imperial authority. From 1830, the emperors banned Christianity, ordering missionaries to leave and forbidding Vietnamese Catholics from practicing their religion. Many missionaries appealed to France's Emperor Napoleon III (1852–1871). Anticipating increasing Western trade with China, Napoleon sought bases nearby and realized that the Christians' plight could legitimize intervention in Vietnam.

In 1858, French troops landed at Da-nang, planning to advance to Hue and seize the Tu-duc Emperor (who ruled 1848–1883). Missionaries had described Vietnam's administration as disorganized and corrupt, promising that "Catholic as well as pagan" Vietnamese would welcome liberation. Despite technological disadvantages, Vietnamese defenders resisted staunchly, containing French forces on the coast. Unable to bring ships into the interior,

The Stele Pavilion at the Tu-duc Emperor's mausoleum, Hue City, central Vietnam

given the lack of deep rivers, the French could not advance inland; lacking firepower, Nguyen forces could not push them into the sea.

In mid-1859, French forces moved to the South, where the rivers are deep and wide, allowing them to move inland and destroy Vietnamese fortresses. By 1861, imperial forces in the South had been crushed. The French began to patrol the rivers and coast to prevent rice from reaching the Center, plunging Hue into famine. In 1862, Tu-duc sent emissaries to French-held Sai-gon to negotiate. In the Treaty of Sai-gon, Vietnam agreed to pay France an indemnity to permit French navigation of the Mekong River to cede three southern provinces and to stop "persecuting" Catholics.

Entrenched in the area around Sai-gon, which they dubbed French Cochin China and ruled as a colony, French officials planned to use the Mekong River to communicate with China. Naval officers steamed up the Mekong in 1866, arriving in China in 1867 and returning to Sai-gon in 1868. But the "river road to China" was impractical, given the rapids in the upper Mekong valley.

Undeterred, the French shifted focus to the Red River, which offered a direct route to China's interior, but they had no rights to its navigation, and the Governor of Cochin China, Jules-Marie Dupré (1818–1881), schemed to provoke a fight. In 1873, he sent Francis Garnier (1839–1873) with four gunboats into the Tonkin Delta with orders not to leave until he had extorted, at the least, commercial freedom on the Red River. Arriving in Ha-noi, Garnier declared the Red River open to commerce in the name of "Civilization and France." He bombarded Ha-noi and cruised throughout the Tonkin Delta, attacking forts and administrative centers. Vietnamese officials, despairing of a military solution, signed the Treaty of Ha-noi in 1874, granting France access to China via the Red River; several northern ports; and a veto over Hue's diplomacy to preclude negotiations with other powers.

French officials soon concluded that Sino-French trade would reach its potential only if France had full authority in northern Vietnam. They provoked a conflict by expanding upon the 1874 treaty, claiming that navigation on the Red River implied rights to police it and demanding that Hue cease tributary missions to China. When Hue refused, Captain Henri Rivière (1827–1883) was sent to Tonkin in 1882 to replicate Garnier's actions. By 1883–1884, he had forced Hue to sign the Convention of the Protectorate, according to which France assumed authority over the Center and the North and reduced the Nguyen monarchs to figurehead status.

VIETNAM UNDER FRENCH DOMINATION

Tonkin (protectorate), Annam (protectorate), and Cochin China (colony) were linked with Cambodia (a protectorate since 1863) and Laos (1893) to make French Indochina. Heading the federal administration was a French governor-general based in Ha-noi, the capital. Under the federal government were the governments of the five "countries" (*pays*): Laos, Cambodia, Annam, Tonkin, and Cochin China. Protectorates were ruled by indigenous officials under French control; the colony by Frenchmen directly. Protectorates were more economical than colonies since the indigenous officials remained in office while French residents "advised" them. Cochin China was ruled directly as a colony since most mandarins had left their posts in the 1860s rather than work for the French. By 1885, however, most officials in the North and Center had been ready to collaborate. In Laos and Cambodia, traditional authorities collaborated through a resident system.

French domination brought socioeconomic change to Indochina, particularly Vietnam. The governors-general strictly enforced existing taxes, imposed new taxes and monopolies, and created an export-oriented plantation economy. The precolonial Vietnamese economy had stressed self-sufficient, village-level agriculture. When Vietnamese forces were defeated, the French granted the lands of the defeated soldiers to Vietnamese and Chinese collaborators. The French also encouraged notables to take private ownership of communal land. Whereas the Nguyen monarchs had taxed lightly and in kind, using the village as the responsible unit, the French taxed family heads heavily, directly, and in cash. People had to sell rice at often unfavorable rates or face imprisonment. Many were forced to borrow from usurers, using land as collateral. Borrowing was often the first step to losing land to the creditor, after which ex-peasants became tenants or wage-laborers for larger, market-oriented owners. Indochina became the world's leading rice exporter, enriching all but the direct producer. From 1900, tension rose between estate owners, who favored the French, and masses of the dispossessed, who blamed France for their losses.

The French regime also encouraged mining and plantation agriculture in products other than rice by building roads, railroads, and ports for exporting minerals and plantation products. It leased exploitation rights to French firms, which recruited the landless as laborers. The industries of extraction— lead, iron, coal—were in the North, their products exported via Hai-phong. Coffee thrived in the central mountains and rubber in the plateaux above Sai-gon. The great rice lands were in the Mekong Delta. Working conditions were deplorable. On rubber plantations, for example, people were housed in barracks and worked long hours—from 3:00 A.M. until dark—for starvation wages. Bosses had the right to punish "troublemakers" by beatings or imprisonment.

Apologists argue that France brought Vietnam the benefits of Western civilization, pointing to hospitals, schools, and roads. Although there is some truth to this, hospitals or schools were available only to a minority of Vietnamese, while the majority suffered from the regime's taxation, brutality, and racial prejudice.

THE RISE OF NATIONALISM

The social tensions created by colonialism, along with its destruction of the imperial order and its underpinnings, stimulated nationalism. During 1885–1954, resistance developed in several stages.

Traditional anticolonialists fought the French in support of the Nguyen Dynasty. Their ideology was Confucianism, their goal to restore the independent monarchy. An ex-official named Phan Dinh Phung (1847–1895), for example, led pro-Nguyen guerrillas in the Center until his death in 1895.

By 1900, most had been killed or captured, and, given Nguyen collaboration, the monarchy as a unifying symbol had been discredited.

The next stage was led by men who had come to prominence after 1900. They were anti-French but, disillusioned with Confucianism, looked to the West and Westernized Japan. Phan Boi Chau (1867–1940), an intellectual of gentry origins, was among the first to recognize that Vietnam had to draw upon Western models to strengthen itself to win independence. He traveled throughout Asia in search of organizational forms and political ideas, participating in many anti-French risings. Phan Boi Chau was captured in 1925 and sentenced to house arrest for life. Afterwards younger leaders emerged as modern nationalists, noncommunist and communist.

The first noncommunist modern nationalist organizations in Vietnam were formed by members of the urban middle class. This small group had arisen after 1900 and comprised clerks, journalists, and lower-level administrators. French-educated, they admired the French conceptions of liberty, equality, and fraternity and were outraged by the difference between legal equality and democratic freedom in France and the discrimination and repression in Indochina. For example, in 1927, Nguyen Thai Hoc (Vinh-yen, 1904–1930) founded the Viet Nam Quoc Dan Dang (Vietnamese Nationalist Party, VNQDD), which sought to overthrow the colonial regime and found a Vietnamese republic. He planned an insurrection in spring 1930 at Yen Bay, planting agents in its garrison who were to poison their officers. The French crushed it, however, decimating the VNQDD leadership and bombing nearby villages in retaliation. By repressing the noncommunist nationalists, France inadvertently opened the way for Marxists to dominate the movement.

The founder of Vietnamese communism was born Nguyen Sinh Cuong but is best known as Ho Chi Minh (Nghe-an, 1890–1969). His father, an ex-mandarin, despised Hue's collaboration and refused to let his son pursue Chinese studies. Instead, Ho studied Western science, geography, and history. In 1911, he left Vietnam by working on a French ship, spending years at sea. In 1918, he settled in Paris and participated in émigré politics. During the Paris peace talks following World War I (1914–1918), he submitted demands for Vietnamese autonomy and democratic rights. Allied leaders ignored him, but these actions made him well known in émigré and French leftist circles.

In 1920, Ho became a founding member of the French Communist Party (FCP) and eventually an agent of the Comintern, through which the Soviet Union (USSR) controlled the world revolutionary movement. By 1923, Ho was studying in Moscow, after which he went to South China to found a

Communist Party. He began to instruct the Vietnamese in Marxism and organizational techniques. In 1930, Ho founded the Indochinese Communist Party (ICP), dedicated to overthrowing colonialism and building socialism in Indochina; it was the ancestor of today's Vietnam Communist Party (VCP).

Many factors account for the ICP's success. The French police imprisoned and executed dissidents. In this context, the ICP had advantages over its rivals. Its agents could go to parts of China held by the Chinese communists or to the USSR for training. It had financial resources provided by the USSR. As a Leninist party, its underground organization was durable. It had a rural reform program and village-level ties; cadres could hide among peasants. Thus, the ICP survived as a working entity until the Pacific War, which created the circumstances for its seizure of power.

Germany conquered France in 1940, and a collaborationist regime was founded in Vichy. Japan pressured French colonial officials. France would retain sovereignty and administer Indochina, while Japanese forces would exploit its infrastructure and resources. As Vichy collaborated with Germany, French Indochina worked with Japan. ICP leaders organized to fight the Japanese and pro-Japanese French collaborators in preparation for a power seizure, founding the Vietnam Independence League (Viet Minh) in May 1941. Dominated by the ICP, it was supported by many noncommunist nationalists. Its guerrillas attacked Japanese or French soldiers in isolation, taking their weapons. The Viet Minh gathered intelligence for the Allies, passing it to America's Office of Strategic Services (OSS) in China in return for weapons. These activities solidified the Viet Minh's reputation as the nationalist opposition to Franco-Japanese rule.

As Japan's prospects declined, Japanese officers launched an anti-French coup in March 1945, imprisoning French officials and seizing the administration. The Japanese invited Nguyen Vinh Thuy, the Bao-dai Emperor (who ruled 1926–1945), to reign over an "independent" Vietnam, hoping to retain control behind the scenes and to appeal to the Vietnamese to help Japan resist an Allied invasion.

Following Japan's surrender announcement of August 15, 1945, its forces throughout Asia collapsed, leaving a power vacuum in Indochina. Who would fill it? French forces had been decimated by the March coup. Bao-dai's regime was tainted by collaboration. The Viet Minh was respected by many Vietnamese as the only organization that had fought for independence, and it had the only broadly based indigenous armed force. Marching into Ha-noi unopposed, Viet Minh cadres occupied administrative offices. OSS men confirm that Ho received a hero's welcome when he read on September

2, 1945, a Declaration of Independence based on French and American precedents. The Viet Minh founded the D.R.V. Bao-dai, lacking support and fearing arrest by the Allies, abdicated. The D.R.V. initially enjoyed broad support based on the Viet Minh's wartime record and nationalist stance. However, despite the nominal participation of noncommunist nationalists, the D.R.V. soon became a Leninist dictatorship.

THE FIRST INDOCHINA WAR

Seeking to return as the colonial power, France initiated the First Indochina War, from 1946 to 1954. French forces outnumbered and outgunned D.R.V. forces, now called the People's Army of Vietnam (PAVN), yet by 1954 the French were willing to withdraw. To see why, one must understand the revolutionary warfare implemented by the D.R.V. The D.R.V. accepted the fact that the French had the stronger conventional force and initially avoided direct confrontations. When the French returned in 1946, it withdrew to the Viet Bac mountains. It began the conflict with small-unit tactics: the booby trap, hit-and-run attacks, and ambushes, allowing the D.R.V. to choose the time and place of confrontations. Though inferior overall in numbers and weaponry, D.R.V. forces were often superior at the points chosen for attack. Gradually, the D.R.V. sought to develop conventional capacities that would bring victory in positional warfare.

To conduct revolutionary warfare, the D.R.V. needed peasant support: it needed intelligence, food and shelter, weapons caches, and recruits. It attracted the well-off peasants by appealing to their nationalism and the poorer ones by implementing rent reduction and land-distribution programs. These gave ex-tenants or laborers claim to land but obliged them to support the D.R.V. Conversely, the D.R.V. terrorized or executed those who refused. French forces controlled the cities and policed the deltas, but despite their technological and numerical advantages were unable to expel D.R.V. cadres from the villages.

France's position declined with the founding of the People's Republic of China (P.R.C.) in 1949. The P.R.C. gave the PAVN access to China, where its soldiers could rest, repair equipment, and load supplies. Fearing wider war, France did not attack Chinese sanctuaries. Soon the PAVN was mounting attacks against large French units. By 1953, French forces were losing on the ground, and Paris was facing domestic opposition to what was seen as *la sale guerre*, a "dirty war" defending colonial interests. To capitalize, the PAVN invaded Laos from the northern mountains; reasoning that the French would either abandon Laos or block the invasion, which would draw forces away from Tonkin and stretch their air power to its limits.

The French responded by building a fortress at Dien Bien Phu, a valley through which the PAVN had to pass to enter Laos. The French believed that their defenses, which could be supplied by air, were impregnable. They believed the PAVN incapable of bringing artillery and anti-aircraft guns to such an isolated spot. But during spring 1954 the PAVN surrounded Dien Bien Phu, cutting supply routes. The PAVN was well armed with Chinese-supplied cannons and anti-aircraft guns that had been disassembled, carried over trails, and arrayed in camouflaged positions around the fortress. The PAVN attacked on March 16, 1954, taking Dien Bien Phu on May 6, 1954.

At the Geneva Conference, France and the D.R.V. signed a truce setting up regroupment zones North and South of the Seventeenth Parallel to separate their forces. There were to be elections in 1956 to choose the form and personnel of an independent Vietnamese regime. Meanwhile, the D.R.V. would administer the northern zone, and France the southern one. The elections would never be held, setting the stage for renewed conflict.

THE SECOND INDOCHINA WAR

During the First Indochina War, America had supported France because of the European priority of U.S. interests after 1945. Fearing Soviet aggression in Europe, President Harry Truman (1945–1953) wanted a strong, pro-Western France. The FCP was the largest party in a multiparty system; losing Indochina might create discontent that it could exploit. Although this factor stayed operative for a time, others arose to reinforce and then replace it. Most important were the Cold War's internationalization and the Truman Doctrine, which sought the USSR's containment. In this context, the D.R.V.'s Leninism became critical for U.S. leaders. Domestic anticommunism also became a factor after 1949. In the McCarthy era, charges of being "soft on communism" ruined careers, motivating politicians to support defending Indochina from perceived communist aggression.

To transmute colonial war into an anticommunist crusade, the French pretended to give the Indochinese states independence in 1949. France made Bao Dai chief of a State of Vietnam (S.O.V.), with like arrangements concluded with pro-Western Lao and Khmer elites. The French claimed that they were helping independent states to defend themselves, but France did not grant its creations real power. For example, the S.O.V. army was composed of Vietnamese draftees commanded by French officers, and they fought alongside French troops. In the war's final years, most of France's expenses were met by the United States.

Weakened and disillusioned, France was prepared to implement the Geneva Accords. President Dwight Eisenhower (1953–1961), wanting to continue the fight for a noncommunist Indochina, knew that Ho Chi Minh, a hero due to his anti-Japanese and anti-French leadership, would win a free election. The United States pressed France to leave in 1955, a year before the elections were to occur; and used Bao-dai and S.O.V. personnel to erect an anticommunist state based in Sai-gon and controlling territory corresponding to the southern regroupment zone. The United States provided economic aid to Bao-dai, encouraging him to accept as prime minister Ngo Dinh Diem (1901–1963). Diem had supporters in Washington, who liked him as an anti-French and anticommunist nationalist; as a Catholic, he might rally his coreligionists.

With U.S. support, Prime Minister Diem organized a referendum in 1955 that allowed him to depose Bao-dai and elevate himself to the presidency of the R.V.N. The United States poured aid and advisors into the South to create a state with an armed force (Army of the Republic of Vietnam, ARVN) that could contain the D.R.V. With U.S. support, Diem canceled the elections scheduled for 1956. There were now two Vietnams: the D.R.V., founded by Ho in 1945 (capital at Ha-noi); and the R.V.N., founded by Diem in 1955 (at Sai-gon). Indigenous support for the R.V.N. was largely limited to the civil servants and military officers who had served France or the S.O.V.; the landed elites of the Mekong Delta; and Catholics, many of whom had fled the D.R.V. Most of the rest of the R.V.N.'s population either supported the communists or wanted to be left alone to rebuild their lives.

The Communist Party, leading the D.R.V., sought to reunify Vietnam under its authority. Its attempts to destroy, and U.S. efforts to save, the R.V.N. constituted the Second Indochina, or Vietnam, War from 1960 to 1975. The R.V.N. was vulnerable, for Diem's misguided policies and arbitrary brutality alienated many southerners, communist and otherwise. In spring 1960 the Party supported the founding of the National Front for the Liberation of South Vietnam (NLF) (which Diemists called Viet Cong), dedicated to destroying the R.V.N., terminating U.S. influence, and reunifying Vietnam. Led by the Party's Ha-noi–based Central Committee, the NLF's rank and file were mostly southerners, which allowed the D.R.V. to deny fostering insurgency.

President John F. Kennedy (1961–1963) continued America's commitment to the R.V.N. but tried to make its responses flexible and appropriate. Among the measures implemented were increased aid and advisors, special forces, and programs to isolate guerrillas from the population. None had much impact. Confident of foreign backing and unwilling to conciliate its nationalist opposition, Diem's regime was corrupt, repressive, and unpopular. The NLF mobilized peasants by exploiting their discontent. It claimed to be carrying on traditions of opposition to foreign domination. It implemented land reform to attract landless and land-poor peasants, the majority in some southern provinces. Like the Viet Minh, the NLF terrorized and eliminated the recalcitrant. By these means, it founded a village-level infrastructure, and the R.V.N. could not destroy it. The NLF's local recruiting was supplemented by the infiltration of cadres, troops, and supplies from the D.R.V. via the Ho Chi Minh Trail, which wound from the D.R.V. through Laos and Cambodia into the R.V.N.

Diem had become so unpopular that ARVN officers decided to oust him. Encouraged by promises of aid from the Kennedy administration, the officers overthrew Diem and murdered him on November 1–2, 1963. The South was ruled by successive juntas until General Nguyen Van Thieu (b. 1923) emerged supreme and had himself elected president in 1967; he would head the R.V.N. until 1975.

By 1963, the R.V.N. held the cities, but most villages were controlled by the NLF. President Lyndon Johnson (1963–1969) intervened directly by bombing the D.R.V. and sending U.S. troops to the South: in 1968, at the height of U.S. involvement, they numbered a half million. U.S. forces used search and destroy tactics against the NLF's (and later PAVN's) main-force units while the ARVN focused on bringing villagers under control. In 1964, the D.R.V. began sending PAVN units to the South. Revolutionary forces (PAVN and NLF) in the South were outnumbered by the United States and ARVN by three to one in manpower, with greater disparities in equipment. The war was stalemated by 1967, making the situation untenable for the United States. Bombing tiny Vietnam had made America an international pariah, and so many U.S. troops were in Vietnam that other global commitments could not be met. Contrary to expectations, bombing the North rallied people around the Communist Party in a perceived common effort against aggression. The U.S. government, conscious of international opinion and fearful of Chinese or Soviet intervention, observed self-imposed constraints: it limited bombing of population centers, at least initially; it did not use nuclear weapons; it did not invade the North. The bombing was also militarily problematic for the United States: the D.R.V. used Soviet anti-aircraft systems that downed more than 1,000 planes and as many pilots.

Eventually U.S. public opinion turned against involvement: before 1967 most Americans had supported the war; afterwards, most opposed it. Following the PAVN's 1968 Tet Offensive, Johnson, fearing an increasingly costly, inconclusive war, stopped bombing the D.R.V. and initiated negotiations in Paris between the United States and the D.R.V., with R.V.N. and NLF participation.

In the context of the Paris talks, President Richard Nixon (1969–1974) began "Vietnamization": withdrawal of U.S. troops while reinforcing the ARVN. The goal was to calm domestic antiwar pressure by bringing U.S. troops home while forcing the Communist Party to settle by denying it the possibility of victory. In 1973, a breakthrough occurred, leading to the Paris Accords. The United States, the D.R.V., the NLF, and the R.V.N. signed a treaty calling for an end to U.S. intervention and for Vietnamese reconciliation through peaceful means, but the parties had not resolved their differences and so provided no viable mechanism by which it could occur.

After American withdrawal, the Vietnamese sides violated the cease-fire, leading to a "postwar war." Congress prevented Nixon from intervening and began reducing aid to the R.V.N., but the ARVN, larger and better armed than the NLF/PAVN, retained the means to defend itself. Its problems were psychological and strategic. ARVN officers were demoralized by their "betrayal" at the hands of the Americans. Unaccustomed to relying on themselves, they felt that the end was inevitable so they focused on feathering their nests and planning their escapes. Strategically, Thieu erred by trying to hold too much territory, spreading troops thinly, making them vulnerable. When the PAVN attacked the Central Highlands in spring 1975, ARVN units retreated in disorder; local defeat became generalized rout. ARVN officers and troops felt the end was near; in the main, they acted to save themselves. They thought that the end had come; and so it had.

THE SOCIALIST REPUBLIC

When the R.V.N. fell on April 30, 1975, the PAVN administered the South until the D.R.V.'s structures expanded. In 1976, Vietnam was reunified, becoming Viet Nam Cong Hoa Xa Hoi Chu Nghia, or Socialist Republic of Vietnam (S.R.V.). Ha-noi, the D.R.V.'s capital, became the national capital; Sai-gon, ex-capital of the defunct R.V.N., became Thanh Pho Ho Chi Minh or Ho Chi Minh City. The Ha-noi–based Dang Lao Dong Viet Nam, or Vietnam Workers' Party (VWP), renamed itself Dang Cong San Viet Nam, or Vietnam Communist Party (VCP). In 1980, a new

The *Quoc Hoi*, seat of the S.R.V.'s National Assembly, Ha-noi, northern Vietnam

Constitution was promulgated to stress the regime's Leninist nature and socialist goals. Government was based on parallel hierarchies of Party and state: policy is set at the Party's higher levels, with application left to the state. The VCP general secretary controls the personnel and agenda of the VCP and the S.R.V.'s state structure. Le Duan held the position until 1986, when he was replaced by Nguyen Van Linh; Linh retired in June 1991; the torch was passed to his protégé, Do Muoi; from 1997 to the present, it has been held by Le Kha Phieu.

At war's end, Vietnam faced dire economic problems. From 1955 to 1975, the R.V.N.'s economy had relied on U.S. aid and the expenditures of American personnel. This ceased in 1975, by which time the South had been devastated, its forests defoliated, its farms cratered. The war also left millions of refugees; hundreds of thousands of demobilized ARVN soldiers; hundreds of thousands of drug addicts; hundreds of thousands of invalids; tens of thousands of prostitutes.

Such problems would have been daunting regardless of the approach, but S.R.V. policies exacerbated problems. Le Duan implemented centralized economic planning; nationalization of industry; and agricultural collectivization. This model had been tried in the D.R.V. in the 1950s and failed to meet the growing population's needs, but Soviet bloc aid had allowed the Party to

Construction worker using *don ganh*, shoulder
pole, to transport crushed rocks, Chau-doc province, southern Vietnam

conceal that failure and ignore its lessons. In 1978, a like program was implemented in the South. Industry was nationalized and run by the State
Planning Commission, which determined the production of each sector and
plant. It coordinated the exchanges among units to ensure that raw materials
were available and that products had buyers. State-appointed managers were
told what to make, where to buy raw materials and at what price, to whom
to sell, and how much to charge. To succeed, managers had to meet quotas;
if a factory ran a deficit, the state would make it up. Since managers did not
face market competition, they were not motivated to maintain quality. There
was much latitude for corruption.

Substandard products were accepted by inspectors for bribes. Industrial
products were too old-fashioned or shoddy for sale in global markets, constraining imports. The USSR provided two billion dollars annually, but most

Urbanite displaying caged roosters for sale, Ho Chi Minh
City, southern Vietnam

of this went into large-scale projects, many of which were troubled by mis-
management or corruption. Collectivization began in 1978, with similar
results. Landholders lost their holdings and became wage-laborers on com-
munally owned farms. Farmers were told what and how much to produce;
the state bought rice at fixed rates for distribution at subsidized prices. The
goal was the socialist one that the state should provide for all, but the system
failed to provide adequately for the Vietnamese of the South, as it had failed
in the North. Farmers had little incentive to produce beyond their subsistence
needs: they could keep only about 20 percent of the harvest, with the rest
going to the state. Increments in production generated by producers' dili-
gence or creativity could be obtained by the state by manipulating quotas
and pricing. Unable to keep pace with a growing population, the state bought
rice from other Asian countries but was unable to ensure decent nutrition.
Lines formed at state stores to buy scarce rations. Malnutrition became
chronic. Some survived by the black market, selling medicines sent by relatives abroad.

Given the VWP's monopolization of political life and the desperation

Hai the Tailor, an independent artisan working in an open-air stall in Ho Chi Minh City, southern Vietnam

created by its economic measures, an exodus of hundreds of thousands of "boat people" began in spring 1978. Leaving was illegal, but officials co-operated in return for bribes. Those who could not afford protection took their chances; many were caught and jailed, some repeatedly. Those who escaped spent months or years in refugee camps in nearby countries before being accepted for resettlement in the West. Thousands drowned or were victimized by pirates, who robbed, raped, and murdered them. Neighboring countries' receptivity waned; they began turning away boats, firing on them or towing them to sea. International outcry finally forced the S.R.V. to meet with the concerned countries. Meeting in Geneva in July 1979, the participants founded the Orderly Departure Program, ODP. Vietnam agreed to end illegal emigrations and begin processing refugees for emigration; Southeast Asian states agreed to accept boat people until they could be resettled in the West; Western states agreed to accept more refugees for resettlement; Japan agreed to pay many of the program's expenses. ODP reduced the flow of illegal refugees but did not stop it.

These difficulties discredited Le Duan's policies. After his death in 1986, the Party's Sixth Congress elected General Secretary Nguyen Van Linh, who launched *Doi Moi* (Renovation), attempting to raise production via market incentives with limited political liberalization. The VCP would remain supreme in politics but would partially withdraw from economics to let the market operate. Under Nguyen Van Linh and Do Muoi, who took control in 1991 due to Nguyen Van Linh's ill health, the state discontinued forced purchases and distribution of rice. The borders were opened to foreign trade, and foreign-investment laws were passed to attract capital. Control over land was returned to farming families via long-term agreements: in return for paying fixed amounts to the state each year, they were allowed to use land for fifteen years with a right to renew the contract. Produce above the fixed fee was theirs to keep or sell. Many large-scale, state-owned projects were abandoned. Emphasis shifted to agriculture and consumer goods, and the state's role in these sectors declined. Factory managers were told that they would have to decide what to make, find and purchase raw materials inside or outside Vietnam, and market goods on their own initiative. If factories were not profitable, bankruptcy became a possibility. Private firms were free to set up businesses and trade domestically and internationally. The result has been rising production and improved living standards. Vietnam is a rice exporter for the first time since the 1930s. Despite these improvements and vast potential, Vietnam is one of Asia's poorest countries. Many years and much investment will be needed for it to catch its neighbors.

The new route to growth is not without hazards. Economic liberalization has rewarded people with capital, knowledge, entrepreneurial skill, and political connections; those lacking these prerequisites have lagged, raising the specter of a new class structure, with elite "red capitalists" (*tu ban do*) at the top and impoverished masses at the bottom. Moreover, since economic liberalization has dismantled much of the public sector, the New Poor, a significant minority, are losing access to health care and education. As industrialization accelerates without effective regulation, ecological costs are mounting: pollution of air and water, destruction of forests, and over-fishing of rivers and coastal seas. Finally, whether economic reform will lead to political liberalization is uncertain. While the 1992 Constitution no longer proclaims Leninism's centrality, it continues to insist on the Party's leading role.

3

Thought and Religion

INTRODUCTION

VIETNAM IS OFTEN DESCRIBED as a Buddhist or Confucian country, and atlases display shaded maps indicating its Buddhist, Confucian, and other populations. In reality, Vietnam's position at a crossroads of civilizations has exposed the peoples inhabiting what is now S.R.V. territory to many traditions, and most pre-colonial Viet held beliefs derived from multiple sources. It is thus impossible to say with certainty the number of followers of particular faiths in any era, past or present.

In addition to Animism (the belief that spirits inhabit nature), which was common throughout Asia, most major religions, including Taoism, Buddhism, Confucianism, Christianity, Hinduism, and Islam have penetrated and are still followed in the lands that constitute the S.R.V. The Viet rarely accepted beliefs or practices wholly as presented to them. They adopted and adapted foreign traditions, blending them with indigenous beliefs and with each other. By Nguyen times Vietnam presented a diverse mosaic; its peoples followed many traditions and did not see them as contradictory. Most Vietnamese followed varieties of Animism flavored with religious Taoism and devotional Buddhism. Scholars and officials, though not so distant from the village world as they purported to be, criticized the "superstitious" nature of such practices, stressing "rational" Confucian ones instead.

ANIMISM

In the early 1900s, one observer noted that "the true religion of the Vietnamese is the cult of the spirits. This religion has no history, because it dates from the origins of the race."[1] This "cult of the spirits," or Animism, denotes beliefs, mostly indigenous, that the world is inhabited by multitudes of spiritual beings.

Pre-colonial Viet believed that spirits inhabited rocks, trees, animals, and the rest of the natural world; and that people should propitiate them to avoid disasters and attract success. Spirits inhabited large trees, oddly shaped rocks, bodies of water, or shaded areas, and villagers tried to propitiate their denizens—or to avoid them entirely. Villagers were careful not to mention spirits by name; by saying the name, one evoked the being and risked its wrath. For example, tigers, seen as vessels of powerful spirits, were called *ong* ("grandfather"). Villagers gave children unattractive names so that spirits would not harm them; the names were changed when the child reached adulthood. In many families, children were referred to by their family ranking instead of by names. Southern families began counting from two, as the firstborn son would likely be of interest to malevolent spirits. Thus, siblings addressed their eldest brother, who was really older brother number one, as *anh hai*, "older brother two."

The spirits of large animals, such as whales, dolphins, and tigers, were venerated. In coastal southern and central Vietnam, villagers notified imperial authorities when a beached whale was found, and, with their approval, buried the animal. The person who found the carcass assumed the role of the whale-spirit's "firstborn son" in the ceremonies, mourning as if his own father had died. Three years later villagers disinterred the bones and installed them in a temple. The Nguyen courts gave villages licenses to conduct these rituals and granted the whale-spirits titles such as *Nam-hai Tuong-Quan Ngoc-Lan Ton-Than* ("Honored Spirit, Jade-Scaled Admiral of the South Sea"). Villagers believed that these ceremonies induced the whale-spirit to protect them and ensure bountiful catches.

Humans were believed to have two kinds of souls: three *hon*, and seven (for men) or nine (for women) *phach* or *via*. Distinctions are made between the *hon*, considered to be more spiritual, and the *via*, more material. Some *via* were thought to be helpful entities, called *via lanh*, ("kind" spirits), while others, *via xau* ("wicked" spirits), were malicious. A person could harbor good and evil *via*, and people known to have *via xau* were avoided. Spirits entered the body at conception or birth, and the day of birth is called *ngay via*, "spirit day." The births of famous men are said to have been occasioned by fragrant breezes, evidence of an auspicious spirit's entry. Spirits might temporarily leave a living person's body if the host suffered a fright, as reflected in the expression *so mat hon* ("so frightened that he lost his soul"). Death was the final separation between spirits and body, with the *via* staying in the corpse's vicinity and the *hon* leaving for the next world—and reincarnation, Buddhists believed.

Since people's spirits survived the host body's death, they, like other spirits, were capable of acting in the world of the living. With a medium's aid, they were asked for advice, protection, and material benefits. Ancestral spirits were the most important since they cared about their descendants' well-being. For an extended family, the proper burial of deceased ancestors and worship of their spirits ensured the latter's welfare and prompted their benevolent intervention. Wealthier lineages maintained inalienable lands called *huong hoa* ("fire and incense") to provide resources for the ancestral cult; poorer families tried to reserve a room or section of the home for an ancestral altar. Ceremonies involving offerings (of food, incense, drink, and betel) and prostration were conducted in the deceased's honor on *Tet* (the New Year) and the *gio*, or death anniversary. Pre-colonial Vietnamese did not celebrate birthdays per se, although children received gifts of money called *tien mung tuoi* ("age-celebrating money") at New Year's celebrations, and a person's sixtieth year (*luc tuan*) was considered an important milestone. Since colonial times, some urban families have taken up the practice of Western-style birthday celebrations complete with cakes and candles. Smaller offerings of fruit, incense, or alcohol were made to mark milestones in family members' lives, such as the birth of children. Ancestor worship was common to Viet of all faiths, including, in attenuated form, Catholics, despite the ecclesiastical hierarchy's prohibition of it.[2] Today, even the most Westernized Vietnamese, in Vietnam or abroad, maintain an ancestral altar in the home before which they burn incense or make offerings. There is currently a revival of ancestor worship in the S.R.V., manifested in ordinary people's efforts to set up altars, repair and visit familial graves, or assemble family members to commemorate *gio*.

The spirits of people who had died far from home, or of those with neglectful descendants, became "wandering souls" (*vong hon*). They might harm anyone they encountered, causing illness or accidents, and villagers protected themselves by erecting altars in fields and along roads; passersby made offerings of flowers or incense to appease the spirit. During the "Feast of Wandering Souls" on the full-moon night of the seventh lunar-calendar month, incense and food offerings in banyan leaf containers were left in outdoor shrines to nourish *vong hon*. Apprehension about *vong hon* persists in the

Animist worshiper near Hue City, central Vietnam

S.R.V., whose highways are lined with altars to appease accident victims' spirits.

At the community level, villagers placated local spirits linked to the village and charged with protecting it. Since about the 1400s, each village has had a *dinh*, or communal house, used for council meetings and rituals honoring the *thanh hoang*, the village's patron deity. As a lineage worshiped its ancestors to obtain family-specific benefits, each village honored its patron deity in hopes of winning support for the village as a whole. Deities were chosen from among many candidates, including village founders, historical figures, and animals. The deity was enshrined in an altar in the *dinh* and honored by sacrifices of pigs or buffalo that were ritually offered to the deity and consumed by the notables.

The imperial states regulated Animistic practices to legitimize imperial rule and prevent *ta giao* ("heterodox teachings") from corrupting morals and promoting rebellion. We have seen how the Nguyen-era courts granted burial licenses to whale-worshiping villagers. The courts also tried to formalize local ancestor worshiping along Confucian lines to encourage filial piety. Filial sons and daughters, it was believed, became loyal adult subjects. Emperors also tried to regulate the worship of villagers' protective spirits. The Nguyen required that villages secure court approval of candidates for a protective spirit. When it accepted a nominee, it issued a "spirit-warrant," or *sac-than*, which named and ranked the deity, described its services, and confirmed its duty of protecting locals in return for worship.

TAOISM

Taoism (*Dao-giao*) originated in China during the struggles preceding the founding of the Qin Empire in 221 B.C.E. Its seminal text is *The Classic of the Way and Virtue*, a collection of works attributed to Laozi, a mythical figure whose name means "Old Master" (*Lao-tu*). Living in turbulent times, the Taoists looked back to a Golden Age, when, they believed, humans had lived in harmony with the Tao, a transcendent principle that acted by combining two properties, "concentration" (*am*) and "expansion" (*duong*). All things derive from a combination of the two, with *am* supplying matter or solidity, and *duong* subtle principle or spirit. Golden Age kings had lived in harmony with the Tao, pacifying the world by "nonaction." As humans became "civilized" and corrupted, rulers and subjects ceased to follow the Tao, instead contending for wealth and power. The solution was to return to the simplicity and harmony with natural forces that had preceded civilization. Taoists longed for a sage-king who would not meddle in people's affairs or provoke futile wars, but who could return humans to their former affinity with the Tao.

However, China's political stage would be dominated by rulers espousing Confucianism while utilizing Legalist administrative techniques. With no sage-ruler to provide a model of Taoist statecraft or ecclesiastical structure to enforce philosophical conformity, Chinese Taoism assumed a popular or religious coloration. Believing that understanding nature allows one to command its powers, Taoist priests explored alchemy and inner hygiene as routes to immortality. They also worshiped deities such as the Jade Emperor, the king of heaven, and practiced shamanism to contact spirits to ask their advice and protection.

Although Chinese philosophical Taoism has had little impact in Vietnam, religious or popular Taoism, resembling spirit worship, was well received from the early centuries of Chinese domination. Taoist concepts of using purification and incantations to manipulate the universe's natural forces or to invoke its spiritual inhabitants appealed to Animistic worshipers. Chinese Taoist masters must have looked like sophisticated practitioners of the same magical or spirit-worshiping arts that Yueh peoples had known since pre-Chinese times. Likewise, the Taoist pantheon's deities blended easily into the Viet spiritual universe. The Jade Emperor (*Ngoc Hoang Thuong De*) and his court became—and remain—common objects of worship in Vietnamese temples. Animist-Taoist blending was so seamless that, in modern times, scholars and even practitioners cannot always tell which practices are indigenous Animism and which are imported Taoism.

By Nguyen times, Taoist masters called *thay*, "father" and, by extension, "teacher" or "master," were entrenched in the Vietnamese scene, serving as healers, mediums, and geomancers. For example, since illness was thought to be caused by spirits, *thay* were asked to identify the culprit and explain how to propitiate it. The victim's relatives invoked the spirit and beseeched it to accept worship and offerings in exchange for leaving the afflicted party alone. Likewise, burial involved selecting an auspicious spot for interment, and masters of geomancy (*phong thuy*, "wind and water") would analyze the relationships among mountains, rivers, and other formations before rendering a verdict.

Confucian rulers looked askance on such "superstitions" (*me tin*) and tried to regulate or suppress them, but popular demand for Taoist ritual and worship ensured their survival. For example, anthropologists have documented Taoist practices among the Perfume River's "boat people" in the 1990s. Despite the opposition of the S.R.V.'s officials, who condemn such practices as superstitious, locals continue to consult Taoist masters as healers, fortunetellers, and mediums.

BUDDHISM

Like Taoism, Buddhism developed abroad before entering Viet lands. In traditional accounts, the historical Buddha was born a prince around 566 B.C.E. in the Sakya kingdom (on the border of modern India and Nepal). His given name was Siddhartha, his clan name Gautama; after enlightenment, he was called Sakyamuni or "Sage of the Sakya" (*Thich-ca-mau-ni*).[3] Finding court life meaningless in the face of omnipresent suffering, he left to seek wisdom. By living simply and practicing meditation, full awareness of reality came to him under a pipal tree, and he became a Buddha, or an "Enlightened One." He spent the rest of his life teaching and founding monastic communities in the Ganges Valley.

His doctrine, or dharma, is based on Four Noble Truths: (1) Life is suffering. (2) The origin of suffering is desire. (3) To end suffering, eliminate desire. (4) Desire can be ended by following the Eightfold Path: Right Understanding, Right Resolve, Right Speech, Right Action, Right Livelihood, Right Effort, Right Mindfulness, and Right Meditation. The Buddha emphasized that, given reality's variable nature, attempts at worldly happiness fail. Only by accepting the Four Noble Truths and following the Eightfold Path can one extinguish the (false) sense of self and its cravings. Early Buddhism thus stressed self-discipline aimed at attaining nirvana (Sanskrit, "blowing out"; Vietnamese, *Niet Ban*), liberation from suffering during one's lifetime and escape from rebirth. The Buddha did not claim to be a savior, prophet, or deity. After his death around 483 B.C.E. disciples interpreted the dharma differently, and rival schools arose.

The school that claims to hold to the original teachings calls itself Theravada, "Way of the Elders." It stresses that nirvana must be sought by following the path laid down by the Buddha, with each person working out his or her destiny. It attracted followers in India and abroad, but to some its seemingly selfish focus on individual salvation meant that only a few could reach nirvana.

In the first century C.E. new interpretations arose in India stressing the Buddha's superhuman nature and emphasizing semidivine previous and future Buddhas as well as bodhisattvas ("wisdom beings"), who had liberated themselves but remained in the world to help others. Buddhas and bodhisattvas were worshiped and asked for help, material and spiritual. Since proponents claimed that their doctrines could save all beings, they called it Mahayana, or Great Vehicle, in contrast to earlier doctrines, which they termed Hinayana, or Lesser Vehicle. (In Vietnamese, Mahayana and Hinayana are *Dai Thua* and *Tieu Thua*, respectively.)

Although Buddhism declined in India after the twelfth century, by then it had spread widely. Theravada Buddhism eventually spread to Ceylon, Burma, Thailand, Laos, Cambodia, and southern Vietnam, where it is still practiced. Mahayana Buddhism penetrated Tibet, China, Japan, Korea, and Vietnam, remaining popular in all of them. Everywhere, Buddhism blended with indigenous customs, beliefs, and practices.

Buddhism entered Viet lands in the first centuries C.E. during Chinese rule, although the precise dates of entry and means of transmission are unknown. The Viet were probably introduced to Buddhism by seaborne monks en route from India to China; terrestrial links with China later became common. While Theravada influence via the sea route or contact with Khmers living in what became southern Vietnam cannot be discounted, Vietnamese

Buddhism mainly derives from Mahayana traditions developed in China. The Viet were not passive recipients, however; they elaborated on received doctrines and contributed to developments in Chinese Buddhism as well.

During the early independence era, from the tenth century until the founding of the Later Le Dynasty in the fifteenth century, Buddhism played a vital role in Viet society and government, sometimes serving as the state religion. Buddhist monks needed to be literate in Chinese to read Mahayana scriptures, and this qualified them for state service at a time when the loyalty of Confucian scholars was suspect in light of the support that some had given to Chinese occupation regimes. Monks also seemed less threatening to rulers, for their severing of family ties (*xuat gia*) and commitment to celibacy suggested that they would not covet the throne. During the early Viet monarchies, monks served as imperial advisors, officials, and diplomats; royally sponsored pagodas in distant corners of the land symbolized royal power's reach and acted as a unifying factor. For monks, political activity was justified by the doctrine that "abstention from the world" (*xuat the*) was compatible with "worldly participation" (*nhap the*); insights gained from withdrawal and meditation could benefit living beings through political activity. Buddhism's influence on political life in this era is reflected by the fact that several monarchs were ordained as monks, either before accession to the throne or after leaving it. In short, the early dynasties derived legitimacy from sponsoring Buddhism and found monks useful in exercising power. Given its prominence at court and in the villages during the first four centuries after Chinese rule ended, later Vietnamese Buddhists consider this a "Golden Age."

From the founding of the Later Le Dynasty in the fifteenth century, Confucianism's revival as state ideology and the increasing role it played in the training and recruitment of bureaucrats meant an eclipse of Buddhism at the imperial courts and reduction in the formal political roles of its priesthood. Nonetheless, some members of the imperial and warlord families were lay practitioners and sponsors of temples and monasteries. Moreover, Buddhism's local influence continued during this period, even growing during the *noi chien* (civil war), given the decline of central power and struggles among military rulers less committed to Confucianism. With diminished access to royal or princely power, Buddhism entrenched itself deeply in the villages, its monks adapting to local society by practicing geomancy, astrology, and healing.

Then, after 1802, the Nguyen emperors, considering Buddhism an impediment to Confucian policies, tried to control its practice. Measures included curbs on building pagodas, limits on the size of the *sangha*, and

Chua Thien-mu, or Heavenly Lady Pagoda, Hue City, central Vietnam

examinations to ensure its doctrinal competency. The Nguyen also supported monasteries and pagodas in the Hue region to concentrate high-level Buddhist personnel and activities in a central location, where, dependent on royal patronage, they could be supervised. It was under Nguyen rule that Hue became a center of Buddhism, and many of its celebrated Buddhist structures date from this time.

While some elite Viet explored doctrines derived from Chinese meditation sects, most Viet practitioners were attracted to devotional and spiritualist aspects. Given the Animistic ability to fuse or blend with other religious beliefs, the Mahayana's multiple Buddhas and bodhisattvas were readily adopted; like Taoist divinities, they were useful for seeking worldly success and advancing the fortunes of departed spirits in the hereafter.

Vietnamese Buddhism's blend with Animism can be seen in the array of statues installed in pagodas. An early colonial-era pagoda in Tonkin, for example, was usually an H-shaped structure hidden behind trees and surrounded by walls. Once inside the walls, practitioners entered the pagoda proper through the right side of the H, as it were, and walked into the bar joining the two sides. At the entrance were statues of *Ho-Phap*, or "Guardians of the Law," the *Thien-Huu* and *Ac-Huu*, who encouraged the good and punished the wicked. The main sanctuary and hall of ceremonies was housed in the rectangular central structure (in the "bar" joining the two sides of the H), in which most of the statuary was displayed. Sakyamuni Buddha appeared as a newborn baby, as an emaciated ascetic, and as a reclining adult. The scenes represent, respectively, his miraculous birth, in which he emerged from his mother's side and walked in the four directions, proclaiming that this was to be his last birth; a period during which he sought wisdom via asceticism; his last sermon, given while reclining on his right side, before entry into final nirvana.

In most pagodas, statues and images devoted to the historical Buddha were overshadowed by those of Amitabha (*A-di-da*), Buddha of the Pure Land of the Western Paradise (*Tinh do*). *A-di-da* is believed to transport petitioners to his Western paradise, where, free of distractions and instructed by Buddhas and bodhisattvas, they practice diligently and attain nirvana. Maitreya (*Di-lac*), a corpulent figure with an exposed torso and smiling face, symbolizing absence of worldly cares, was also prominently featured. He is the "Future Buddha," who waits in the Tushita Heaven for the end of Sakyamuni's reign, when he will descend to earth to teach the dharma anew. Pagodas also housed statues of the Bodhisattva Avalokitesvara, "the Lord Who Looks Down" in compassion for worldly suffering. A male figure in early Indian Buddhism, Avalokitesvara's identity changed in East Asia, where compassion is often considered a "feminine" virtue. While most Chinese visions of Avalokitesvara range from gender-neutral to female, Vietnamese emphasize the female *Quan The Am*, the "Perceiver of the World's Sounds," who responds to suffering beings' cries. She often appears as a thousand-eyed, thousand-armed deity, symbolic of attentiveness and helpfulness.

Statues of non-Buddhist deities were also found, including Taoism's Jade Emperor. Smaller buildings attached to the sides at the rear of the main structure housed statues of Buddhism's eighteen *arhats*, or saints. As a deterrent, statues of the Kings of Hell inflicting on sinners tortures appropriate to their sins were displayed. A separate room was reserved for cults devoted to a pagoda's deceased abbots, whose cremated remains might be housed in *stupa* outside the pagoda but within its grounds. Another room housed shrines to deceased lay followers whose relatives had paid a sum called *hau* so that the monks would conduct rituals to ease their suffering in hell and speed felicitous reincarnation.

Buddhism played a political role during the Indochina Wars, particularly the Second. Claiming that Diem favored Catholics at the expense of the R.V.N.'s Buddhist majority in regulating religious practices, selection to state posts, and aid distribution, activist monks mobilized urbanites for anti-R.V.N. protests. Blaming the United States for the war, which they described

The Bodhisattva *Quan The Am* with Pipal or Wisdom Tree as backdrop, Chau-doc City, southern
Vietnam

as one pitting Vietnamese against Vietnamese while devastating their home-
land, they advocated the R.V.N.'s overthrow and national reconciliation under a coalition government to include the NLF, Buddhists, and other
nationalists. The movement garnered a large urban following, including
many who were not necessarily devout but supported the monks as symbols
of resistance to foreign influence and the Diem regime. In May 1963, R.V.N.
policemen shot into a crowd of demonstrators, killing nine. In protest, monks
went into public places, had themselves drenched with gasoline, and lit
matches, meditating as they were consumed by flames. Such scenes appeared
in the international media, outraging public opinion. President Kennedy
urged President Diem to negotiate with Buddhist leaders, but Diem cracked
down: thousands of students and demonstrators were arrested; many were
beaten by the police. In a raid on Xa Loi Pagoda in Sai-gon, for example, a

number of monks were killed. The resulting outrage contributed to the Kennedy administration's decision to support the ARVN in its November 1963 coup d'etat.

Conflicts between state and *sangha* in the R.V.N. did not end with Diem's death. In spring 1964, Buddhist leaders institutionalized their political role by founding the Unified Vietnamese Buddhist Religious Association (*Giao-hoi Phat-giao Viet Nam Thong-nhat*). It grouped Vietnamese Buddhists under a central hierarchy, which divided southern Vietnam into seven zones, each of which was subdivided into provincial-level, district-level, and village-level administrative units. As the head of the Association's policy-making body, the Council of the Buddhist Hierarchy, Thich Tri Quang militated against politicians supporting escalation of the war and in favor of those supporting neutralism. Finally, the Buddhist movement, never so unified as its name suggested, was suppressed by force in 1966–1968, its key figures silenced by imprisonment or exile. While Buddhist-inspired opposition to the American-supported regimes in Sai-gon continued at a lower level until 1975, Buddhists would never again bring such sustained pressure against any Vietnamese government. Despite the Association's opposition to the R.V.N. and the United States, Buddhism has not fared better than the other organized religions under the S.R.V.

CONFUCIANISM

Confucianism derives from the thought of Kong Fuzi (551–479 B.C.E.), a Chinese thinker roughly contemporaneous with the early Taoists. Like them, Confucius (as he is known in English) was troubled by the times in which he lived. He believed that his historical studies had revealed the answer to contemporary problems and sought ministerial rank to put things right. He never attained sufficient authority to put his ideas into practice, however, and withdrew to become a teacher, a role in which he found enduring influence.

Confucius taught that ancient rulers had practiced the Way of Virtue, and the people had followed their positive examples. He described these rulers' attributes as *ren* ("benevolence"; Vietnamese *nhan*). The problem, Confucius believed, was that his contemporaries had forgotten how to act in such a fashion. For this he blamed the reigning kings: they pursued wealth and power rather than virtue, setting bad examples. Scholars who knew the Way of Virtue—Confucius and his disciples—had to teach kings how to return to the Way. The people would follow a virtuous ruler's example, as reeds bend before the wind. To help rulers and people act virtuously, Confucius argued that people must accept fixed roles within a social hierarchy: "Let the ruler rule as he should and the minister be a minister as he should. Let the father act as a father should and the son act as a son should." If each would meet the obligations of his or her role—for example, if rulers would practice *ren*—harmony would be restored. The teachings of Confucius and his disciples, along with older texts on which they relied, were eventually canonized as the Four Books and the Five Classics.

Confucianism was adopted by Chinese states, becoming their official doctrine from Han times (206 B.C.E.–222 C.E.) onwards. While the organization of Chinese states owed much to Legalist statecraft, Confucianism provided the rationale for imperial rule. As Confucianism evolved in China, it blended with other ideas regarding parallels between the human and natural worlds. A universal reason, it was believed, permeated and regulated natural phenomena, including the movements of the celestial bodies and the changing of the seasons. A virtuous emperor united the natural and human worlds by allowing this principle (*ly*) to pass undiminished through his person and then to permeate all people. Such a ruler, the Son of Heaven (*Thien-tu*), held a "Heavenly Mandate" (*Thien-menh*), a cosmic sanction that could be passed to his heirs as long as they were virtuous; and reflected on his officials when acting in their official capacities.

Thus, while the emperor was not, strictly speaking, divine, his family's claim to power rested on his role in linking the natural with the human worlds, ensuring prosperity, peace, and harmony on earth. Chinese emperors participated in rituals intended to maintain this harmony, making sacrifices to heaven and earth, appeasing the agricultural gods to ensure fertility and prosperity. The Confucian canon also became the curriculum on which candidates for administrative positions were tested. As such positions brought wealth and honor, generations of scholars poured over the canon, and Confucianism permeated Chinese society, particularly in education and family life.

Confucianism entered Viet lands during Chinese domination as the doctrine of state, imposed by Chinese officials and their local collaborators. With the rise of independent Viet monarchies in the tenth century, Confucian scholars, associated with China's occupation, were reduced to competing for influence with Buddhist monks, royal relatives, and militarists. Confucianism was but one of three doctrines on which rulers relied: with Buddhism and Taoism, it constituted the *tam giao dong nguyen*, the "three teachings from one source."

It was not until the Later Le Dynasty in the 1400s that Viet rulers adopted Confucianism as state ideology and initiated a Chinese-style bureaucracy and legal codes. The use of examinations on the Confucian canon for training and selection of officials encouraged men to master the Confucian doctrines, and for the next 400 years, elite thought was more heavily influenced by them. Reinforced by the state, Confucianism reached the masses, and family life was influenced by its ideas about the virtues of male domination, ancestor worship, and filial piety, although older practices, including those giving a relatively higher place to women than was the case in China, were not lost. The zenith for Confucian orthodoxy, bureaucratic procedure, and the influence of scholar-officials came under the early Nguyen Dynasty, just before Confucianism and the state that it legitimized began to face Western imperialism.

Even in Nguyen times, however, Confucianism's hold was firmer on the elite than on the common people, who were still attached to Mahayana Buddhism, popular Taoism, and Animism. Despite the Confucians' pretensions to rationalism and humanism, imperial Confucianism, in Vietnam as in China, admitted many religious practices—for example, the emperor's role as First Plowman, who opened the first furrow of the planting season.

Confucianism's sway among the elite began eroding with the Nguyen failure to deflect French aggression during the nineteenth century. In this context, many ex-officials led anti-French resistance movements based on Confucian concepts of monarchical loyalty (*trung quan*). When these movements failed to restore independent Confucian monarchy, it became obvious to politically conscious Vietnamese that the Confucian model of state and society could not generate the power to resist Western aggression. To make matters worse, the many Nguyen princes willing to serve as "puppet emperors" degraded the monarchy and Confucianism. Finally, with the ending of the civil service examinations in 1918, Confucian studies were divorced from bureaucratic appointment.

By the 1920s Confucianism's influence had faded, and many Vietnamese opposed to colonialism and the social evils that it fostered found Marxism an attractive alternative. Marxism served as a political religion, providing an historical explanation of Vietnam's crisis and promising liberation through revolutionary action. Still, even today many Communist Party members retain some attributes of Confucian scholars of old: a paternalistic attitude toward the people based on a sense of mission as carriers of a superior doctrine. Confucianism per se, however, never again exercised its former influence on Vietnamese public life, despite the efforts of scholars such as Tran Trong Kim to restore it; or those of Diem, who offered a refurbished Confucianism as an anticommunist national identity. Its residual effects can be seen in the continuing importance placed on the family and education.

CATHOLICISM

Introduced by missionaries in the 1500s, Catholicism is the most recent world religion to have a significant impact on Vietnamese life. The Viet elite found the new religion shocking in its worship of a single creator-deity to the exclusion of ancestors, village genii, and the emperor; the Le monarchs and the Trinh and Nguyen *chua* banned it. However, the severe *du cam dao*, or "edicts of interdiction" against the "heterodox teaching" (*ta giao*) of Catholicism, were often waived in practice, for the Nguyen-Trinh conflicts had created a context in which foreign support or technology might be decisive.

Catholicism's appeal was enhanced by the fact that missionaries learned Vietnamese and presented doctrines to peasants in ways the latter could understand. Their emphasis on the allegedly miracle-working powers of the saints or curative properties of holy water attracted villagers seeking supernatural "insurance." Further, the missionaries served as community leaders, distributing aid and helping reclaim land from the sea. By Nguyen times, Catholicism had had considerable success among the peasants of the North, where overcrowding and poverty were acute; its influence in the Center and South was more limited. By the French conquest, about 5 percent of Vietnamese (half a million people) were Catholics, and it was mainly among the masses that converts were found.

The missionaries, Viet priests, and their followers were resented by the unconverted Viet. The Le monarchs and the Trinh and Nguyen *chua* were alarmed by the missionaries' tendency to isolate the Catholic from the non-Catholic Viet, often founding separate Catholic villages. Moreover, the missionaries forbade followers to worship their ancestors and village deities. Since the dynasty regarded ancestor worship as training for political loyalty and regulated the worship of village deities, it was worried by the Catholics' refusal to participate fully. Many peasants were offended by the Catholics' refusal to contribute to communal festivals and rituals, which expressed the villagers' solidarity. When Catholics refused to contribute because of the "superstitious" nature of the ceremonies, the non-Catholic villagers had to increase their contributions to compensate. The material difficulties of non-Catholic villagers also increased when the Catholics withdrew to form their own communities. In such cases, the remaining villagers faced crushing taxation, for the monarchy did not take account of their reduced numbers.

Feuding arose between Catholic and non-Catholic villages and villagers over land ownership, water rights, and the like. After centuries of erratic efforts to stamp out Catholicism, the Nguyen Dynasty's Minh-Menh, seeking to safeguard Vietnam's independence and preserve (as he saw it) its Confucian morality, began issuing anti-Catholic edicts in the 1830s and enforcing them vigorously. His policies backfired, for the limited numbers of executions of missionaries (most of whom, by this time, were French) and Vietnamese Catholics under him and his successors would give France a justification for invasion.

The conquest further drove a wedge between the followers of the traditional faiths and the Catholics, for the French used the "persecution" of Catholics to rationalize attacks on Vietnam and called upon missionaries and Vietnamese Catholics for support. Some Vietnamese Catholics aided the French, deepening the chasm between the Catholics and the followers of traditional faiths. Many of the Vietnamese insurgents who resisted France's conquest condemned all Catholics as pro-French collaborators. After "pacification," French officials looked more favorably upon missionary work than had the independent Nguyen courts. Thanks to this privileged position under the colonial regime, the number of Catholics continued to grow, although many Vietnamese priests resented subordination to missionaries and chafed at charges that Vietnamese Catholics followed a "foreign religion" and supported colonialism.[4]

The Vietnamese Church supported the August Revolution of 1945, and many Vietnamese Catholics joined the Viet Minh, at least until 1949, when its Marxist-Leninist orientation hardened. By then, many Vietnamese Catholics left the movement, turning to the French for protection or charting a middle course. With France's defeat at Dien Bien Phu in 1954 and the partition of Vietnam at the Seventeenth Parallel, more than 800,000 northern Catholics fled South.

During French times, there had been one ecclesiastical structure for all Vietnam, subordinate to the Vatican but (by the 1900s) with a largely Vietnamese clergy. After the 1954 partition and throughout the Second Indochina War, the Catholics of the South remained under the Vatican, whereas those of the North came under a "patriotic" Catholic hierarchy, which was controlled by D.R.V. authorities and expected to cooperate with Party programs. By the 1960s, there were approximately 750,000 Catholics in the D.R.V., with close to 1,500,000 residing in the South due to the migrations of 1954–1956.

Catholic refugees provided a reliable base for Sai-gon's anticommunist regimes, particularly for Diem, who was a Catholic himself and saw to it that his coreligionists were well treated by the state. Catholic support was a mixed blessing, however, for the R.V.N.'s favoritism of the Catholics alienated the South's non-Catholic majority. While precise statistics are lacking, southern Catholics were well represented in the first waves of refugees who left Vietnam after the R.V.N.'s defeat in 1975. There are now about 5,000,000 Catholics in the S.R.V., with the increases mainly resulting from natural growth rather than conversions.[5] Although restoration and construction of churches supports S.R.V. claims of religious freedom, the reality is more complicated, as this chapter's concluding section indicates.

THE NEW SECTS

Many Vietnamese responded to the crisis of colonialism by adopting sectarian religions that combined and reinterpreted existing traditions. The most significant were the *Cao Dai* and *Hoa Hao*.

Cao Dai

Cao Dai beliefs draw upon Taoist, Confucian, Buddhist, Animist, and Catholic traditions, the last being critical for organization. *Cao Dai* means "High Platform," a supreme deity derived from the Taoist tradition. The formal name is *Dai Dao Tam Ky Pho Do*: "Great Way of the Third Amnesty of God." *Cao Dai* asserts that the Supreme Being had proclaimed two previous Ways to salvation: to the West through Moses and Jesus, and to the East through Laozi and Sakyamuni. Caodaists do not reject these doctrines but believe their "Third Amnesty" to be superior.

Caodaism began in 1919, when the *Cao Dai* supposedly manifested itself to Nguyen Van Chieu, a lower-level administrator in Cochin China, telling him to proclaim a new religion, the icon of which was an eye from which sunrays emanated, symbolizing omniscience and omnipresence. Chieu, timid by nature, preached for several years but attracted few followers. Then in 1924 he attended a séance in Sai-gon with Vietnamese who were merchants and officials in the French hierarchy. Caodaists believe that the Spirit ordered those attending to proclaim the doctrine widely. Among them was Le Van Trung, who became a devout believer. Chieu withdrew from an active role, and the dynamic Le Van Trung assumed the title of Great Master of the *Cao Dai*, reorganized the movement along Catholic lines (including a papacy, cardinals, bishops, monks, and nuns), and began intensive proselytizing.

Given the crisis provoked by colonialism, such a "neo-traditionalist" faith, which drew upon familiar elements but presented them in a new and dynamic

Local *Cao Dai* temple in Sa-dec City, southern Vietnam

way, was attractive, especially to peasants in the Mekong Delta. By 1926, it boasted 20,000 followers; at the height of its influence in the late 1950s and early 1960s, it had more than 1,000,000.

Cao Dai first steered a middle path between the Viet Minh and the French but eventually allied with the latter in return for promises of aid and autonomy. After the First Indochina War, the *Cao Dai*'s autonomous status and independent military power were crushed by Diem's forces in 1955 when the *Cao Dai* joined other sects in a failed anti-Diem coup. Many *Cao Dai* members, however, embittered at Sai-gon's actions, supported the NLF in the Second Indochina War, which has earned them limited tolerance in the post-1975 era.

Hoa Hao

Phat giao Hoa Hao ("*Hoa Hao* Buddhism") was founded by Huynh Phu So from Hoa Hao Village in the western Mekong Delta. A sickly child, So was sent by his parents to a local sorcerer for treatment. He learned the magical practices and millenarian views common among the region's Buddhist monks and Taoist masters but returned uncured after the master's death in 1939. He later experienced a seemingly miraculous recovery before his family altar and began healing and proselytizing in the area.

So's doctrines were a simplified devotional Buddhism mixed with Animist and Taoist practices and emphasizing the imminent ending of the world. *Hoa Hao* eschewed elaborate temples and paraphernalia. Its family-based rituals were limited to four daily prayers before a table draped in a red cloth and adorned with flowers, water, and incense. So criticized expensive funerals, gambling, and the use of alcohol and opium. He soon had more than 100,000 followers, who admired his apparent miracle-working ability and found the doctrine's simplicity and economy attractive; by the end of World War II, the *Hoa Hao* had more than 1,000,000 believers.

Like *Cao Dai, Hoa Hao* became politically active. So's apocalyptic prophecies and appeal to the Mekong Delta's peasants aroused the suspicions of the colonial regime, which exiled him to Laos. Japanese occupation forces returned him to Vietnam, protecting him while exploiting his anti-French nationalism. At the end of World War II the *Hoa Hao* controlled territories in the southwestern delta and sought to hold them against the returned French administration and its challengers, the Viet Minh. Since the *Hoa Hao* appealed to the peasantry and refused to enter the Viet Minh–dominated anti-French alliance, So was assassinated, presumably by Viet Minh, in 1947. This drove So's followers into the arms of the French, who supported the *Hoa Hao*'s new leaders against the Viet Minh until the end of the First Indochina War. When Diem was installed in Sai-gon in 1955, *Hoa Hao* leaders resisted his curtailment of their autonomy and influence. After a failed coup d'etat, *Hoa Hao* forces were decimated by Diem's forces. This confrontation reduced *Hoa Hao*'s political role, though its religious influence among the delta's peasantry lingers.

RELIGION IN THE SOCIALIST REPUBLIC

After the Second Indochina War, the S.R.V. took power in a reunited Vietnam. The Communist Party, which guides the S.R.V., is doctrinally atheist and wary of any group capable of challenging its rule. In a sense, the party assumed the role of Vietnam's Confucian-inspired dynasties, which believed that they had a monopoly of political wisdom and attempted to regulate religious practice. However, the modern party-state apparatus is more capable of interfering in the lives of its citizens than were the imperial states of yore. In practice, the Party—while encouraging a secular-scientific worldview and outlawing customs that it considers superstitious, wasteful, or degrading—has not waged violent mass campaigns to root out religious belief per se, as was the case in the Soviet Union.

Church-state conflicts in contemporary Vietnam have more to do with perceived institutional threats to the Party's power by the organized religions: Catholic, Buddhist, and sectarian. The Party infiltrates these organizations and tries to control their activities. Tension often derives from the Party's insistence that the religious organizations recruit and promote "patriotic" (procommunist) clergy. The religious organizations try to satisfy the Party's demands while maintaining their institutional autonomy and integrity. The religious organizations are paradoxically warned to limit their activities to religious matters, avoiding any political role.

Yet the Party also demands that they mobilize support for policies proclaimed by the Party and state organs on matters as unambiguously "political" as taxation and conscription. When religious leaders resist the Party's direction on issues deemed political by the Party, the security services do not hesitate to imprison monks or priests. The Party justifies such actions by pointing to alleged security risks posed by the supposedly illegal actions or foreign contacts of particular individuals rather than in terms of conflicts between church and state or between religious and Leninist viewpoints. By avoiding direct challenges to religious organizations or their belief systems, the Party keeps believers in the officially controlled institutions, where they can be more easily monitored, and does not risk driving them underground.

It is too early to discern *Doi Moi*'s long-term impact on Vietnamese religious practice. It appears, however, that the loosening of social controls, increases in prosperity, and disillusionment with Marxism-Leninism are resulting in more participation in traditional religious activities. For example, pagodas in large cities openly celebrate major Buddhist holidays, and these are well attended in a festive atmosphere by practitioners. Likewise, it is again common to observe elaborate funeral processions in the streets of major cities, despite official criticism and legal limitations of them in the recent past. In rural society also, Buddhist monks remain active, and pilgrimage sites such as famous pagodas are avidly visited by the faithful.

Ancestor worship is also experiencing a revival, perhaps as a way of preserving a sense of belonging to a larger extended family as the nuclear family becomes more common in urban areas. The continuing influence of popular Animism is evident in the plethora of shrines to accident victims along the S.R.V.'s highways. Furthermore, some traditional beliefs live on in official propaganda. For example, the Ho Chi Minh Museum in Hue City, in addition to exhibits illustrating the life of the late president, has a solemn-looking room decorated in red in which a bust of Ho Chi Minh rests on an "altar" and in front of which visitors leave "offerings" of flowers and incense. The continuity with worship of patron deities is obvious. In sum, despite the Party's official atheism, traditional religious beliefs, practices, and organizations give every appearance of maintaining or even strengthening their influence.

NOTES

1. Leopold Cadière, *Religious Beliefs and Practices of the Vietnamese*, trans. Ian W. Mabbett (Clayton, Victoria, Australia: Center of Southeast Asian Studies, 1989), 6.

2. In 1968, the Vatican began to allow Vietnamese Catholics to have ancestral altars. Even without them, ancestor worship had remained widespread among Vietnamese Catholics.

3. The "family name" *Thich* is taken by Vietnamese monks to symbolize that, upon ordination, they leave their birth families (*xuat gia*) to enter that of Sakyamuni Buddha.

4. Although Catholicism was held by many pre-colonial and colonial era Vietnamese to be a foreign faith, it was no more so than Confucianism, Buddhism, or Taoism. Whereas traditional faiths had had more time to adapt and were no longer perceived as foreign, Catholicism, a relative newcomer spread by foreign clergy associated with European powers, had not yet been able to do so.

5. There are also about 30,000 Protestants in the S.R.V., mostly minority peoples of the Central Highlands, where American missionaries were active during the wars.

4

Literature

VIETNAMESE LITERATURE may be separated into three categories according to whether it was originally written in *chu Han*, or Chinese characters; in *chu nom*, or vernacular characters; or in *quoc ngu*, or romanized script. As the last is the most widely used form at present, it will be the focus of this chapter.

IN CHINESE

As the Yueh peoples had not developed a writing system by the time of the Chinese occupation, they first expressed themselves in writing in Chinese. Since the few Vietnamese to have learned Chinese during this period were either involved in government (Chinese was the language of administration) or religion (it was needed to read Mahayana sutras), most of the texts produced were historical chronicles or Buddhist treatises. Few of these works have survived, but those that have suggest that Chinese influences predominated.

With the advent of independence in the tenth century, Chinese remained the language of administration as well as literary expression, and Chinese influence on forms and styles continued. Nonetheless, a sense of Viet identity began to pervade the works, and they may be considered part of the Vietnamese literary tradition and not merely a provincial form of Chinese literature. Moreover, given this stress on establishing an independent identity vis-à-vis the northern neighbor, Viet writing in Chinese was often indirectly aimed at Chinese and not only Viet readers.

While the Viet Tran (1225–1400) and Later Le (1428–1788) dynasties followed Chinese precedent in publishing Chinese-style dynastic chronicles, the texts reflected concerns to establish the ancientness and thus the independent origins of Viet monarchical traditions. For instance, *Dai Viet Su Ky Toan Thu* (*The Complete History of Great Viet*), published under Le patronage in 1479, traces Vietnamese history back to the semilegendary Hong Bang Dynasty. It was intended to demonstrate the existence of Viet imperial houses predating the Chinese conquest, implying that the present dynasty was legitimately continuing a time-honored tradition of independent dynastic rule.

Viet political and military leaders also often used Chinese to address their northern counterparts directly, acknowledging nominal vassalage to China but stressing a separate identity. For example, the scholar and military strategist Nguyen Trai (1380–1442) composed Chinese-language works to this end. Nguyen Trai contributed to Le Loi's defeat of the Chinese Ming Dynasty's occupation in 1428, leading to the founding of the Le Dynasty that year. The battle won, Le Loi, who became the first emperor of the new dynasty under the reign title Le Thai-to (ruled 1428–1433), asked Nguyen Trai to compose a victory proclamation. His *Binh Ngo Dai Cao* ("Great Proclamation of the Pacification of the Wu"), a masterpiece of Vietnamese literature written in Chinese, begins by referring to Dai Viet's unique geography and culture as well as to the independent dynasties that ruled its people from the tenth to the fifteenth centuries:

> Our country Dai Viet has long since been [a] land of old culture, with its own rivers and mountains, ways and customs, different from those of the north. The Trieu, Dinh, Ly and Tran built up our independence and stood as equals of the Han, T'ang, Sung, and Yuan. We had known both days of greatness and times of decline, but never had we lacked heroes.[1]

It then recounts the hardships suffered under Ming occupation and the glorious struggle to expel the Chinese and reestablish independent Viet rule. The outcome of the battle was, the author asserts, in accord with heaven's will as attested by the restored harmony of the natural world after the Viet victory. Thus Chinese-derived imagery had so impregnated the minds of the Viet elite that it was even invoked to justify anti-Chinese resistance. Like many literati, Nguyen Trai despised the courtier's life, full of intrigues and corruption. After the founding of the Le Dynasty, he withdrew to the countryside to commune with nature and compose poems in Chinese but also in the "southern script," which will be the topic of a subsequent section of this chapter.[2]

THE FOLK TRADITION

In addition to the texts in Chinese, which were largely incomprehensible to the common people even if read to them, the masses produced a rich corpus of sayings, folklore, and tales, much of which would eventually be recorded in Chinese, vernacular characters, or *quoc ngu*. Before turning to the Vietnamese literature in vernacular characters, let us consider several examples of this popular culture.

The origins of the folk tradition cannot be precisely dated since it was not initially recorded in writing, but it must pre-date the Chinese Conquest and stem from rural society with its Animistic traditions. Many folk stories purport to describe the origins of particular practices or institutions. One story explains the origins of rice farming and comments as well on the "proper" roles of men and women. In ancient times, there had not yet been tiny grains of rice as we know them now; nor had it been necessary to grow and harvest rice. Rice grains had been as large as a person's head and had grown without human intervention; when mature, they would come to people's houses and present themselves for cooking. In one household, a wife had not finished her chores when the grain presented itself. Angry at being caught with her work unfinished, the woman struck the grain with her broom, breaking it into tiny pieces. As punishment for her laziness and violence, rice henceforth appeared as tiny grains, which had to be laboriously cultivated and harvested. We note also the ethical content of this and other such stories: humans are generally punished for the failure of a particular individual to meet her responsibilities, here defined in terms of domestic chores assigned to women.

Likewise, many stories spoke to the relations between humans and animals, questions of great interest in a rural context. One such story recounts how tigers came to have stripes. One day long ago, a peasant and his buffalo were plowing the fields. Suddenly a tiger appeared and asked the buffalo how it was that he, a large and powerful animal, did the bidding of the smaller, weaker human. The buffalo replied that the humans had a powerful talisman called "intelligence" that made the animals obey them. The tiger demanded to obtain this talisman for himself so that he could summon his prey to appear before him rather than hunting for his food. The frightened peasant agreed to return home to get his "intelligence" for the tiger to examine, on the condition that the tiger allow himself to be tied to a tree to prevent him from eating the buffalo. The tiger agreed, and the peasant tied him to a tree, passing the ropes around his body many times. When the peasant returned, he brought not any talisman but rather armfuls of hay, which he placed at the base of the tree to which the tiger was tied and ignited. Howling in pain, the tiger was saved only when the ropes burned through, allowing him to escape into the forest. But the ropes had burned deep black marks into his flesh, which we can see even today as the tiger's stripes.

In sum, the masses built up a storehouse of lore derived from their experiences as village dwellers and petty producers; it would eventually incorporate elements from world religions, Viet elite culture, and other sources. The elite Viet authors would in turn enrich their own creations by drawing upon the forms and idioms of popular culture, particularly for the vernacular works that are our next topic.

IN VERNACULAR CHARACTERS

Beginning in about the thirteenth century, Viet scholars developed a second writing system, an indigenous character-based vernacular (*chu nom*, or "southern script") that adopted and adapted Chinese characters to express Vietnamese-language sounds. Rejected by most Viet dynasties, which retained Chinese as their official medium, it was taken up by many members of the elite, who, while continuing to read and write in Chinese, used *nom* in their literary pursuits until the early twentieth century. Aside from giving the pleasure and pride of writing in one's native language, *nom* allowed authors to produce works that drew upon the popular traditions described above. Furthermore, it permitted them to produce works that could be understood and memorized by the masses when read to them, thus becoming part of the popular oral tradition. *Nom* works could bring an author a degree of influence or renown that Chinese-language ones, with their limited elite readership, could not.[3]

In part because of the ravages of the Ming occupation—the invaders destroyed or removed many Viet texts and the blocks for printing them—the earliest body of *nom* texts that we have dates from the early post-occupation era and is attributed to Nguyen Trai. In this collection of 254 *nom* poems, called *Quoc Am Thi Tap* (*Collected Poems in the National Language*), composed after his retirement from court life, Nguyen Trai gives vent to his disenchantment with politics and expresses his preference for a rural life of rustic pleasures and quiet contemplation.

Despite his alienation from court life, Nguyen Trai's philosophical orientation remained Confucian-influenced as evidenced by another major *nom* work attributed to him, the *Le Trieu Tuong Cong Nguyen Trai Gia Huan Ca* (*Familial Instructions Put in Verse by Minister Nguyen Trai of the Le Court*).

This didactic poem of 976 lines stresses the obligations of children vis-à-vis their parents, and wives vis-à-vis their husbands. Such admonitions were by then standard fare among the upper class of the time, but the *Gia Huan Ca* is noteworthy for its emphasis on compassion for people in distress. For example, in describing the way that the poor suffer in wartime, the author encourages his children not merely to meet their familial obligations but to help the poor with material support and kind words as if they were members of one's own family.

Nguyen Trai's *nom* poetry is also notable for its openness to popular culture's proverbs, tales, and expressions. He was, therefore, if not the originator, at least an eminent early practitioner of the fruitful trend of cultural borrowing from the "rice-roots" by *nom* poets, a trend that would culminate in the nineteenth-century "novels in verse."

The Later Le Dynasty that Nguyen Trai helped to found reached its apogee under its fourth monarch, Le Thanh-tong, who reigned from 1460 to 1497. Chinese remained the language of administration, but Le Thanh-tong wrote extensively in *nom* and encouraged his entourage to do likewise. The collection of over 300 *nom* poems, written by the emperor and his collaborators, is known as the *Hong Duc Quoc Am Thi Tap* (*Collected Poems of the Hong Duc Era in the National Language*). The *Hong Duc* poems treat many subjects, but two themes are outstanding: the elevated conception of the monarch's role, demonstrating Confucianism's influence among the official elite; and efforts to make the cultural borrowings of the Chinese-style court relevant to Vietnamese villagers with their homegrown traditions.

With the passing of Le Thanh-tong, the Later Le Dynasty began its slow decline, and the rise of the military houses to de facto power would lead to centuries of turmoil and civil war. The spectacle of the Le monarchs' captivity and the seemingly endless conflicts between military houses forced members of the elite to choose their masters carefully or to withdraw from politics altogether if they had not the stomach for it.

This political context left its mark on Nguyen Binh Khiem (1491–1585), the dominant figure among sixteenth-century poets. Like Nguyen Trai, Nguyen Binh Khiem abandoned an administrative career for the life of a rural recluse. His collected poems, *Bach Van Quoc Ngu Thi Tap* (*White Clouds Poetry Collection in the National Language*), express his Confucian humanism tinged with Taoist wisdom regarding the vanity of worldly riches and power. The best life, he suggests, is lived close to nature and devoted to simple pleasures. He did not completely turn his back on politics, however, for his retreat attracted many writers and officeholders who sought his advice on all manner of topics, including political ones. His poetry often obliquely criticized those who used their positions to exploit those under their control. For example, one of his short poems compares corrupt officials to rats eating the crops of hardworking peasants.

The seventeenth and eighteenth centuries witnessed advances in *nom* literature, in part because the writers' forced retreat from politics thrust them back into the world of the villages. Although Chinese literature and Chinese-language works authored by Viet still provided much of the subject matter for Viet *nom* poets, writers increasingly gave their Chinese materials a Viet treatment, drawing upon the oral tradition for their vocabulary as well as form. For example, the oral tradition had long been poetic one that employed six-eight (*luc bat*) or seven-seven-six-eight (*song that luc bat*) verse.[4] This facilitated the composition of lengthy works that could be easily memorized, so *nom* writers began experimenting with these forms in this period. This confluence of Chinese themes and Viet forms would make the seventeenth and eighteenth centuries an age of *nom* masterpieces, of which we here consider but a few.

The *Chinh-phu Ngam* (*Complaint of a Warrior's Wife*) was first written in Chinese by Vietnamese author Dang Tran Con (1710–1745), who derived his themes from Chinese poetry. The result was so similar to Viet folk poetry that many Viet authors attempted *nom* translations and adaptations. Among the many existing versions, Phan Huy Ich (1750–1822) created a seven-seven-six-eight *nom* versification that is among the best known and most often cited. As the title indicates, the work is a *ngam*, or lament, a style intended to be read in a low, plaintive voice. This produces a mournful impression upon listeners that was particularly effective in this case, given the work's subject, the suffering of a wife whose husband has been sent off to war. Beyond the dissection of pain suffered by the couple in question, the work describes the broader impact of the sufferings engendered by warfare, criticizing at least implicitly the powerholders in this era of seemingly endless conflict.

Another famous *nom* poem employing the *ngam* style is *Cung Oan Ngam Khuc*, or the *Lament of a Royal Concubine*, by Nguyen Gia Thieu (c. 1741–1798). Nguyen Gia Thieu was an aristocrat related to the Trinh lords. He showed little inclination for officeholding, resigning a command in 1783 and retiring to his lakeside villa in Thang-long (i.e., modern Ha-noi). When the Tay-son armies seized the North in 1786, he refused their offers of positions and lived out his life as a reclusive scholar, drinking wine, fishing, and composing poems, of which the *Lament of a Royal Concubine* is his masterpiece. The *Lament* tells the story of an imperial concubine who briefly enjoys the monarch's favor but is then discarded by him and forced to live out her life in isolation. This theme allows the author ample opportunities to express his disappointment with the political system of the day and more generally to make a Buddhist-inspired critique of the vanity of worldly aspirations, be they for material wealth or political power.

The chaos and insecurity that derived from the Le dynastic decline, the Trinh-Nguyen conflict, the Tay-son interregnum, and the Nguyen reconquest also influenced the life and literary career of Nguyen Du (1765–1820), considered to be the greatest Vietnamese writer of all time. Nguyen Du had been a high-level official of the Le Dynasty who reluctantly accepted service with the Nguyen Dynasty after its defeat of the Tay-son. Thus out of necessity he served a master whom he could not consider legitimate, and this theme of the emotional conflicts arising from divided loyalties and compromise solutions would pervade his *nom* masterpiece, *Doan Truong Tan Thanh*. The title means "Severed Intestines, A New Telling," but it is widely known, by reference to its main characters, as *Kim Van Kieu* (*Kim, Van, and Kieu*), or simply as *Truyen Kieu* (*The Tale of Kieu*). The story, derived from a sixteenth-century Chinese novel and set in ancient China, is based on the Buddhist concept of karma, in which actions in a previous existence influence events in present and future lives. In the story, the heroine has committed unspecified sins in a former existence and must expiate them in the present lifetime by suffering calamities before she can find happiness.

Thuy Kieu is the oldest daughter of the Vuong, a respectable family of modest means. She and her sister, Thuy Van, are described as beautiful and morally pure. Thuy Kieu falls in love and promises to marry a scholar named Kim Trong, but before they can be married, Kieu's father is arrested by local officials and tortured. Desperate to save her father, Kieu tells her younger sister to marry Kim Trong in fulfillment of Kieu's promise to him, sells herself in what she supposes to be marriage to a wealthy merchant named Ma Giam-Sinh, and uses the money to buy her father's freedom. However, instead of making her his wife, Ma Giam-Sinh forces Kieu to work as a prostitute in a brothel. After a time, she wins the heart of one of the regular patrons, Thuc Sinh, who takes her from the brothel and makes her his second wife. When Thuc Sinh's first wife, Hoan Thu, learns of the arrangement, she dispatches ruffians who kidnap Kieu and force her into service as Hoan Thu's maid; the cowardly Thuc Sinh dares not reproach his first wife for treating Kieu so brutally. Kieu runs away and takes refuge in a Buddhist nunnery. Although the head nun, Giac Duyen, cares for Kieu, she mistakenly entrusts her to an older nun, Bac Ba, who tricks Kieu into marrying her nephew. The nephew then forces Kieu to work in a brothel again. Kieu's fortunes seem to turn for the better when she meets Tu-Hai, a rebel against the reigning dynasty. She becomes his wife and enjoys her revenge when Tu-Hai, who establishes his rule over a large territory, allows Kieu to punish her tormentors. But Tu-Hai's reign is short-lived. The imperial official sent to subdue him uses a ruse to obtain his submission in return for the promise of an official position. Believing the offer to be bona fide, Kieu urges Tu-Hai to accept, but once he has surrendered, the official kills him and forces Kieu to marry a local chieftain. Kieu tries to kill herself but is saved by Giac Duyen, the kindly nun who had tried to help earlier. At last, Kieu is reunited with Kim Trong, who is now married to Kieu's sister, Van. Kieu agrees to marry Kim Trong but, feeling that her experiences have left her impure, makes him agree that their relationship will remain platonic.

While the plot may seem repetitious, Nguyen Du elevates the work to high art by the beauty of his poetry and his penetrating descriptions of the emotional states of the characters as they move through trying situations. As such, the work speaks to the deepest feelings of the Vietnamese, who consider its verses relevant to almost any situation that they encounter. This was, no doubt, why it was so beloved in the nineteenth century and why it remains so today. Indeed, in the last fifty years, with multiple foreign occupations, wars, revolution, and now life under the S.R.V., millions of Vietnamese have had to come to terms with the same emotional predicament as Nguyen Du and his heroine, Kieu: serving masters other than those to whom they feel that they rightly owe loyalty. Even today, almost all Vietnamese can quote lines from the poem at will, and many still use the text as an oracle, selecting verses at random in hopes that they will shed light on the outcome of events.

One of the last *nom* masterpieces was *Luc Van Tien* by Nguyen Dinh Chieu (1822–1888). Nguyen Dinh Chieu was born in southern Vietnam and passed the local civil service examinations in 1843. He subsequently moved to central Vietnam to prepare for the higher-level competitions, held at Hue. Before he could begin the testing, he learned that his mother had died, and so he returned home to assume mourning duties. On the way, he fell ill, losing his sight. His blindness meant the end of his hopes for a career in administration, and he began teaching and practicing medicine. When the French invaded southern Vietnam in 1859, Nguyen Dinh Chieu supported the anti-French guerrillas; after the Treaty of Sai-gon and the defeat of the resistance, he criticized those who collaborated with the colonial regime and refused the latter's efforts to buy his support. Nguyen Dinh Chieu composed *Luc Van Tien* in six-eight verse around 1860 by dictating it to his students, who transcribed it in *nom*. As the following summary will suggest, *Luc Van Tien* is autobiographical in certain respects.

Set in the mythical country of So, understood to be a state in ancient China, the poem begins as Luc Van Tien travels to the capital to compete in the examinations. En route, he saves a woman named Nguyet Nga, who has been kidnapped by bandits, and wins her love. Van Tien never makes it to the capital because he must return home to mourn his mother's death. He cries continually and loses his sight, becoming easy prey for villains, including the parents of another woman, with whom Van Tien's parents had been discussing marriage. The prospective in-laws, fearing that the blind scholar would be a burden to them, abandon Van Tien to die in a cave. Nguyet Nga, believing that Van Tien has died, vows to honor his memory by refusing to marry anyone else. When Nguyet Nga rejects a powerful suitor, the latter induces the king of So to send her as tribute wife to the king of the nearby state of Phien. Nguyet Nga attempts suicide rather than violate her pledge of fidelity to Van Tien, but she is saved by a bodhisattva and sheltered by a sympathetic older woman. However, unknown to Nguyet Nga, Van Tien has been supernaturally saved from his cave, recovers his sight, passes his examinations, and enters So's political elite. The king of So asks him to lead a force against neighboring O-Qua. While leading the army to victory, he is reunited with Nguyet Nga. After their marriage, Van Tien is offered the throne of So by its king, who wants to retire. Finally, Van Tien's tormenters come to bad ends: his intended bride's father dies of shame, while her mother and the woman herself are eaten by tigers!

Some modern writers have criticized *Luc Van Tien* for the predictability of its action and the lack of depth of its characters. To be sure, Nguyen Dinh Chieu's plots were unoriginal and his characters were little developed. In context, however, such criticisms miss the point. The work was beloved by contemporary Vietnamese (and remains so today), who appreciated it as a lively, albeit predictable, adventure story with an important and edifying message. In trying times, *Luc Van Tien* reaffirmed traditional values by encouraging virtuous behavior through positive and negative examples: virtuous acts are rewarded, and evil ones are punished. It thus spoke directly to Vietnamese audiences searching for a response to the perennial problem of how to respond to invasion and the French occupation, recommending the emotionally satisfying response of resistance.

Unlike Luc Van Tien, however, Nguyen Dinh Chieu never regained his sight, and Nguyen Vietnam was vanquished by its invaders. The success of the French invasion was the beginning of the end of *nom* literature, and the rise of literature in romanized Vietnamese, to which we now turn.

In Romanized Vietnamese

Quoc ngu, or romanized script, was invented by Catholic missionaries in the sixteenth and seventeenth centuries and was long the exclusive property of Catholic missionaries, indigenous priests, and the Viet faithful. It entered wider usage in the nineteenth century under the colonial regime, which introduced the printing press, encouraged the publication of books in *quoc ngu*, and even made it the language of administration in some areas. It was also taught in schools as a means of giving basic instruction on Western subjects while alienating Viet from their Sino-Vietnamese heritage and reducing their exposure to potentially subversive Chinese-language materials. In this context, Vietnamese intellectuals soon began creating literary works in *quoc ngu*, adapting French literary styles and concerns in the process.

Under Colonialism

The first steps in *quoc ngu*'s popularization were taken in association with the colonial regime by Catholic Vietnamese scholars, Huynh Tinh Cua (1834–1907), and Truong Vinh Ky (1837–1898). Huynh Tinh Cua, fluent in Vietnamese, Chinese, and French and literate in *quoc ngu*, worked for the French in Cochin China as a translator and became the editor of the officially sponsored *Gia-dinh Bao* (the *Gia-dinh Newspaper*), the first Vietnamese-language newspaper, which began in 1865. He also produced a *quoc ngu* dictionary, a book of Vietnamese proverbs and folk sayings, and a collection of short stories called *Stories for Fun*.

Truong Vinh Ky was, like Huynh Tinh Cua, a talented linguist who found employment with the colonial state, serving as editor of the *Gia-dinh Bao*, interpreter for Franco-Vietnamese diplomatic missions, and instructor at interpreters' schools. He also wrote widely, publishing more than 100 works on history and languages, as well as dictionaries and translations of Chinese novels and *nom* "novels in verse." The latter works allowed Vietnamese who lacked training in Chinese or *nom* but had learned *quoc ngu* to have access to the Sino-Vietnamese cultural heritage as contained in such works as *The Tale of Kieu*. Through their editorship and publications, Huynh Tinh Cua and Truong Vinh Ky contributed to the popularization and modernization of *quoc ngu*, showing that it could be used to express all kinds of ideas and subject matter, from classical to scientific.

During the first two decades of the twentieth century, French policies gradually created a new Vietnamese urban elite, one that was literate in *quoc ngu* and often in French as well. In the interests of satisfying this elite's yearnings for modernization and education while "inoculating" them from the revolutionary ideas being popularized by activists such as Phan Boi Chau, the regime increased its emphasis on defending its "civilizing mission" by supporting *quoc ngu* publishing efforts.

In 1913, on the eve of World War I, a Frenchman named Schneider founded the *quoc ngu* weekly entitled *Dong Duong Tap Chi* (*Indochinese Journal*), which was published from 1913 to 1916. The paper fulfilled the authorities' intentions of making propaganda for their policies while criticizing anticolonial activists. However, its chief editor, Nguyen Van Vinh, and staff assigned themselves a broader mission as well: to popularize *quoc ngu*, to disseminate Western knowledge in general, and to reexamine the Asian cultural heritage in light of the new knowledge. In particular, Nguyen Van Vinh used the review to criticize Chinese characters, which he considered an impediment to civilization, and to encourage the dissemination of *quoc ngu*. One of the most effective means to do so, the editors found, was the publication, often in serialized form, of *quoc ngu* translations of Chinese novels such as the *Romance of the Three Kingdoms*, which were popular with Vietnamese readers. Nguyen Van Vinh translated a number of Western works into *quoc ngu*, including Victor Hugo's *Les Misérables*. It would be hard to overestimate the impact of the *Dong Duong Tap Chi*, through which *quoc ngu* became increasingly popular, particularly in the urban milieu. Furthermore, it was through its pages that many Vietnamese readers had their first contact with classical and modern novels from the West as well as from China.

However, given the politicized context of World War I, the regime decided to sponsor another newspaper, one that would hold more firmly to the political goals that had inspired the founding of the *Dong Duong Tap Chi*. Thus was born *Nam Phong*, or *Southern Wind*, a trilingual monthly (Chinese, *quoc ngu*, and French) that would appear for seventeen years (from 1917 until 1934). Its editor was an ex-librarian and former *Dong Duong Tap Chi* staff member named Pham Quynh. There is no doubt that Pham Quynh took his duties as pro-French propagandist seriously, publishing *quoc ngu* articles praising French imperialism in Vietnam as a noble crusade to uplift a "backward" people, and he has been bitterly criticized by later Vietnamese nationalists on this account. Nevertheless, *Nam Phong* contributed to the popularization of *quoc ngu* and to the dissemination of knowledge of modern literary genres, particularly the novel. Indeed, in 1921, Pham Quynh published in its pages the first Vietnamese-language analysis of the novel as a literary form. Its bias toward the French novel notwithstanding, the work was important in introducing the theory of the novel to Vietnamese writers and interesting them in its possibilities. Vietnamese writers were not long in taking up the challenge of the new literary forms and styles that the journalists had brought to their attention. The 1920s and 1930s were a time of great experimentation with these new forms.

Western-style poetry was the first genre to be seized upon, with French romanticism and free verse stimulating a movement for *tho moi*, or "new poetry," free verse in *quoc ngu* as opposed to the stylized forms hitherto employed in Chinese and *nom* poetry. The transition between the traditional styles and new poetry was made by Nguyen Khac Hieu (1881–1939), whose pen name was Tan Da. Confucian-trained and French-influenced, he wrote in a great variety of styles and was the dominant figure in Vietnamese poetry during the 1920s and 1930s.

Vietnamese authors also began experimenting with the new prose forms described in *Nam Phong* and the other early newspapers and reviews. Among the first short story writers in Vietnam were Nguyen Ba Hoc (1857–1921) and Pham Duy Ton (1883–1924). Both addressed issues that concerned educated urban Vietnamese of the day: the transformations wrought by colonialism and their impact on Vietnamese institutions. In Nguyen Ba Hoc's "A Family Story," for example, two brothers take different paths in life. While the elder son follows the traditional route of Confucian studies and finds his opportunities have been foreclosed by the French regime, the younger one takes up French studies and finds a well-paying position but is corrupted by the excesses of the Western lifestyle. Their stories did not condemn the changes out of hand, recognizing that French-stimulated economic growth could mean prosperity for an increasing number of Vietnamese, but they encouraged readers not to become obsessed with wealth and position to the extent that they neglected their familial obligations or exploited their fellow Vietnamese.

Immediately after the publication of Pham Quynh's essay on the novel, the first novels in *quoc ngu* began to appear. Although scholars do not agree who deserves the honor of having produced the first true Vietnamese novel, three early authors deserve mention: Nguyen Trong Thuat (1883–1940), Hoang Ngoc Phach, and Ho Van Trung, alias Ho Bieu Chanh (1885–1958).

Nguyen Trong Thuat, a *Nam Phong* staff writer and close associate of Pham Quynh, derived the plot for his 1925 novel, *Qua Dua Do* (*The Watermelon*) from a well-known fable. Set in ancient times, the novel recounts the story of a faithful minister who is wrongly accused of a crime and exiled to a deserted island. Determined to make the best of a bad situation and believing that all wrongs will be righted in the long run, the minister finds some watermelon seeds and plants them. When the fruits mature, he sells them to people on passing ships, becoming wealthy. The business attracts settlers, and the island becomes prosperous. The king learns of the minister's innocence, invites him to return, and rewards him with positions and honors. Although it is possible to interpret the work as mere escapist fare or as a reassertion of traditional values, one can also read in it the conservative message that the Vietnamese should make the best of their colonial status while working for a better future. One may assume that the editors of *Nam Phong* interpreted *Qua Dua Do* in the latter sense, for their organization, *Hoi Khai Tri Tien Duc* (Association for Intellectual and Moral Development) awarded Nguyen Trong Thuat a literary prize for it.

Hoang Ngoc Phach, an education student at the University of Ha-noi, published *To Tam* (*Pure Heart*) in 1925. It immediately became a smashing success, particularly among young people, while provoking debate about the proper behavior for youth and literature's role in providing role models. *To Tam* tells the story of a young Ha-noi male student named Dam Thuy, who falls in love with a young woman whom he nicknames To Tam. Although she returns his feelings, they accept that their relationship can never lead to marriage because Dam Thuy's parents have already arranged for him to marry a woman whom he does not love. When To Tam refuses the proposal of another promising young man, her mother and Dam Thuy press her to reconsider. Finally, when her mother falls seriously ill, she relents and marries the young man but is so unhappy that she sickens and dies. Although Dam Thuy is so wounded by the death of his true love that he also becomes ill, he recovers with the help of his older brother, accepts his parents' choice of a marriage partner, and eventually recovers his health completely.

Despite its unoriginal plot, a virtual pastiche of Chinese and French romance novels, *To Tam* did deal with issues arising from the social and cultural changes provoked by colonialism, particularly with the pressures felt by young people torn between their desires for independence and romantic love and their familial responsibilities. Its answers to the questions, however, were consistent with the conservative tendencies favored by the *Nam Phong* group. Dam Thuy returns to his family, marries the woman that his parents had selected for him, and recovers from his doomed affair. The author's intended message was apparently that Dam Thuy's and To Tam's problems were caused by their flirtation with Western values of individualism and romantic love, not by the strictures of the traditional family. Nevertheless, many young Vietnamese saw Dam Thuy and To Tam as victims of the practice of arranged marriages, identifying so intensely with their plight that a number of brokenhearted young men and women committed suicide by throwing themselves into Ha-noi's lakes after reading the novel.

Ho Bieu Chanh was an official in French Cochin China, eventually working his way up to provincial governor. His real passion, however, was literature. In the early 1920s, he began producing *quoc ngu* translations of French romantic novels, and by 1924 he had written *Tinh Mong* (*Awakening from Dreaming*), which, though influenced by French romanticism, was an original work. Over the next decades, he would write hundreds of short stories and novels that won him a devoted readership, particularly among southerners. *Tinh Mong*, which by virtue of its early appearance and modern construction is arguably the first Vietnamese novel, explores adultery's impact on a southern family. Yen Tuyet, the teenage daughter of a local official, is seduced and impregnated by Truong Xuan, her cousin. Desperate to preserve appearances, the family "hires" an impoverished young scholar named Ky Tam to marry Yen Tuyet. However, despite his poverty, the groom refuses monetary compensation for the marriage and proves to be of such noble character that the couple, despite the unfortunate circumstances of the union, develops a genuine mutual affection and agrees to make the marriage a real one. In terms of the political tendencies displayed by his writings, Ho Bieu Chanh falls well within the parameters established by the *Nam Phong* group. Although he criticized aspects of the colonial society, overall his work encouraged a return to traditional morality, a message manifested by his traditional "happy ending" format, in which good and evil receive their just deserts. In *Tinh Mong*, as we have seen, the poor scholar's virtues of compassion and piety rescue the family from an unfortunate situation of its own making.

Although the enthusiasm for the new forms was widespread among urban intellectuals, not all agreed with the conservative political message that Pham Quynh and other French-sponsored journalists had attempted to inculcate and that some of the early writers had adopted. In contrast to the *Nam Phong* group's collaborationist stance, the opposition writers took two main tendencies, both of them nationalistic: those who advocated an anticolonial but noncommunist reformism, and those who favored left-leaning or communist-led anticolonialism and social revolution.

The noncommunist reformist writers gathered in the early 1930s into the *Tu Luc Van Doan*, or Self-Reliance Literary Group, a name chosen to mark their distance from the French-sponsored *Nam Phong* circle. Their leader was Nguyen Tuong Tam (1906–1963). Known by his pen name, Nhat Linh; he was a former art student at the University of Ha-noi who had also taken scientific degrees in France. His chief collaborator was Tran Khanh Giu (d. 1946), known as Khai Hung, a mandarin's son and the graduate of a French *lycée* who worked as a teacher. One can measure the duo's talent by noting that authorities on Vietnamese literature have disagreed on who was the better writer; each has been called the greatest writer of his generation.

Under Nhat Linh's editorship, the *Tu Luc Van Doan* published several influential magazines and newspapers, including *Phong Hoa* (*Manners*), *Ngay Nay* (*Today*), and *Chu Nhat* (*Sunday*), in which they called for the modernization of Vietnamese society. Their concerns were summarized in *Muoi Dieu Tam Niem* (*Ten Points to Consider*), a manifesto issued by member Hoang Dao. The manifesto urged Vietnamese youth to modernize themselves by adopting Western ways; to believe in progress and hold to high ideals; to work for the improvement of society; to encourage the greater participation of women in society; to strengthen themselves physically through exercise; to acquire a scientific framework; to seek genuine accomplishments instead of chasing after positions and honors. In addition to their proposals, which often ran afoul of official censorship, the publications were innovative in their use of humor and satire to make their points, a feature that endeared them to readers, particularly to urbanites, who were their primary audience. Self-Reliance Literary Group members also expressed their modernizing vision by publishing widely in all of the new literary genres, including poetry, short stories, and novels. It was in the last genre that the group, particularly Nhat Linh and Khai Hung, had their greatest influence, establishing the novel as *the* genre of Vietnamese literature and creating a direct and clear *quoc ngu* prose style, liberated from its reliance on Chinese loan words and literary allusions. The group dominated the literary scene throughout the 1930s, and their books are still enjoyed today; indeed, they are experiencing a revival under the more liberal context created by the post-1987 reforms.

Among Nhat Linh's best-known novels are *Nho Phong* (*Confucian Manners*), *Doan-tuyet* (*Rupture*), *Lanh-lung* (*Loneliness*), and *Di Tay* (*A Trip to the West*). In *Doan-tuyet*, Loan, a modern-minded young woman, falls in love and plans to marry Dung, a well-educated young man who has been disowned by his mandarin father for his political activities. (They are presumably revolutionary and anti-French; but the author was constrained by censorship from being more specific.) However, Loan is forced by her mother to marry Than, the son of the family's creditor, and finds herself persecuted by Than's family, which objects to her Westernized ways. In an argument, Than beats Loan, and she draws a knife to defend herself, killing him by accident. She is acquitted when her lawyer paints Loan as the victim of an oppressive family system. Loan becomes a career woman, working in education and journalism. Dung, learning of these events from afar, attempts to contact Loan through intermediaries, and she is delighted at the prospect of renewing their relationship. In *Doan-tuyet*, as in many of his other works, Nhat Linh expressed the yearning of urban youth to be free of the constraints of the traditional family while urging them to struggle for independence.

Khai Hung's most celebrated novels include *Gia-dinh* (*Family*), *Thua-tu* (*The Inheritance*), *Tieu-son Trang-si* (*Righteous Warriors of Tieu Mountain*), *Nua Chung Xuan* (*Mid-Spring*), and *Hon Buom Mo Tien* (*Butterfly Soul Dreaming of a Fairy*). Although many of his novels advocated social and particularly familial reform along the lines of Nhat Linh's novels, Khai Hung's works also evinced a pronounced romanticism, particularly *Hon Buom Mo Tien*, a short and immensely popular novel published in 1933 and set in a Buddhist monastery located near Ha-noi. It tells the story of a young male student from Ha-noi named Ngoc, who spends several months in the monastery visiting his uncle, the superior monk. He is strangely attracted to one of the monks, who is in fact a young woman named Lan who has disguised herself as a man to take refuge in the monastery. Although the novel does allude to the lack of opportunities available for women in rural society, its focus is on the relationship between the two protagonists as they fall in love but decide not to marry since Lan has pledged her life to the service of religion. Intrigued by Buddhist teachings and inspired by Lan's sacrifice, Ngoc declares that he will no longer consider only his biological relations to be his family but will broaden his vision to include all of humanity, whom he pledges always to serve.

The *Tu Luc Van Doan*'s predilection for romanticism, pronounced in Khai Hung's *Hon Buom Mo Tien*, caused its members to be anathema to the writers of the next group, those who wrote under the inspiration of Marxist ideas or under the direction of the Communist Party.

Popular or Realist Literature

While the Self-Reliance authors waxed hegemonic during most of the 1930s, they were challenged in the latter half of that decade by writers influenced by Marxist ideas of class struggle, anti-imperialism, and antifeudalism. Many of these writers were from the lower levels of the new urban and rural classes and were thus closer to the poor workers and peasants than were Self-Reliance Group members. In contrast to the often romanticized focus on middle- and upper-class characters that one finds in the Self-Reliance novels, the works of the class-conscious writers realistically depict the experiences of the popular masses. Hence Vietnamese refer to this as "popular" (*binh dan*) or Realist (*ta chan*) literature. Among the most influential Realist authors were Nguyen Cong Hoan (1903–1977), Vu Trong Phung (1912–1939), and Ngo Tat To (1894–1954).

A prolific writer of short stories as well as novels, Nguyen Cong Hoan was at his best describing the travails of the northern peasants at the hands of local officials. He addressed this theme in a number of novels, including his best-known work, *Buoc Duong Cung* (*Impasse*), published in 1938. *Impasse* recounts the struggles of a Tonkinese peasant named Pha who falls victim to a plot hatched by a powerful landlord named Lai. Lai is an opium-addicted landowner who, wanting to take possession of Pha's meager holdings, schemes with Pha's neighbors to plant illegal alcohol on Pha's land. Because the production of alcoholic beverages in competition with the administration's monopoly is a serious crime in colonial Indochina, Pha is arrested and taken before the district magistrate. He suffers greatly at the hands of the magistrate's underlings, who beat and rob him before finally allowing him to plead his case before the magistrate. Even when Pha is allowed to meet the magistrate, the latter demands bribes before considering the case. Although Pha is set free, he has been forced to mortgage his land to meet his expenses. When he resists the seizure of his property by agents of Lai, his creditor, Pha is arrested again. It is noteworthy that in the course of the narrative Pha undergoes a metamorphosis: early in the story, he is passive and accepting of his fate, but in the end—and partly as a result of conversations with a leftist acquaintance—he emerges with a clearer vision of the system that oppresses him, and he curses his captors as he is led away in chains. Later communist writers would point to Nguyen Cong Hoan's *Impasse* as a transitional work leading to socialist Realism.

Vu Trong Phung's life and literary career were short but productive. Having lost his father to tuberculosis when he was only seven months old, Vu Trong Phung was raised by his impoverished mother and performed manual labor as a youth; he later supported himself by working as a printer and a journalist, the latter profession allowing him to devote himself to writing after 1930. His published work, which includes documentary reporting (e.g., *Ky Nghe Lay Tay*, or "The Profession of Marrying Frenchmen") as well as fiction (e.g., novels such as *Lam Di*, or *To Be a Whore*), gives evidence of his familiarity with the realities of working-class life under the colonial regime. One of his favorite topics, which he handled with biting sarcasm in one of his best-known novels, *So Do* (*A Fortunate Life*), is the corruption of the French authorities and of the Vietnamese who aggrandized themselves under their patronage. In *So Do*, a young Vietnamese of humble origins called Red-Haired Xuan works at a French Club, returning tennis balls to the wealthy players. Adept at flattering superiors and conniving against competitors, he rockets up the social ladder in colonial society, becoming successively a tennis champion, a shop manager, a medical doctor, and even a Buddhist reformer! In the end, he is awarded medals by the French administration for agreeing to deliberately lose a championship tennis match! What kind of society has flourished under the French regime, the author seems to be asking, that allows such opportunists to enjoy success at the expense of others?

The third Realist writer is Ngo Tat To, a Confucian scholar who became one of the Realist school's most effective members. Born and raised in the countryside of northern Vietnam, he was familiar with the problems encountered by the peasants and made their plight the leitmotif of his 1939 masterpiece, *Tat Den (When the Light's Put Out)*. The story illustrates the French taxation system, which increased the amounts imposed on the peasantry while demanding that they pay in cash instead of in kind, as under the imperial regimes of yore. In particular, the author stresses that the system gave leeway to the regime's local agents, the Vietnamese officials at the district, canton, and village levels with whom the peasants had to deal, and criticizes the corrupt practices these officials employed to enrich themselves at the peasants' expense. In *Tat Den*, a resourceful peasant woman called Chi Dau (Elder Sister Dau) sells all of her belongings, her dog and its puppies, and even her own daughter to raise money to pay her husband's head tax in order to rescue him from the clutches of the local officials, who brutally beat and painfully bind their victims until their taxes are paid in full. Nor is this all: even after Chi Dau has purchased her husband's freedom, the local officials make her pay her husband's brother's head tax even though the man has died, stating that the tax records had been finalized while the man was still alive and the bill must be paid in order to close the dossier of the year's taxation. Because of *Tat Den*'s portrayal of peasants who do not hesitate to take action against the forces that oppress them (e.g., Chi Dau's determined response to her family's crisis), Ngo Tat To was widely praised by later communist writers who considered his *Tat Den* to be the masterpiece of Vietnamese Realism, a worthy precursor to their own Resistance literature.

Resistance Literature

Under the Communist Party, literature in *quoc ngu* assumed a largely uniform and strongly political character during the two Indochina Wars (1946–1954 and 1960–1975) and the first decade of unified rule (1976–1986). This can be considered a single period, characterized by what may be termed Resistance literature. With the August Revolution and the outbreak of the First Indochina War, it was no longer sufficient for writers to portray, in realistic terms, the sufferings of the peasants at the hands of mandarins as the Realists had done. Following Soviet and Chinese precedents, the call went out for Vietnamese writers to produce a revolutionary socialist Realism in which, for example, the struggles of peasants and other oppressed classes could be shown to be part of the larger struggle for liberation under the aegis of the Communist Party. Literature was, in short, to serve the Party's goals of mobilizing the people for revolutionary struggle in all its facets, including anti-French or anti-American resistance, land reform, and industrializing the D.R.V. and then the S.R.V.

The most successful writers of this period included a "first generation" comprising writers of established reputations who rallied to the revolutionary ranks, including Nguyen Cong Hoan, Ngo Tat To, and Nguyen Huy Tuong (1912–1960). Joining them were "second generation" Resistance writers— that is, those who matured artistically during the First Indochina War, including Nguyen Dinh Thi (b. 1924), Nguyen Van Bong, and Dao Vu. The Resistance writers' ranks were completed by the addition of authors of the "third generation," those who came to intellectual maturity during the Second Indochina War, including Chu Van, Anh Duc, and Nguyen Minh Chau. Representative works will illustrate how these writers met the challenge put before them by the Party's literary establishment.

The central issue addressed by the Resistance writers, of course, is the Resistance itself—that is, the military struggle against the French and later the Americans. Nguyen Van Bong's 1953 novel *Con Chau* (*The Buffalo*), which describes life in a village in the D.R.V.'s liberated zones during the First Indochina War, shows how the struggle in rural areas was portrayed. The narrative describes the efforts of the village's inhabitants and their Party leaders to maintain production and provide for the welfare of village residents in the face of French attempts at sabotage. The novel's title refers to the fact that the French forces tried to destroy the material basis of the resistance by shooting the villagers' buffalo, which were vital in field labor, as transportation, and as provider of fertilizer. Although many village residents, old and young, male and female, participated in the struggle, the two main characters are a poor peasant turned guerrilla fighter named Tro and the local Party secretary and military leader, a cadre named Chuc. Benefiting from Chuc's guidance, Tro becomes a skillful guerrilla fighter, displaying courage and a profound hatred for the colonialists. Chuc is presented as a model Party cadre and guerrilla leader, the heart and soul of the village's efforts.

Resistance writers were also asked to depict the struggle in the urban areas of the country that were, in the First Indochina War, occupied by the French.

Nguyen Huy Tuong's novel *Song Mai Voi Ha-noi Thu Do* (*Forever with Hanoi the Capital*), for example, portrays the lives of the Vietnamese who found themselves in French-occupied urban zones for most of the war and had to choose between serving the Resistance or the French and allied Vietnamese forces. Several upper-class intellectuals, including a teacher and an artist, join the Resistance in hopes of finding more meaningful or exciting lives, and they come to support it wholeheartedly as a result of the political consciousness and sense of commitment that they develop. The lower-class figures presented in the novel—soup merchants, ironworkers, bicycle repairmen—support the Resistance, and they are well led in their efforts by dedicated underground Party members. These figures, who are presented in a positive light, are contrasted with others—for example, Tan, son of a wealthy businessman with ties to the French, whose main regret is that the war is destroying the beautiful capital, previously a source of pleasure to him. Postponing any political commitment, he tries to enjoy the capital's remaining pleasures. As the narrative develops, and Vietnamese forces fight to retake the capital from the French, each of the above figures is forced to chose sides, with the majority of the members of the popular classes and even bourgeois intellectuals supporting the Resistance. However, wealthy figures whose backgrounds tie them to the French, such as Tan, the businessman's son, go over to the French side. Paradoxically, although Nguyen Huy Tuong gives his characters little scope for moral choice by attributing their political allegiances to their social origins, he praises those characters who devote themselves to the revolutionary cause.

As even such a brief summary indicates, Resistance works tend to engage in stereotyped characterizations and predictable narratives. Many foreign observers as well as Communist Party officials have called attention to the generally poor quality of Resistance literature, as broadly defined here, and critics are hard-pressed to name a single work of great artistic value. Indeed, U.S.-based Vietnamese literary historian Hoang Ngoc Thanh asserts: "Regardless of the efforts of the Party to indoctrinate artists and writers with Marxism and Leninism for the development of a revolutionary realist literature, the [D.R.V.] has produced so far no literary work of real great value, among the various genres in general and the novel in particular."[5] One can only suggest that while many Resistance writers were genuinely committed to the revolutionary cause in its early years, the increasing constraints of producing works on the topics and in accordance with the formulas handed down by the Party's literary establishment sapped their creative forces in the long run. Witness the explosion of creativity that followed the partial and provisional lifting of these strictures under Nguyen Van Linh's Renovation policies, initiated in 1987.

"Marking Time" Literature

Of course, not all of the writers of this era lived in the Resistance zones or served the revolutionary cause. What of the writers who lived under French protection during the First Indochina War and under the American-supported southern regimes during the Second? While space constraints preclude an extended discussion of their work, which some historians have characterized as a literature without commitment, one that "marked time" while waiting for the conflicts of the age to be settled by others, it may be briefly described as follows.[6]

In the First Indochina War, the French and their S.O.V. allies held most of the urban areas and significant portions of the larger deltas, including those of the Mekong and Red River. Thus, anticommunist and noncommunist intellectuals had the option of fleeing the Resistance zones and living out the war under France's military umbrella. In these areas, Vietnamese intellectuals had a renewed access to Western culture, particularly French but now including English and American as well. In response to the urbanites' curiosity about life in the Resistance zones, memoir writing enjoyed a vogue, with a wave of published accounts by people who had lived in the Resistance zones during World War II or the early First Indochina War, sharing (mostly) their experiences of disillusionment with the Viet Minh, particularly after the increase of Chinese influence after 1949. There was a paucity of creative writing, which has led some scholars to describe literature outside the Resistance zones as having been "in cold storage" during the years 1946–1954.[7] Several new publishing houses were founded, however, in response to the popular demand for translations (into *quoc ngu*) of Chinese novels as well as for reprinted editions of popular pre–World War II novels such as those of the *Tu Luc Van Doan*.

During the Second Indochina War, the U.S.-supported Republican regimes controlled the urban areas of southern Vietnam as well as roughly half of its countryside. Intellectuals in these regions enjoyed a freedom of thought that was relatively greater than that of their northern confreres, despite repression of outright dissent and the official sponsorship of anticommunism, linked strongly to Catholicism, particularly during the Diem era (1955–1963). In this context, a new literature arose giving voice to the Vietnamese of the South and the problems they faced because of the war. Many writers suffered agonizing dilemmas, caught as they were between their fear of communism and their revulsion toward the omnipresent destructiveness of the anticommunist effort by U.S. and R.V.N. forces. Le Tat Dieu, Nguyen Thi Thuy Vu, and Tran Thi Nha Ca are examples of authors in this category. Others turned away from the crisis entirely, producing novels with romantic and individualistic tendencies. A number of southern intellectuals became fascinated with the existentialism of French philosopher Jean-Paul Sartre, and this interest was reflected in philosophical discussions as well as in creative writing, particularly in the poetry of, for example, Thanh Tam Tuyen. Other intellectuals busied themselves with scholarly activities, producing historical and literary studies that are still of value to researchers today: Vuong Hong Sen's works on early Sai-gon, for example, or Toan Anh's research into Vietnamese popular culture.

Renovation Literature

Although the Party's preference for socialist Realist literature stressing the oppressed masses' heroic struggles under the socialist banner has remained pronounced, the relative liberalization brought about by renovation policies formalized by the Party's Sixth Congress in 1986 allowed some writers to experiment with new themes and styles and to address a number of formerly taboo topics. As General Secretary Nguyen Van Linh put it in a speech to a writers' group shortly afterward, "Speak the truth. Whatever happens, Comrades, don't curb your pens."[8] When writers responded eagerly to this opportunity, producing novels, short stories, and essays critical of the regime and its literary policies, conservative Party officials objected, and, following the Seventh Congress in 1993, there was a reassertion of the Party's authority over literary matters and a restatement of writers' obligations to produce a "wholesome" and "socialist" literature. The new policies, though not as restrictive as those in place before 1986, have produced uncertainty, as writers and editors cannot be sure what is permitted and what is forbidden.

It is nonetheless possible to describe the period from roughly 1987 to the present as the era of Renovation literature. According to one Western literary critic, Renovation literature is characterized by a "high degree of criticism of everyday reality"; focus on the individual rather than the collective experience; frank treatment of the "decline of traditional morality"; and a "willingness to take a fresh look at important issues in the past."[9] Five outstanding contemporary writers—Duong Thu Huong, Le Luu, Bao Ninh, Le Minh Khue, and Nguyen Huy Thiep—have addressed these themes in their major works.

Duong Thu Huong was born in Thai-Binh province in northern Vietnam in 1947 into a revolutionary family. She volunteered for army service in 1967 and was stationed as a "cultural worker" with the PAVN in the Central Highlands of what was then the R.V.N. Her faith in the cause began to waver in the post-war period, however, as she began to question whether the "liberation" experienced under the S.R.V. was worth the suffering endured by its wartime supporters. Since she began to publish in 1980, she has enjoyed popular and critical acclaim in Vietnam and abroad. Two of her novels, *Ben Kia Bo Ao Vong* (*On the Far Bank of Illusions*), published in 1987, and *Nhung Thien Duong Mu* (*Paradises of the Blind*), published in 1988, were immensely popular in Vietnam. With more than 140,000 copies sold, they were best-sellers by the modest standards of developing countries. They also earned her official disapproval. *Nhung Thien Duong Mu* was impounded by the authorities soon after publication. Her masterpiece, *Tieu Thuyet Vo De*, which would be translated into English and published in 1995 in the United States as *Novel without a Name*, was refused publication in Vietnam. She has also suffered repeated interrogations, expulsion from the Party in 1990, and imprisonment in 1991.

Based on Duong Thu Huong's observations of combat, *Tieu Thuyet Vo De* tells the story, in pseudo-autobiographical fashion, of a male PAVN soldier named Quan. In contrast to the focus on the heroic masses that characterized the official Resistance literature, her novel stresses how the grand struggles led by the Party devastated the physical and emotional lives of its followers. The battle scenes focus not on heroic actions of exemplary cadres but on the human cost of the war for the D.R.V.'s soldiers, who suffered horribly under the American bombing and from the incompetence of their own leaders. For example, in one scene, Quan's unit, a PAVN main-force unit fighting in southern Vietnam around 1970, engages in deadly but confused nocturnal combat with a presumed "enemy" unit, which is later identified by the soldiers as one of their own. The PAVN authorities never acknowledge the error, and Quan is horrified to read an account in the official press that describes the encounter as a "glorious victory" by revolutionary forces.

Tieu Thuyet Vo De does not stop at reevaluating wartime sacrifices. Duong Thu Huong also casts a critical eye on material and social life under the D.R.V. During his leave, Quan travels from southern Vietnam, where his unit operates, to his village near Ha-noi. In D.R.V. territory, he rides a train and observes the abject poverty of the passengers, one of whom is described as relishing a tiny piece of moldy bread. This image is contrasted with that of two other passengers, high-ranking Party members who are well-fed, half-drunk, and smoking foreign cigarettes. Quan cannot help overhearing a scandalous conversation about the role of Marxism under what was then the D.R.V. Its function, they boast, is to inspire the "ignorant" masses to greater sacrifices on the battlefield and lead them to accept the privations that permit the Party elite's privileged (or "civilized," in the speaker's words) lifestyles. When another passenger takes offense and summons the conductor, who questions the men, they arrogantly brandish their Party identification cards, and he backs down apologetically. By juxtaposing the enormous sacrifices of the soldiers and the people with the mediocrity and corruption of their leaders in the context of generalized poverty, Duong Thu Huong questions the value of the revolutionary struggle and the nature of the resulting society. Both of these questions, as we have seen, are characteristic of the Renovation approach.

The second Renovation author, Le Luu, was born in Hai-hung province, northern Vietnam, in 1942 and served in the Second Indochina War as an army signal man and correspondent in central Vietnam. Since then he has worked as the editor of *Van Nghe Quan Doi*, an official PAVN literary organ, and he won the prestigious National Award for fiction in 1987. He has written a number of novels, most of which reflect his military experience. His masterpiece is *Thoi Xa Vang*, which has been translated into English as *A Time Far Past*. *Thoi Xa Vang* spans the Indochina wars as well as the early postwar era by following the life of Sai, a studious and likable village boy from northern Vietnam, as he grows from adolescence into his fifties.

As a boy, Sai is married by his traditionally minded parents to a girl named Tuyet, with whom he has little in common and whom he comes to despise. Although he loves a village girl named Huong, who returns his affection, they are kept apart by his family's insistence that he honor the commitments they have made with Tuyet's family. The author here critiques the continuing domination of the individual by the traditional family, but the story is more complex and the criticism broader than that, for Sai's relatives, some of whom are powerful figures in the local and regional Party hierarchies, prevent him from renouncing the marriage for fear that the stigma of divorce would hinder Sai's career and damage the family's future position. Abandoning a promising academic career, Sai volunteers for the army, not because of a spirit of patriotic self-sacrifice—as would have been the case in Resistance novels—but because service in a faraway region would allow him to escape from his oppressive domestic situation.

After the conclusion of the war and the reunification of Vietnam, Sai returns from the South as a wartime hero but finds it difficult to adjust to the peacetime environment with its stress on careerism and materialism. Divorced from Tuyet at last, he tries to rebuild his life, marrying a Ha-noi woman named Chau, who, unknown to Sai, is in love with a married man, and pregnant by him. When Sai's relationship with Chau deteriorates, he divorces for a second time and returns to his native region, where he finds a measure of personal happiness and professional satisfaction by reestablishing a platonic relationship with Huong, his old flame, and by working as a district-level official, in which capacity he resolves a number of local economic problems.

Le Luu's *Thoi Xa Vang* is thus characteristic of Renovation fiction in that it reexamines the historical events of the Indochina Wars, presenting them not as noble struggles of the whole people for liberation but as periods of suffering and separation after which soldiers are able to reintegrate themselves into society only partially and with difficulty. The book is also notable for its criticism of everyday reality and its analysis of the decline of traditional morality. The protagonist's family, traditionalist in its organization and ruthless in manipulating the revolutionary political structures, selfishly forces Sai to marry a woman whom he does not love and then forbids him to divorce despite the couple's unhappiness. While Sai accedes to the family's wishes to arrange the marriage, he protests passively by refusing to speak to his wife, later joining the army to temporarily escape the situation. The work also portrays some Ha-noi residents who divorce freely and take advantage of their lunch breaks to conduct love affairs!

Ha-noi native Bao Ninh, born in 1952 and, like Duong Thu Huong and Le Luu, a veteran of the Second Indochina War, fits the Renovation style by virtue of his reexamination of the combat experience of the Second Indochina War and his dissection of the difficult postwar lives of its veterans. His best-known work, published in Vietnam in 1990 as *Than Phan Cua Tinh Yeu* (*Love's Fate*) has been reissued in Vietnam under the name of *Noi Buon Chien Tranh* and translated into English as *The Sorrow of War*. It is a best-seller in Vietnam and widely read abroad in translation. It earned its author a literary prize in Vietnam in 1991 but also brought criticism from military and political authorities in Vietnam, who found his descriptions of the wartime experience shocking and subversive. *Noi Buon Chien Tranh* recounts the wartime and postwar experiences of veterans by using a first-person narrator named Kien. Kien and his fellow combatants participated in the war's latter stages, which led to the "liberation" of the South. They suffer immensely in the fighting and perceive no real meaning in it; they intoxicate themselves with local herbs so that they can continue to perform their duties without breaking down psychologically. Even when the war is over, they do not feel that they have won anything; they continue to struggle to come to terms with their experience. They are haunted by the war's ghosts—by visions, for example, of the mutilated and maggot-infested corpses of young women found by the soldiers. With Bao Ninh, Vietnamese literature has traveled a long way from the glorification of victorious attacks by courageous guerrillas and their sagacious leaders, the stock in trade of the Resistance authors. *Noi Buon Chien Tranh* is also notable for its author's innovative use of a stream-of-consciousness narrative technique, dream sequences, and flashbacks, which contrast with the chronological narration employed in Resistance novels.

Le Minh Khue, born in Thanh-hoa province in 1949, joined the PAVN at the age of fifteen and served in a youth brigade along the Ho Chi Minh Trail in southern Vietnam. She has since worked as a reporter and is currently editor of the Writers' Association Publishing House in Ha-noi. She is a prolific writer of fiction, including novels and short stories, winning a Writers' Association award for her work in the latter genre in 1987. Like much of Renovation fiction, her work is driven by an intense feeling of disillusionment as the ideals of the revolution, which demanded so much sacrifice in wartime, have seemingly been abandoned in the postwar period. One Western critic has described her work as creating a "language of lost ideals."[10]

A summary of two of her short stories will give the reader an idea of how this language fits the description of Renovation literature. Her 1990 story, "A Small Tragedy," presents a critical viewpoint on the D.R.V.'s leadership during the Second Indochina War. Set in the postwar period, the story uses the first-person narrative of a female reporter whose uncle is a high-ranking local official named Tuyen. When she travels with a group of reporters to the region formerly under Tuyen's authority, her companions, unaware of her relationship to Tuyen, talk about the fate of young people assigned to wartime labor projects by him. In one case, many were killed when they fell into a sinkhole beneath the soil on which they were working for a construction project. Tuyen had been warned about the instability of the soil but had paid it no mind, promoting the project with the usual fanfare. In another instance, they recount, he ordered youths to fill in bomb craters during the daytime despite the likelihood that they would be targeted by American warplanes; more than 100 were killed when a plane bombed the area. The reporters note ruefully that although the tragedies were common knowledge in the area, no official action was taken against Tuyen, and the newspaper accounts of the bombing only mentioned that anti-aircraft crews had shot down one of the planes. Here Le Minh Khue breaks sharply with the heroic treatment of Party officials typical of the Resistance school. The local leader presented in her account is cynical, corrupt, and incompetent, but he prospers in spite of his faults because of the failure of the D.R.V.'s system to hold its officials accountable. Vietnamese readers would note, of course, that the situation still remains the same, the wartime-era political system being unchanged in its essentials.

Her 1992 story, "Scenes from an Alley," critiques everyday life in contemporary Vietnam, in particular the decline in traditional morality. The alley is inhabited by several families whose reactions to an accident are presented for the reader's consideration. Mr. Quyt and his wife rent a room to a Westerner, who drinks heavily, frequents prostitutes, and drives recklessly when inebriated. When the Westerner hits a local girl with his car and kills her, he is forced to pay the girl's mother, Mrs. Tit, $1,000, a small fortune by local standards. Having become a "millionaire," Mrs. Tit, who used to scavenge scrap metal and sleep on the street, buys a house in the alley, sets up a business, and takes to wearing a gold chain and flower hat, all of which make her newly attractive to the local men, who begin courting her. Mr. Quyt, the Westerner's landlord, bribes local officials to allow the Westerner to stay on as a tenant and even closes his eyes to the fact that his wife has begun to sleep with the guest, suggesting that he values the rent money more than conjugal fidelity. Another neighbor, Mr. Toan, begins encouraging his aged father to take his naps outside by the road, hoping that their family too will enjoy the "good fortune" of having one of its members killed by a foreigner! This short piece of fewer than ten pages is one of the most devastating critiques of day-to-day reality in modern Vietnamese fiction.

The final Renovation author—and, in the almost unanimous opinion of readers, critics, and other Renovation authors, the best writer of them all—is Nguyen Huy Thiep. A native of Ha-noi who spent much of his youth in the mountainous provinces bordering the Red River Delta, Nguyen Huy Thiep is the only major Renovation writer who does not have a military background. He was trained as a history teacher and worked in that capacity in the D.R.V.'s northern highlands during the Second Indochina War. He is currently an entrepreneur and restaurant owner in Ha-noi, where he continues to write novels, short stories, and plays, which have created a sensation since they began to appear in the mid-1980s among readers, most of whom loved them, and Party officials, many of whom condemned them.

For Vietnamese readers, much of the appeal of Nguyen Huy Thiep's work lies in the original way that he breaks down conventional modes of thinking and writing about historical topics. In a short story called "Chastity," for example, he depicts one of the Tay-son movement's leaders, Nguyen Hue, as a brutal and perverted figure. In a play called *Love Remains*, he presents the nationalist leader Nguyen Thai Hoc as a revolutionary martyr. Both characterizations run counter to the Marxists' interpretations of these figures: the Tay-son movement is seen as a harbinger of the communist one, and Nguyen Thai Hoc's party competed with the early communists for nationalist leadership. Since the Communist Party still draws legitimacy from its interpretation of history, it is obvious how dangerous such revisionism can be in context.

Nguyen Huy Thiep has also fascinated Vietnamese readers with his almost clinical dissection of social reality under the S.R.V., presenting slices of daily life that almost everyone knows to be true but which are rarely spoken of, even in private. Such is the case with his 1987 masterpiece, *Tuong Ve Huu* (*The General Retires*). The general is introduced as having joined the PAVN at a young age to escape an unhappy familial situation. As in Le Luu's *Thoi Xa Vang*, a military hero has joined the service not out of patriotism—invariably the case in the Resistance stories—but to escape unpleasant personal circumstances. He nevertheless serves honorably and finds meaning in his military career, but it has not prepared him for the retirement to civilian life, which is the setting of the novel. The general stays for a time with his wife, his son (the story's narrator), and his son's wife and children. None of their relationships seem to work. The general's wife, for example, is senile and relegated to a compound behind the family house. His daughter-in-law is intelligent but ruthless: for example, to keep the family out of poverty, she takes home aborted fetuses from the hospital and grinds them up as dog food for guard dogs, the sale of which is the family's main source of income. To the general's consternation, his son refuses to take a stand against the practice or to assert himself in any way. Even social rituals (a wedding and a funeral) that are presumably intended to bring people together turn out disastrously, with guests getting drunk and behaving crudely. Perhaps seeking a return to the moral certainties that his military career had provided, the general returns to visit his old camp, where he dies and is buried.

Despite its withering criticism of the present society, it is worth noting—and this is true throughout Nguyen Huy Thiep's published works—that *Tuong Ve Huu* avoids direct, moralistic condemnations of the S.R.V.'s policies or officials. Part of this is simple prudence, of course, but it is consistent with Nguyen Huy Thiep's artistic vision, which eschews moral certainties and even straightforward narrative, preferring ambiguity and leaving open the possibility of multiple interpretations.

PROSPECTS FOR THE FUTURE

Contemporary Vietnamese literature is in transition. For the major creative talents working in the S.R.V. who have tasted the relative freedoms of the

Renovation era, there can be no turning back to the literature of the Resistance period. The Vietnamese public, by its enthusiastic reception of Renovation writers, has also demonstrated that it finds such fiction compelling, if controversial, which certainly could not be said of any of the old-style socialist Realist works. It is by no means certain that the Party will continue to allow writers the relative freedoms of the Renovation period, as the conservative turn taken in the early 1990s suggests. Vietnamese authors of the highest caliber have learned to adapt to this situation of uncertain and shifting literary freedom by adopting narrative devices that allow them to tell their stories to perceptive readers while maintaining "deniability" vis-à-vis the Party and state hierarchies.

NOTES

1. Cited in Nguyen Dinh Hoa, "Patriotism in Classical Vietnamese Literature," in *Essays on Literature and Society in Southeast Asia*, ed. Tham Seong Chee (Kent Ridge, Singapore: Singapore University Press, 1981), 310–311.

2. His contributions to the founding of the Le Dynasty and wishes to remain aloof from politics notwithstanding, Nguyen Trai was accused of poisoning the dynasty's second emperor, Le Thai-tong. Although the accusations were probably false, his criticisms of high-level corruption had won him no friends at court: Nguyen Trai and three generations of his family were put to death.

3. It has been estimated that 3 to 5 percent of the Vietnamese population in pre-colonial times had mastered Chinese characters. Since one would learn Chinese characters before taking up *nom*, an additional step that not all chose to make, we may assume that knowledge of *nom* was less widespread, perhaps 1 to 3 percent. Access to the oral tradition was thus essential for authors seeking wider fame or influence.

4. That is, verses with a line of six words alternating with a line of eight words; or verses with two lines of seven words followed by a line of six words and a line of eight words.

5. Hoang Ngoc Thanh, *Vietnam's Social and Political Development as Seen through the Modern Novel* (New York: Peter Lang, 1991), 190.

6. Maurice M. Durand and Nguyen Tran Huan, *An Introduction to Vietnamese Literature* (New York: Columbia University Press, 1985), 132.

7. Ibid.

8. Cited in Dana Sacks, "Le Minh Khue's Language of Lost Ideals," *Crossroads* 13, no. 1 (1999): 4.

9. Dana Healy, "Literature in Transition: An Overview of Vietnamese Writing in the Renovation Period," in David Smyth, ed., *The Canon in Southeast Asian Literatures: Literatures of Burma, Cambodia, Indonesia, the Philippines, Thailand and Vietnam* (Richmond, Surrey: Curzon Press, 2000), 46–47.

10. Sacks, "Le Minh Khue," 3.

5

Art and Architecture

INTRODUCTION

A VISIT TO ONE of the numerous galleries that have now opened in Ha-noi or Ho Chi Minh City may lead one to note the seemingly overwhelming influence of Western schools of painting such as Cubism, Abstractionism, Futurism, or Fauvism on Vietnamese artists, and to conclude that their works are mere imitations of European masters' and that the Vietnamese are incapable of genuine creativity and lack any original aesthetics. This would be a great error. Vietnamese art and architecture in their modern expressions are but the offspring of thousands of years of tradition rooted in the immense bird-and-sun-engraved bronze drums of Dong-son, in the wooden sculptures of But Thap (or Ninh Phuc) and Thay pagodas, in the popular Dong Ho prints, or in the ceramics of Bat-trang. They are inspired by the agrarian background of Viet culture, trees with roots plunging deep into the rivers and mountains and sky of Vietnam, and blossoms most fragrant in the traditional surroundings of the village and its activities. Mythological tales of princesses and dragons; historical epics of sister queens, peasant-kings, child-prodigies, heroes all, and literary characters from the *Tale of Kieu* have long inspired Vietnamese arts and aesthetics. Nevertheless the art and architecture of Vietnam have also been strongly affected by the colonial era, which introduced Western artistic concepts, expressions, and methods such as figurativism, perspective, and oil painting, thus inaugurating the era of Vietnamese modern art.

PRE-COLONIAL ARTS

Pre-colonial Viet art found its expression in bronze casting, stone and wood sculpture, block printing, pottery, lacquerwork, and architecture, the last considered the premier of all arts. Given the limitations of the scope of this book, only a few of these methods will be discussed: pottery, wood-block prints, lacquerwork, and architecture. Unlike in Europe, in Vietnam no distinction was made between fine arts and handicrafts. Vietnam was an agrarian society that did not begin industrializing until recently; most of the objects produced in premodern times, whether meant for the peasant's needs or the elite's enjoyment, came from the hands of master crafters. These were artisans who had acquired the knowledge and expertise from their ancestors, secrets transmitted from generation to generation and kept within the confines of a village specialized in a particular craft.

Throughout the Red River Delta sprang up villages reputed for one particular product: the village of Vac for its bamboo and paper fans; the village of Bat-trang for its ceramics; the village of Ngu Xa for its bronze casting, in particular, the bells used in pagodas and temples; the village of Dong Ky for its firecrackers (since New Year's fireworks were outlawed in the mid-1990s by the S.R.V., the village has switched to wood carving); or the Chuong village for its conical hats. At the beginning of the twentieth century, labor became so specialized that some villages would use one particular element only in a product and then sell it to another village, which would take up the next step; this process formed an artisanal chain of production. For instance, the making of conical hats starts with the village of Tao Dung, which makes the crowns. This is followed by the village of Canh Hoach, which produces the frames that are then rimmed in the village of Don Thu. The village of Chuong finishes the process by sewing the palm leaf frond onto the whole frame. There are villages in the Red River Delta that have thrived solely on handicrafts (e.g., the Van Phuc village for its silk and brocade, the village of Quat Dong for its embroidery) and have been able to produce for numerous local markets as well as the markets of the capital, Ha-noi, with its thirty-six streets. Each of these streets bears the name of the particular merchandise sold in exclusivity there: *Hang Bac* is the Silversmith's Street, *Hang Chieu* is the Grass Mat Street, and *Hang Trong* is the Drum Street, but it also sells wood-block prints. Nowadays, the products sold in these streets no longer correspond to the original names. For instance, in the Flaxseed Street (*Hang Gai*) one finds mostly silk fabric and clothes, and in Flower Street (*Hang Bong*), clothing articles.

In central Vietnam, the stone carving of Quang-nam and Da-nang and the wood carving and embroidery of Hue are famous. In the Mekong Delta, by contrast, because of the dispersed settlement pattern, clusters of different handicrafts (*xom nghe*) would gather along rivers and arroyos: wooden clog making, boat crafting, and tofu making in the province of Vinh Long; brick making and sugar refining in the province of Binh Duong; carpentry and silk raising and weaving in the province of An-giang, famous for its silk from Tan Chau; and stone sculpting in the region of Buu Long, province of Dong-nai.

The pre-colonial art and architecture of Vietnam were, in large part, products of anonymous and unrecognized artisans who catered to the daily needs of the peasant and the luxury consumption of the elite. They provided for the social and religious activities of these two groups from materials that surrounded them, such as bamboo, persimmon wood, palm leaf, clay, ivory, mother-of-pearl, gold, and silver. The skills of the artisans were undeniable as far back as the first millennium B.C.E., when bronze casting techniques led to the crafting of the gigantic bronze drums of Dong-son (the name refers to the area where the artifacts were first found), decorated with representations of animals, the sun, and tall humans in feather headdresses harvesting rice, racing boats, or hunting. Whether in wood carving (with or without mother-of-pearl inlay) and wood-block printing, in stone sculpting, in shaping delicate ceramics, or in silk and brocade weaving, over the centuries the Viet artisan has produced remarkable objects. Some of them have survived the passage of time and can be found in museums or in family collections, but most have been destroyed by the climate or the ravages of war.

Though springing from the soil of Vietnam, pre-colonial art and architecture have absorbed and integrated Buddhism, Confucianism, and Taoism while never losing touch with their rural and Animistic roots. The fusion of external elements with domestic sources has provided an inexhaustible well of inspiration to the artisans, as reflected in the dragons and unicorns on the curved roofs of temples and communal houses, in the Buddhist deities on sculpted lintels or as statues in pagodas; in the lotus, phoenix, turtle, and crane represented on lacquerware, ceramics, and bronze objects; and in the simple buffalo boy or village musicians and dancers represented on paper prints.

CERAMICS

According to archaeological findings that unearthed engraved diamond-patterned pots, the making of ceramics (*gom*) in Viet lands dates to Neolithic times, but it only truly took off during the independent monarchies in the eleventh and twelfth centuries. In this era, celadon-glazed ceramics made of fine white clay were produced in northern and central Vietnam, often decorated with the lotus motif or having a lotus shape, reflecting the influence of Buddhism. Urns with six handles for suspension, dragon-spouted pots, and animal-handled (e.g., parrots, shrimp) vessels were crafted during this time. In the fifteenth century, the use of ivory glaze over cobalt motifs (rooster, white elephant, crane, pelican, and flowers) on ceramics dominated, with an ornamental brushwork that became more skillful and elegant. The crackled glaze technique was applied by the crafter to create cracks that would then be brushed with colored ink (black or otherwise) to suggest landscapes, relief, or movements. By the seventeenth century, high-quality Vietnamese ceramics were sold throughout Asia as far as Turkey and Japan. In the latter they were called "Kochi" pottery (Japanese transcription of the word "Giao Chi"), and some of the pieces were favored for the tea ceremony. Figural ceramics of piglets, parrots, and ducklings made of crude brick clay and used as children's toys were much in demand, whereas ornamental ceramics of dragons and unicorns went to decorate temple roofs. Numerous pottery centers emerged in the Red River Delta, such as Bat-trang, Tho Ha, and Chu Dau, which produced diverse hue-glazed ceramics (e.g., green or brown monochrome glazes or gray-yellow ones); and in the Mekong Delta, such as Lai Thieu and Bien Hoa, which made glazed as well as unglazed everyday objects like jars and pots, bowls and plates, cups and incense burners, as well as small coffins for burying children, head supports, jardinieres, and terra-cotta roof tiles for pagodas and temples. The most famous ceramics center, and one that is still in existence and actively producing, is Bat-trang in the North.

Bat-trang, located about ten miles from Ha-noi, has been active at least since the fifteenth century and remains a thriving ceramics center, serving domestic and foreign markets. Thanks to nearby sources of kaolin, clay, and oxides, Bat-trang artisans did not have to go far for the primary materials that are used in making ordinary items such as rice bowls, cups and plates, pitchers, and building bricks, as well as refined, luxurious, carefully crafted objects such as flute-necked vases, delicate teapots and their accompanying cups, wine ewers, incense burners, and, in former times, the tiles that covered the floor of the Nguyen royal tombs in Hue.

Once taken from the ground, the clay is ground to a powder and mixed with water to form a thick paste, which is then thrown on a potter's wheel to be molded. Once the desired shape is attained, the potter brushes it with a glaze that, in Bat-trang's case, is typically ivory in color. Other tints can

Artisan using potter's wheel to fashion vases in
Bat-trang pottery center, northern Vietnam

also be attained, depending on the oxides used. The Bat-trang brushwork is
recognizable for its lightness and spontaneity and its blurred, uneven inten-
sity. The wares are fired in kilns that previously used wood but have switched
to coal. Vietnamese glazed and unglazed wares are not the only ceramics that
can be found in local markets; they compete with stoneware and earthenware
produced by the Highlanders or by Cham and Khmer of the central and
southern plains.

LACQUERWARE

Lacquerwork (*son mai*) is of ancient existence, as testified by the lacquered
items dating back to the third and fourth centuries B.C.E., which have come
to us almost intact. Lacquering was used for the preservation and decoration
of wooden items like betel boxes, tea trays, bowls, and cups, although it had
also been applied to ceramics and leather, even silver and gold. Traditionally

Artisan painting pottery at Bat-trang ceramics center, northern Vietnam

it allowed only three colors: black (*than*), derived from the oxidation of the
resin, red (*son*), from the use of vermillion, and brown (*canh gian*—literally,
the color of "cockroach wing"), from the mixing of black and red. Throughout the country, communal houses, pagodas, and temples had lustrous lacquered pillars and beams; statues of the Buddha and Taoist deities and
national heroes; ancestral altars, along with their votive items, like ancestral
tablets and candleholders, were equally lacquered, allowing them to survive
humidity and termites. The lacquer itself is a substance obtained from the
sap of the lacquer tree (*Toxicoderdron succedanea*), cultivated in the hilly
forests of Phu Tho province in the North. After a long process of successive
fermentation, heating, and mixing with other products, the secrets of which
vary according to each crafter, the varnish is applied to perfectly sanded
wooden items in multiple layers, each of which is left to dry, then polished
to a shine. Traditional materials such as crushed eggshell, wood ash, gold,

and silver are used to impart colors and relief. Over the centuries, and in particular during the heyday of Buddhism from the eleventh to the fifteenth century, lacquer artisans perfected the techniques and produced marvels like the beautiful vermillion- and gilt-lacquered miniature boat of the Keo pagoda or the polychrome lacquered *Quan Am* statue of the But Thap pagoda, shining from its centuries-old patina. During the French colonial period, thanks to the introduction of a new technique known as chiseling, lacquerers began to use a wider palette of colors, the painters' medium of choice along with oil and silk painting.

PAINTING

Painting, whether in the scroll form or as murals in premodern times, did not generate the same interest among Viet literati and artists as it did for their Chinese counterparts, who deemed it as high an art as literature. The tools (e.g., silk, paper, ink and brushes, woodblock) were there, but the circumstances were not favorable. It was not that the artistic impulse and creativity were lacking, only that they translated differently in the Viet context. Where a Chinese artist would paint roof beams and supports, the Viet counterpart would carve them. Where a Chinese artist of the Tang or Sung Dynasty would compose portraits or landscapes, the Viet artist would turn to folk prints, although there are a few nineteenth-century examples of Vietnamese silk painting.

Wood-block printing may be considered a major art form because of its creativity, the profusion of its production, and its unique themes and their treatments. Wood-block printing was a folk art that produced prints (*tranh dan gian*) meant for the peasant's enjoyment during festive times such as the New Year (*tranh Tet*, or Tet images) or the Mid-Autumn Festival, when even the poorest person could buy a few bright prints to adorn a humble abode. Villages such as Sen Ho, Nam Du Thuong, and Binh Vong used to specialize in wood-block printing, but Dong Ho (Bac-ninh) and Hang Trong (Hanoi) are the most renowned of them all for their colorful prints. In this handicraft as in the others, the whole family participates in every step of the wood-block printing process, with each person assigned a specific task. It begins with the drawing of the motif on paper, which is then glued to a block made of persimmon wood. The precise carving is then carried out by the artisan. The finished block becomes a family heirloom, passed on from generation to generation. It is inked and a piece of paper carefully pressed onto it. Outlines appear that are then filled in with different opaque and contrasting colors, which may also be printed from other blocks. The paper used for the printing is dyed, using plants like the yellow *Sophora japonica* and also minerals. A coating of diluted mother-of-pearl shell powder is applied to the paper to give it a unique sheen. Gold and silver touches can also be added, especially for religious paintings.

The themes are immutable but varied, springing from familiar rural surroundings as well as from mythological and historical sources, but all carry a symbolism meant to convey wishes of prosperity, happiness, and longevity; to impart moral, historical, or religious lessons; or to satirize. Above all, they display a sense of humor, even a sharp witticism, from the part of the peasant-artisan. Thus one may find the usual prints centering on flowers and fruits, with the lotus as the symbol of purity, harmony in marriage, and numerous progeny, or the peach as the symbol of spring, of marriage, and, above all, of longevity. Animals like the sow and her piglets represent abundance of wealth or of children; the rooster is seen as the symbol of courage, charity, and trust; and the toad is a symbol of success in examinations. There are illustrations of village scenes and activities (e.g., buffalo herding, wrestling, dancing), of chubby boys and girls carrying baskets of fruits or fish—scenes that evoke the peace and prosperity hoped for by all peasants at the New Year. To ensure the home's protection from demons and wandering evil spirits, prints of ferocious warrior-spirits are pasted to the door of the house. Other prints illustrate the favorite themes of resistance and heroism: the Trung sisters riding elephants, swords in hand, leading the charge against the enemy in the first century; the buffalo boy who became emperor (Dinh Tien Hoang); and Tran Hung Dao, who defeated the Mongol armies at Bach Dang in the thirteenth century. The prints often display a sharp humor, mocking students by representing them as frogs mindlessly memorizing lessons, or a certain eroticism, as in the print of a peasant boy harvesting coconuts while a scantily clad peasant girl awaits him at the foot of the tree. During the French and American wars the D.R.V. used this medium for its propaganda. Nowadays, only a few families still carry out the tradition of popular prints.

Modern Painting

When Vietnam entered the colonial dominion of France, the government introduced French aesthetics and art embodied in the *Ecole des Beaux-Arts de l'Indochine* (Indochina School of Fine Arts—ISFA), which opened in 1925 in Ha-noi. It was founded on the erroneous conception that Vietnamese people, like their colonized brethren, the Khmer and the Lao, were incapable of artistic concepts and could rise only to the level of handicrafts, and the school was meant to train generations of artisans who would keep handicrafts alive by producing them for the mother country—that is, for France. Despite that faulty premise, and thanks to the leadership of its first director, Victor Tardieu, a French painter and artist who appreciated Viet traditional art, an entire generation of Western-trained urban artists was born who were introduced to the world of oil painting, to new trends that were emerging in Europe in the twentieth century such as Cubism or Fauvism, and to European conceptions of anatomy and perspective.

While introducing the Viet to this new world, the French artists and teachers who presided over the ISFA, particularly Joseph Inguimberty, discovered Viet traditional art and techniques such as lacquerwork. This traditional technique, applied to objects of worship and for everyday use, found a new life as Inguimberty and his students made use of it as a medium of expression as rich as oil on canvas.

The first generation of modern artists, who graduated from the school in 1930, comprised such trailblazers as To Ngoc Van, Nguyen Gia Tri, and Tran Van Can. They studied classicism and romanticism and followed the poetical realism trend in their works. This trend inspired the artists to represent people interacting with nature in an idealized, harmonious setting, to create concrete images as vessels of the artist's sentiments and ideas; they experimented with impressionism and Fauvism; they were inspired by masters ranging from Renoir to Monet to Gauguin. Although the artists mastered oil painting, they often preferred to work in mediums such as silk painting, lacquerwork, and wood-block engraving as they continued to explore agrarian themes such as village dances, harvests, or festivals. The pre-1945 world that they depicted was an innocent one where life seemed to flow unchanged, as shown in engravings by Dinh Luc (e.g., *The Pagoda Gate*) or lacquerwork by Hoang Sung (e.g., *A Market Day in the Highlands*); women of this prewar time, as they appeared in the silk painting of Mai Trung Thu (e.g., *Young Woman of Hue*) or Le Van De (e.g., *Young Woman by the Pond's Bridge*), were of the upper class, often portrayed as languid and melancholic and idealized as willowy silhouettes straight out of *Kim Van Kieu*.

As an artist and a teacher, To Ngoc Van was among the most influential of the first generation of painters. With a style that continually evolved, he contributed a large body of work that covered numerous themes, from landscapes of famous sights like the Ha Long Bay to village scenes to portraits, especially of women. He is most noted for two paintings, *Young Woman and Lilies* and *Two Young Women and Child*, which have come to epitomize the Ha-noi woman of the 1930–1940s, urbane, refined, and graceful through his use of bold colors contrasted with restrained, minimalist lines.

Nguyen Gia Tri, his classmate, was among the first to master lacquer painting. At its best, his work combined techniques from the West and the East, using the multiple layers in lacquer painting to convey depth and illusion, the smoothness to bring a liquid but light impression to the scene, and the limited range of colors (black, gold, silver, vermillion red, and brown) to provide a distinct and unique dimension. As one can see in his *Spring Garden* or his *By the Surrendered Sword Lake*, Nguyen Gia Tri's favorite theme was that of the *ao dai*–clad city women, refined and demure, shown at their leisure against a background of lush gardens brimming with tropical blooms, existing in a dream world as conveyed by the artful use of shining red and gold in his lacquer painting and by the fluid silhouettes of the women.

Bui Xuan Phai, through his two favorite media, oil painting and pastel sketches, was inspired by the traditional village scenes of festivals and gatherings, by the local folklore and mythology, and by Vietnamese literature and *cheo* popular theater. He was also a passionate chronicler of Ha-noi and its thirty-six neighborhoods, which he showed evolving throughout the seasons in his works collectively known as *The Old Streets of Hanoi*.

All these artists left behind this sybaritic world when the war began and launched themselves into paintings that would no longer speak of self and of the inner world but of the heroism of a whole people. People like Nguyen Do Cung, for example, who had introduced Cubism into Vietnam, forsook their former passions to follow a narrow ideological path in arts when war hit home. The First Indochina War split the artistic world along the lines of the political division of Vietnam, forcing all of them out of their inner world and into the chaotic and deadly world of the war. With the partition in 1954, Vietnam witnessed the emergence of two schools of arts, one in the North and the other in the South. Through the choice of themes and techniques, the "southern school of arts" displayed a greater awareness of the West and its influences from the 1950s to the 1970s. In contrast, the more isolated "northern school of arts" turned inward, returning to its village roots and ancient folklore. Both schools chose as their main forms of expression oil painting, lacquer painting, and, to lesser extent, silk painting.

During its thirty years of relative isolation, the D.R.V. regime viewed the notion of "art for art's sake" as decadent, and "self-indulgent" artistic expressions such as nudes and abstraction disappeared from public view. Arts took on a more "pragmatist" approach, as they had to serve the country during its dire hours of need. Return to the peasant roots and the realities of the worker's everyday life was emphasized as the country took the socialist road. Thus was opened the College of Industrial Arts in 1958, while the

French-founded Fine Arts School was renamed Vietnam School of Fine Arts in 1949. As the war became increasingly pressing, themes such as heroism, dedication, and hard work were reflected in the artistic expressions of the time, specifically in painting, as the artist was turned into a "soldier" at the vanguard of the struggle against imperialism. In short, art became propaganda. Soviet-style Socialist Realism, as a school of expression, dominated all: it was supposed to serve the people and not the individual or the artist, to present ideas and not feelings, and to inspire people to act selflessly. Works by artists like Nguyen Sy Ngoc, Tran Van Can, and Nguyen Tu Nghiem reflected the spirit of the time. To Ngoc Van took the lead by embracing revolutionary themes, and his works—for example, *Uncle Ho at Work in Bac Bo*, *Soldiers and Porters at Rest*, and *In Search of the Enemy in the Forest*—emphasize the social over the personal. Scenes of battlefields, of the contribution by all classes and ethnic groups to the war effort, and of the havoc wrought by the bombing of villages were all expressed by artists in oil paintings, lacquerwork, wood-block engraving, and silk paintings. Languid silhouettes, sensuous forms, a lone melancholic rider, and beauty for beauty's sake were all renounced in favor of robust shapes, determined attitudes, muscular arms and legs, ruddy complexions, agrarian and industrial group activities, and themes like industry, socialism, and the military. In order to realistically capture the movement, the light, and the energy of their subjects, painters accompanied the troops into the jungles, went on night marches with them, slept in rice fields, and endured the pain and hardship of combat; worked with the peasant; or went underground with the miner. Throughout these works, an optimistic spirit emanated that banished despair, sadness, and melancholy as destructive, bourgeois emotions. Tran Van Can, a master at oil and lacquer painting, one of the leaders of Socialist Realist painting, was able to use silk, a medium usually reserved for ethereal topics, to deal with themes as mundane as industrialization and to project through works like *The Forge Producing Plowshares in a War Zone* a fiery sense of energy and enthusiasm as well as a palpable impression of volume.

Along with oil paintings that presented Socialist Realism–inspired themes, the artists of the North, cut off for decades from the outside world, sought inspiration by returning to the village and the traditional popular arts of silk painting, lacquer work, wood-block printing, communal-house carvings, and ancient ceramics as well as in landscapes and the activities of the minorities in the highlands and mountains. Nguyen Tu Nghiem is a perfect illustration of this tendency. He experimented with every medium and was successful in all. Witness, for example, his lacquerwork *Soldiers Playing the Flute*, where for the first time the color green was used successfully, or his wood-block engraving, *The Guerrillas of Phu Luu*. Nguyen Sang, a painter from the South who had participated in the battle of Dien Bien Phu, stood out for his anti-colonial message conveyed by the choice of his themes (atrocities committed by French troops); strong brush strokes; sparse colors; and linear, angular, and stark figures, as expressed in his paintings *Admission to the Party, The Bo Market*, or *The Enemy Burned My Village*.

In the South, the National College of Fine Arts—which opened in Saigon in 1954 with artists that had trained at the former ISFA—trained generations of artists (e.g., Nguyen Trung and Nguyen Than) who were widely exposed to Western influence. International trends in painting such as Cubism, abstraction, or Futurism had enormous impacts on the style of southern painters, although their inspirations remained rooted in the Vietnamese world. These Western schools of painting coincidentally suited the Vietnamese artistic temperament, which leaned toward poetry in painting and often refused to differentiate the poet from the painter. Such were the influences informing the work of the members of the Young Painters Association, among them Nguyen Khai, Dinh Cuong, Nguyen Thi Hop, Ho Thanh Duc. Women in the paintings of the southern school were often represented in the white *ao dai*–clad silhouettes of schoolgirls and as elongated, ethereal, upper-class women with tapered, lily-white hands, floating by the river, strolling to the market, or coming home from school.

Descriptive realism, as represented in portraits of individuals in the still life, was not widely adopted, although there are a few exceptions, of which Le Huy Tiep and Do Quang Em are talented examples. Do Quang Em's painting is unique in style and themes and has often been referred to as belonging to the school of hyper-realism. Throughout the war and continuing into recent years, his works—all on the themes of self and family members—appear, minutely painted, in a gold-ochre atmosphere, lit in a sort of nimbus, with the characters sitting or lying on bamboo beds or chairs and as if floating in another dimension, uncluttered by any objects except one or two rudimentary traditional utensils, and wrapped in a meditative inner world all their own.

Along with lacquerwork, silk painting has been the medium of choice for Vietnamese painters—though one extremely tricky to master, as colors can quickly be diffused throughout the entire fabric. The master of silk painting in the 1930s and 1940s was Nguyen Tien Chung. His work could transcend the fickle nature of silk to project taut images in which colors are carefully controlled to evoke an impression of tranquil force and measured peace. He masterfully exploited the tendency of silk to permit a softening of features and an uneven but striking dimension that neither oil nor lacquer painting can provide. His work often depicts the figure of a young woman deep in reflection, leaning on a cushion, clad in a velvety *ao dai*, her face perfectly oval and hands finely tapered. During the wars, silk was scarce, but Vietnamese artists continued to turn to it as their favorite medium whenever possible. Works from the prewar period that exuded a dreamy, sensuous quality ceded to those that conveyed a robust quality, a martial air reflective of the time. Nguyen Tien Chung, famous for his sensuous, romantic painting, also projects rhythmic force and dynamism in his landscapes, as can be seen in his work *Harvest*, which presents an immense golden field with an almost infinite horizon, limited only by distant hills. Silhouetted against the sky, bamboo hedges stand and peasants bend, busy harvesting the paddy or performing other tasks.

Vu Giang Huong's work, *A Liaison Post on the Truong Son*, which takes as its theme the liaison work carried out by women during the war, showed a few young liaison women, arms at shoulders, standing outside a dimly lit cave. The impression that viewers have is that of strong, independent, healthy women, unafraid, contributing their share to the war effort.

Of a later generation, Do Thi Ninh's watercolor on silk work is dominated by dynamic strokes and bursts of color that bring a powerful energy to her painting. In her *Thay Pagoda* painting, the eye is drawn to the vegetation, giant areca and banana trees pushing forth in large strokes of translucent green that practically dominate the ancient roofs of the pagoda, with nary a human silhouette to disturb the immutability of the scene.

With the return of peace and the reunification of the country in 1976, along with its opening in 1986 under *Doi Moi*, Vietnam saw the emergence of a profusion of artists who are now free to travel, to experiment, and to express themselves, no longer yoked to the necessities of wartime service. The first individual exhibition of a single artist, that of the well-known painter Bui Xuan Phai, opened in 1984. Artists from throughout the country were allowed to present exhibits of their works without fear of being accused of narcissism or of being "lackeys of the West." Artistic debates raged over the necessity for Vietnamese art, specifically painting, to detach itself from Vietnamese tradition in order to renovate itself.

Painters of the war generation, like Bui Xuan Phai (1921–1989) or Nguyen Phan Chanh (1892–1984), yielded to those of the younger generation, who have chosen to express themselves diversely. Rather than forsaking traditional expressions like lacquerwork, however, the younger artists are infusing them with new themes and techniques, opting for abstract expression or Fauvism while using a profusion of colors. Individualism and even artificiality have blossomed, and a profusion of galleries have sprung up in the cities, particularly in Ha-noi and Ho Chi Minh City, where censored artists of yore (e.g., Nguyen Than and Nguyen Trung) and rising ones (e.g., Tran Van Thao, Viet Dung, Dang Xuan Hoa, and Bui Minh Dung) take turns presenting their latest works. Nguyen Than's painting evokes Chagall and Dali, as it seems to create a world where a dreamlike element is dominant and yet where sadness seems to seep out. In *Autumn Love Letter*, the viewer looks out and beyond a wooden door frame half-immersed in water, upon the surface of which golden leaves are reflected. A white horse is ridden by a melancholic eye staring into the emptiness as the horse drinks from the lake.

Bui Huu Hung, a Ha-noi man and former soldier, expresses himself through lacquer painting, suffusing his work with themes of loss, tragedy, and destiny. Using Vietnamese historical, mythological, or folkloric figures, the painter evokes the sadness of a doomed dynasty or the mother's sorrow of losing her soldier son, ghosts from the past haunting the present. His portraits, often lit from below, stand in an empty landscape of mist and incense smoke, evoking an eerie sense of the nether world and of the weight of the past. Shifting to another world, an aquatic one (water is a favorite element in Vietnamese painting), there is Tran Luong and his *Under the Water* series, with its real and unreal sea creatures, jellyfish, anemones, and urchins undulating in the current.

A number of these artists have chosen to present their works through exhibits throughout the world, gaining experience and recognition while earning a living from the sale of their works. Such has been the approach of the young artist, Le Thiet Cuong, one of a cluster of young painters and sculptors who have emerged over the past decade, including Nguyen Tan Cong, Le Van Nhuong, Dang Hong Van, and Hoa Bich Dao. While still evoking rural themes of villages and famous landscapes of Vietnam, these artists present them through a fresh prism detached from social pressures and moral obligations. Take, for instance, the theme of Ha-noi's suburbs as viewed through the eyes of Hoang Dang Nhuan: in his *My Faubourg*, for example, the curved roofs of the houses are like boat sails of vibrant purple, vermillion, and cobalt blue rising in the gray winter sky of Ha-noi. Or take Le Thiet Cuong's abstract oil painting entitled *Herding the Water Buffalo*: in a wide, flat, blue landscape seemingly dotted with faint puffs of clouds floats the buffalo like a kite in the sky, tended by a brown, peasant-garbed boy holding the tether. The painting evokes a feeling of lightness, joy, and de-tachment. Chinh Le, a young female lacquer painter, is known for her Zen-like work, suffused with a certain mysticism, tranquility, and reflection that can be found in her lacquer entitled *Van Canh*. By contrast, and in testimony to her range, the joyfulness of youth is expressed in her *New Year*, a work resplendent with vermillion-clad persons, golden turtles, and pink lotuses, a painting that resonates with the vibrancy of the New Year and its rituals.

The Vietnamese arts, after a period of enforced slumber, have now revived thanks to strong outside demand and to the state's patronage. Artists are producing for domestic as well as international markets. Traditions that seemed perilously close to extinction are being learned again by younger artists, and artisan secrets that were seemingly about to die out with the last artisan in a given village are being carefully recorded for posterity. Once again artists can debate the merits of tradition over modernity, of abstractionism over realism.

ARCHITECTURE

Architecture in Vietnam, being born in the alluvial terrain in the Red River Delta, was initially limited in its choice of construction material: wood and brick over stone, which was not available in abundance as in Cambodia. Wooden monuments could not last forever but became victims of Vietnam's humid and hot climate and rich fauna. The historical condition of constant wars of resistance against invasion also contributed to their destruction, leaving behind little to match the splendors of Angkor Wat or the Bayon in Cambodia. Thus, only foundations remain of the ancient capital of Co Loa of the kingdom of Au Lac, or of citadels and palaces mentioned in historical texts. Stylistically and conceptually, traditional architecture in Vietnam bears the imprint of Chinese civilization as well as Indian civilization, as reflected in the Cham monuments that have survived time and war, mostly in central Vietnam at My-son or Po Nagar. However, only Viet—that is, *Kinh* traditional architecture, as embodied in the Hue palaces, in the citadels, temples, and pagodas, and in the peasant's habitation—will be discussed here. It should be noted that most of the monuments that can be seen nowadays are but new incarnations of their old selves, which have been restored incessantly as the result of war and intemperate climate.

Vietnamese architecture was influenced by China, although in this as in all else it adapted to the particular climate and landscape with its greater humidity and heat and, above all, to the Viet identity. The closer to the people, the more intimate and reflective of the Viet the traditional architecture was; the further away from them, the more Chinese the palatial architecture became. The buildings had a simpler quality, devoid of pretension but graceful in curves soaring to the sky and in lines symmetrical to the horizon. Depending on its function, Viet architecture can be divided into

Temple at Co Loa, northern Vietnam

three categories: religious, military, and civilian. However, it can be said that religious beliefs permeated all three, and in any case geomancy dictates the choice of the site and the orientation of the building along with its integration into the vegetation and landscape.

The typical Chinese-influenced edifice (palace or temple but not individual residence) adopted by Viet architects usually includes four sections: a stone terrace, a horizontal foundation and main body made of timber or brick, brackets, and an overhanging roof with curved ends crowned with mythical unicorns, dragons, or phoenixes and covered with glazed or enameled tiles. The successive edifices are symmetrically aligned on an axis, interspersed with gardens and pools, giving an overall impression of stately calm and grace. As they adopted these features, Viet architects modified them to harmonize with the different natural environment and mentality of the people: the roof's ends are deeply curved, like sea waves reaching to the sky, and richly decorated; the proportions and the scale, though smaller and lower, are adapted to the setting, following the horizon in their architectural lines. The wooden beams and brackets, along with panel friezes, are richly carved in relief, with friezes being inserted between the columns and the roofs.

Religious architecture involves pagodas (*chua*), communal houses (*dinh*), and deified national-hero temples (*den*). The Viet pagoda is a religious edifice that is meant for the practice of Buddhism, whereas the *dinh* and *den* are built for the worship of Taoist and Confucian deities in addition to numerous village guardian spirits and deified national heroes. Typically, a Viet pagoda is usually walled in, and the main entrance and the bell tower are placed farther in front, where a beautifully decorated portico announces to the visitor the name of the religious complex (traditionally written in Chinese characters but nowadays spelled out in *quoc ngu*). The main building, topped by a saddlebag roof, is in the shape of the letter H, with a wide frontal entrance. In the central room can be found the statues of the Buddha (as a child, as the historical Buddha, and as the Buddha of the future), flanked by bodhisattvas and arhats. The transversal wings are used for housing minor deities (e.g., of the earth, of war), guardian spirits, judges of the afterworld, and so on. Lacquered wooden columns rise to the roof and bear the supporting beams. Viet pagodas, unlike the Chinese ones, seldom have paintings because the carving of columns and beams is used as a decorative technique. Among the pagoda's edifices is the tower, derived from the Indian stupa and multi-storied (five, seven, or nine stories), an example of which can be seen at the Heavenly Lady Pagoda in Hue, which dates back to the seventeenth century.

The *dinh*, or temple and communal house, is both a civil and religious edifice. It serves as the worshiping place of the village's guardian spirits, the gathering locale for the entire village during festivities and rituals and the meeting site for the council of notables. Not vastly different in architecture from the *chua* it was, however, built on piles, a reflection of its Southeast Asian past, reminiscent of the communal houses of the mountain minorities. The *dinh* includes two parallel buildings, the principal one being a sanctuary that is not open to the public. Constructed in the shape of an inverted T, it houses the imperial decrees that conferred an official status on the village, that named it, or that bestowed imperial ranks to the guardian spirits worshiped by the village at an altar inside the sanctuary. The building is open only for the annual festivities and village notables' meetings. The *dinh* is always richly decorated with gold and vermillion lacquered parallel sentences, with embroidered standards, ceremonial parasols, and ceramics; it is the very symbol of the village and its standing. Among the most ancient *dinh* are the Dinh Bang temple and that of Tho Ha.

The *den*, the national or regional hero deities temple, is in the shape of an H or an inverted T and is always preceded by a courtyard fronted by a wall meant to protect it from evil spirits (hence the representation of the tiger). It differs from the *chua* in the sense that it has no Buddhist statuary, or at least none visible to the public; its rooms contain a number of altars bearing offerings and incense burners along with a rack of ceremonial halberds and swords. In the temples by the seaside near fishing villages, conse-crated whale or dolphin bones are encased in a glass box and carefully cleaned every year during the purification ceremonies. *Den* abound in Vietnam as monuments for the worship of national heroes; small and large, they dot the landscape—the Trung Sisters temple; the temple of the founder kings Hung Vuong, and the Marshall Tran Hung Dao *den* that are found all over the country and to which people still throng to worship and celebrate on the deity's day.

In the Red River Delta, the cradle of Vietnamese civilization, innumerable temples and pagodas rival each other in beauty and grace. This is true also for the capital itself, as Ha-noi is dotted with Buddhist pagodas, national hero and Taoist temples, like the Trung Sisters temple; the *Bach Ma* ("White Horse") temple dedicated to Cao Bien, a patron deity of Ha-noi and the founder of the Dai La kingdom; and the Ngoc Son temple near the Lake of the Surrendered Sword. Of note there are the *Van Mieu*, or Temple of Literature, and the unforgettable One-Pillar Pagoda (*Chua Mot Cot*), both from the eleventh century. The *Van Mieu*, following a North-South axis, is an enclosed complex of several courtyards, porticos, pavilions, and lotus ponds in addition to two rows of eighty-two stelae bearing tortoises that carry the names of 1,306 doctoral laureates inscribed in stone. The temple was dedicated to Confucius, and its grounds served as a royal college. The *Chua Mot Cot* was built in the shape of a lotus blossom, with its curved roofs emerging from the square-shaped pond on a straight stem pillar, the edifice itself being held aloft thanks to brackets sunk into the column and with a stone staircase bridging the pond and leading up to the pagoda. Both have been rebuilt so often that they have somewhat lost the patina that centuries confer to old buildings.

Outside the capital, one of the most important religious monuments is the Ninh Phuc or But Thap pagoda in Bac Ninh province, renowned for its architecture as well as for the richness of its carving, in both wood and stone. This is reflected in the innumerable Buddhist statues—in particular, that of the magnificent gold and vermillion lacquer *Quan The Am* statue, represented sitting on a lotus, with her thousand arms and thousand eyes and her huge nimbus, a masterpiece of Vietnamese statuary. Another example is the ema-ciated Buddha, who is represented sitting on a lotus, gaunt and skeletal; this is the Buddha before enlightenment. The pagoda itself, built somewhere between the thirteenth and seventeenth centuries and dedicated to *Quan The Am*, is a structure that includes eight buildings, some reflecting a strong Chinese influence (the Thien Dien pavilion with its stone bridge and bal-ustrade), and others more Viet in their features. Upon entering the portico, one encounters the one-story bell tower followed by the temple complex: pavilions with their roofs deeply curved at the corners and a number of stupas, the tallest an octagonal, four-storied building made entirely of stone. In the same province can also be found the more ancient and equally important Buddhist architecture of the Van Phuc Pagoda.

The existence of Vietnamese military architecture with its varied edifices is explained by the constant necessity for the country to defend itself against invasion and the concomitant construction of numerous citadels. The most famous one, Co-loa, the shell-like structure snaking up into the sky from the third century B.C.E., was the capital of the Au Lac kingdom, but its only remains are three-rampart foundations. The Ho citadel, built in the fourteenth century, is described as being of rectangular shape, each facade closed by an arched gate, with the external walls, the arches, and the foundations built of enormous stone blocks; it is no longer extant. The citadels of Hanoi, Hue, and Sai-gon—of more recent (nineteenth century) and partially French-inspired construction (built according to the Vauban model)—are also of note, with their square, octagonal, or pentagonal shape, their watchtowers and gated entrances, and their enclosed walled buildings several stories high. The one that has survived is the square-shaped citadel of Hue, which is, in fact, a citadel within a citadel, inside which resides the imperial city. Another type of military architecture is the defensive wall: the Dong Hoi wall, constructed in 1631 by the Nguyen princes to interdict the entrance to the South by the Trinh lords, was a formidable monument twelve miles long, from the Dau Mau mountain to the mouth of the Nhut Le river; dozens of feet high, mounted with cannons and stone mortars; and with an inside parapet wide enough to allow elephants and horses to circulate.

The civilian architecture includes imperial palaces as well as habitations of peasants and mandarins, infrastructure, and so forth. Unfortunately, very few of these edifices remain. The imperial palaces in Hue, for instance, built relatively recently in the nineteen century, followed the same pattern as the Qing capital in Beijing, but they have been ravaged so repeatedly by war and flooding (most devastatingly during the Tet Offensive in 1968 and as recently as spring 2000 by serious flooding) that they stand nowadays as the sums of successive repairs. These edifices reflect the division into three parallel sections common to habitations. The main section, acting as a principal nave, is wider and higher than the other two. Conceptually they are not very different from their Chinese counterparts, with their symmetric pattern, enclosing walls, successive courtyards, pavilions, and elevated terraces rising by the bank of the Perfume River. Vietnamese elements are contributed by the rich wood carving of the supporting beams and pillars (lacquered in vermil-

Gate at the Imperial City, Hue City, central Vietnam

lion and gold) and of the doors, which feature panel friezes encrusted with mother-of-pearl or ivory and bearing illustrations of flowers and mythical animals and stylized Chinese characters, often in parallel sentences and poems composed by the emperor himself. Civilian architecture also includes covered bridges, remarkable by their harmony, of which a rare surviving instance can be found in the village of Say Son, province of Son-tay. This covered bridge dates back perhaps as far as the ninth century and bears Chinese influences in terms of style, standing on stone arches and topped by a beautifully curved wooden roof. Its survival is especially extraordinary, as this type of construction was usually among the first to be destroyed during invasion.

Unlike the religious and military buildings that were built to last, Viet habitation is impermanent because it is made of perishable material like bamboo, wood, palm leaf, and mud. Nevertheless, its careful construction followed age-old principles, and the house itself was often said to be a temple as well as a habitation because it houses the ancestral altar. Its construction as well as orientation (on a North–South axis, facing East) strictly follow rigid rules. Unlike their mainland Southeast Asian counterparts (e.g., Thailand, Laos, or Cambodia), the house (or *nha*) in Vietnam—from the Red River Delta to the narrow plains of central Vietnam to the Mekong Delta—is generally not raised but built directly on the ground. Throughout the country, the steep roof (of palm frond or terra-cotta tile), which is saddle-, ridge-, or straight-sloped, may differ slightly in terms of its inclination or in the number of slopes (usually four). The house in general may use materials like bamboo or wood for its frame, palm leaf for its matting walls (or cob for the latter), some stone for the pillars to rest on (in the affluent houses), and bare, pounded earth or tiles for the floor. A basic structure with logs and/or bamboo poles to support the roof is set up first, with a frame tied to them. The more elaborate houses have a complex system of cross beams and roof support. Next comes the roof, followed by the walls. There are usually one to three front entrances and barred windows (when the walls are made of wood), usually shaded by a veranda. Although there are stylistic variations depending on the wealth of the owner and hence on the materials used, the disposition of the house and the rooms is basically the same.

The traditional house, understood as an ancestral home, may consist of a single building or several, with the principal edifice divided into one main room and two side rooms. In the poorer houses, there may be only a single room. The main room, considered also as the men's area, contains the ancestral altar (sometimes three, in an elaborate house) placed centrally against the rear wall, a wooden polished (often carved and mother-of-pearl inlaid) plank or bed, which serves as the reception place for guests to sit on, and storage jars. Of the two side rooms, one is used by the parents and as a storage space for the precious family mementos and possessions, and the other is a bedroom for the children. The kitchen, with its three-pronged open hearth, is to be found in a rudimentary shed in the back of the house, perpendicular to the main building; it is also used as a storage space for the sauce jars, pots, and pans. In the rear, there is a garden of fruit trees and herbs, at the foot of which lies a pond used for washing and for raising ducks and fish. A well provides potable water, which can also be scooped out of large earthenware jars set out for the collection of rainwater. There may be additional sheds for utensils and animals. More modern homes are generally masonry houses, usually multi-storied with a shaded terrace on top in the city but single-storied and straight-roofed in the countryside. Recently, however, the construction of multiple stories, symbolic of wealth, is spreading quickly, even in the countryside.

Because of the lack of space in the city, the disposition of the three rooms is often compressed, with the rooms succeeding one another along a single axis. If a family's means permit there is generally a courtyard with a tiny pool decorated with rocks and trees to bring some relief in the hot summer months.

6

Cuisine

INTRODUCTION

JUST AS PRE-COLONIAL VIETNAM was a crossroads of cultures and religions, it was also a place where Asia's and the world's foods, utensils, spices, and modes of preparation and consumption blended, with the Viet selecting those that appealed to them and creating a unique "food culture."

The nearly 1,000-year period of Chinese domination contributed to the Vietnamese assimilation of staples such as soy sauce, bean curd, and noodles; as well as of techniques of food preparation and consumption including stir-frying and deep-frying with the wok and the use of chopsticks. The Mongol invasions during the thirteenth century contributed to Vietnam's food culture as well, particularly in northern Vietnam. From this horse-riding and herding people, the Vietnamese enhanced their taste for meat dishes, manifested in northern specialties such as *pho* (beef and noodle soup) and *thit bo bay mon* ("Seven Dishes Beef"), and adopted the technique of cooking meat on a "Mongolian hot pot," or *lau*. The Southward Movement, or *Nam tien*, which carried Viet settlers from the North to what is today central and southern Vietnam between the sixteenth and nineteenth centuries, brought them into sustained contact with the Indianized cultures of the Cham, the Khmer, the Thai, and the Malay peoples, who contributed their knowledge of spices, attained through international trade, and their fondness for curried dishes.

Viet lands also participated in the Columbian Exchange, the movement of plants, animals, and technology from the "New World" of the Americas to the "Old Worlds" of Africa and Eurasia. European explorers and traders from the 1500s introduced to Dai Viet, directly or via third countries such as China, New World staples such as peanuts, potatoes, corn, and tomatoes, which were quickly adopted and assimilated. Vietnamese assimilation of Western foods was most intense during the nearly 100 years of French colonization (1862–1954), when many Vietnamese, particularly members of the urban elite, developed a passion for French coffee, bread, butter, ice cream, and pastries. By contrast, the shorter American involvement left relatively little imprint on Vietnamese food culture. Ho Chi Minh City, for example, has several establishments that serve American foods such as hamburgers and fried chicken, but they cater to a primarily foreign clientele.

UTENSILS AND MANNERS

Vietnamese cooking equipment and eating utensils are few and have changed little from pre-colonial times. Refrigeration was impossible, and most fresh foodstuffs were taken from the family garden or pond or purchased from the local market on the day of consumption. Foods were cooked on a brick or clay stove. Charcoal or wood was the preferred fuel because each gives a steady, moderate heat; poorer households resorted to straw or dried leaves, which are less desirable since they generate an intense, short-lived heat. Cooking methods included grilling, baking, boiling, and steaming. The basic cooking implements were a large, curved-bottomed pan called a *wok* in China and a *chao* in Vietnam, a wooden chopping block, and a large iron cleaver; from colonial times onward, some southern cooks replaced or supplemented the *chao* with a French-style sauté pan. Pre-colonial households also used a bronze or earthenware casserole (*noi*) and elongated "kitchen chopsticks" (*doi dua bep*) for cooking rice. Meats and vegetables were cut into bite-size morsels in the kitchen before serving, and cutlery was not used at the table. Given the limited equipment and preference for copious amounts of chopped fruits and vegetables, food preparation was a labor-intensive and time-consuming process.

Well-to-do families took their meals while seated upon a low table or tray called a *phan*, with food placed at its center. No tablecloths or covers were used, and the tables used by elite families were made of beautifully carved wood. Rice was served in individual bowls (*bat* or *chen*), while other prepared foods were served in communal bowls placed at the center of the table on a raised tray called a *mam*. Diners held their individual bowls in their left hands and their chopsticks in their right hands. Poorer families usually spread a bamboo mat called a *chieu* on the floor, put a *mam* in the center of the *chieu*, and crouched around it with their individual bowls in hand.

Pre-colonial Vietnamese used chopsticks (*doi dua*) made of wood, bamboo, or ivory to pick up solid food, and ceramic spoons (*thia* or *muong*) to scoop up liquids such as soups. Young children unable to manipulate chopsticks ate solids as well as liquids with spoons. Given the prevalence of soups and broths, drinks of any kind were not served during meals but were made available before or after for those who wanted them.

Etiquette governed food consumption. The basic conventions, most of which are observed today in attenuated form, may be summarized as follows. The daughters or daughters-in-law usually sat near the casserole and put rice in the individual bowls for everyone; in wealthy families, servants would perform this task. Family members were not to start eating until the senior male of the household (usually the father or grandfather, occasionally the great-grandfather) had begun the meal by serving himself from the dishes presented on the *mam*. Nobody was to leave until the meal had been completed, at which time they had to ask the senior male's permission to do so. In some elite households, the senior male was served individually by his wife or daughters and ate apart from the family. Diners were not to move food directly from the communal bowls to their mouths but had to put it in their individual rice bowls first, using the larger end of their chopsticks for this purpose. When not in use, chopsticks were placed on the edge of one's bowl or by its side. They were never placed upright, sticking out of the food, as this calls to mind incense sticks and symbolizes funerals.

CEREALS, FRUITS, AND VEGETABLES

Rice has long been the staple of Viet cuisine. Indeed, the verb "to eat" in modern Vietnamese is *an com*—literally, "to eat rice," but it is used whether or not rice will actually be consumed at the meal in question. There are two basic kinds of rice: glutinous, or "sticky," rice (*gao nep*), which is prepared by steaming, has been the staple of the non-Viet highlands peoples; ordinary rice (*gao te*) has played that role for the majority Viet. However, the Vietnamese also consumed limited amounts of steamed glutinous rice, which they call *xoi*, mainly for breakfast, on festival days, at funerals, or at weddings. Rice was consumed in other forms as well. Rice flour was used to make noodles (*bun*), cakes, and rice paper for wrapping vegetables or fish in dishes such as *chao tom*, a shrimp and sugarcane delicacy. Rice was also fermented in a fish or shrimp base to produce condiments such as *mam tom* (shrimp paste). Finally, it was distilled to make a variety of wines and liquors. (The general name for alcoholic beverages is *ruou*, followed by a specific term as in *ruou nho*, "grape wine," or *ruou bia*, "beer.") It must be emphasized, however, that in pre-colonial and particularly in colonial-era Vietnam, Vietnamese farming families were often too poor to eat the rice that they grew, in which case the common practice was for the household to sell most of the rice crop immediately after the harvest, saving only enough seed grain for the next planting and perhaps a small amount for consumption on special occasions. In such cases, the daily rice was replaced in the diet by corn, the second most important grain, or tubers such as potatoes, sweet potatoes, and manioc.

Pre-colonial Vietnamese consumed a wide variety of fruits and vegetables. The most important fruits were bananas (*chuoi*), oranges (*cam*), grapefruits (*buoi*), lemons (*chanh*), mangoes (*xoai*), papayas (*du du*), jackfruit (*mit*), durion (*sau rieng*), and pineapples (*dua*). They were served in many ways—raw, cooked, and dried—and eaten before, between, during, and after meals. Unripe fruits were also used. Green papayas, for example, were sliced thinly and served with shrimp in a salad called *goi du du*. The list of uses to which fruits are put has been constantly expanding because the Vietnamese have been exposed to foreign cultures and new technologies. For example, most of the above-named fruits are now used to flavor ice creams. Lemon juice, diluted by ordinary or carbonated water, spiked with sugar or salt, and poured over ice, is now a popular beverage in southern Vietnam.

In addition to the fruits themselves, Vietnamese made use of edible flowers. "Floral cuisine," still enjoyed today, utilized, for example, the grapefruit tree's flowers, from which an oil was extracted and used for flavoring desserts. Lotus seeds were used as a stuffing for main dishes such as chicken or were cooked in syrup and eaten for dessert. Jasmine flowers flavored candies and teas.

The most widely used vegetables and legumes were soy (*dau nanh*), convolvus (*rau muong*, a "floating plant" that flourishes on the lakes of Vietnam), aubergine (eggplant) (*ca*), potatoes (*khoai Tay*), sweet potatoes (*khoai lang*), onions (*cu hanh*), shallots (*cu he*), garlic (*toi*), mustard (*rau cai*), mint (*rau hung*), and ginger (*gung*). Among the most important of these were soy, convolvus, and aubergine. Soy shoots were eaten fresh from the garden, used in prepared dishes, and added as a topping on soups such as *pho*. Soy beans were processed to make soy milk (*nuoc dau* or *sua dau nanh*), a popular beverage, now commonly heated or iced and sweetened with sugar; curdled soy (*dau phu*), extensively used in soups and as a main dish, often to replace meat or fish in vegetarian cuisine; and to produce a spicy sauce called *tuong*, second only to *nuoc mam*, a fermented fish sauce, as a condiment. Convolvus

Vegetable merchant (in hat) bargains with customers, Ho Chi Minh City, southern Vietnam

was harvested by farming families, particularly in the North, who made it a staple because of its cheapness and availability. Inventive cooks developed many attractive ways of serving it: boiled and eaten with a *nuoc mam* or *tuong* dip; in freshwater crab soup; or thinly sliced as a salad. Given its association with the home, family, and village life, this seemingly humble plant arouses considerable emotion, as expressed in a folksong: "As long as the sky, water, and clouds endure, there will be lakes of convolvus and jars of soy sauce."[1] A similar role was played by the eggplant, which was often salted and stored in large pots until needed. Like the convolvus, eggplant was considered to be a reliable staple to which a family could turn in hard times, as one would turn to a true friend when in trouble.

On the topic of vegetables, it must be mentioned that, under the influence of Buddhism's teachings on abstaining from taking the lives of sentient beings, many pre-colonial Vietnamese practiced vegetarianism (*an chay*) at least part of the time. Abstinence from consumption of animal products (including milk and eggs) was (and remains) the rule in most Vietnamese monastic orders, and monks and nuns were required to follow a vegetarian diet (e.g., boiled vegetables and salted grilled sesame, with soy sauce replacing fish or shrimp sauce) year-round. Some modern lay practitioners follow suit and abstain from eating animal products on a permanent basis. Many more abstain during limited periods: for example, on Buddhist holidays, before visiting a pagoda, or to give thanks for a safe journey or successful examination performance. Although the daily vegetarian diet at monasteries may seem austere by modern Western standards, for lay practitioners, giving up animal products did not necessarily mean abandoning tasty and varied fare. Vietnamese cooks developed vegetarian alternatives to many dishes. Meat, fish, or fowl were replaced by peas, tofu, green bananas, or coconut meat. A skilled chef can prepare tofu in such a way as to make it almost indistinguishable from duck or other delicacies. A modern innovation is the "vegetarian takeout" restaurant. Located near major pagodas and advertising with placards featuring lotus flowers (symbolizing enlightenment) and the words *do an chay* ("vegetarian food"), these places prepare vegetarian delicacies that can be taken home and consumed by lay practitioners or used as offerings at the pagoda.

MEAT AND MEAT PRODUCTS

With most of Vietnam's arable lowlands given over to rice production, and with little large-scale animal husbandry or hunting, meat and meat products played a relatively small role in the daily diets of most Vietnamese. Many peasant households, taking maximum advantage of the scarce resources at their disposal, raised fowl such as pigeons, chickens, and ducks, which provide some of their own sustenance by scavenging. The fowl were valued for their flesh and eggs as well as for their internal organs, especially the intestines. The flesh of ducks, for example, was the main ingredient in many dishes, including a rice-based soup called *chao vit*; fertile duck eggs (*hot vit*) were boiled and eaten out of the shell with a garnish of fragrant knotweed (*rau ram*); and curdled duck's blood (*tiet canh*), garnished with *rau ram* and served with sliced meats, was considered a delicacy.

Elite cuisine utilized the larger domesticated animals, including goats, oxen, water buffalo, dogs, and pigs, among which the last was the most widely consumed.[2] Pigs were nourished with rice bran (*cam*) and duckweed (*beo*) and were prized for their role in religious sacrifices (e.g., as offerings to the village genies) as well as in consumption, particularly on special occasions such as the New Year's Festival. Among the many ways of preparing pork in pre-colonial Vietnam, roast pork (*heo quay*) was a prized main dish; pig's intestines were the main ingredient in a spicy rice-based soup called *chao long*; and seasoned ground pork was wrapped in banana leaves and boiled to produce a portable snack called *gio*, of which there were many varieties and uses. Dog meat also played a role in pre-colonial cuisine, but it was a delicacy that was rarely eaten, even among the elite. Hunting and trapping were not highly developed as professions in pre-colonial Vietnam, but elite cuisine did make use of the flesh, bones, blood, and internal organs of larger mammals, such as deer, as well as those of larger reptiles, including iguanas, pythons, and cobras. Smaller mammals, such as bats and mice, were a welcome addition to the diets of peasant households.

FISH AND CRUSTACEANS

Having more than 1,000 miles of coastline and countless rivers, lakes, canals, and rice paddies at their disposal, pre-colonial Viet made fish, crustaceans, and batrachians (frogs and toads) an essential part of their diets, much more important than the meats and meat products discussed above. Most freshwater fishing was carried out with rudimentary tools on a part-time basis by the members of farming families that derived the bulk of their sustenance from agricultural activities. Crabs, shrimp, and tiny fish were hunted in shallow waters with small bamboo baskets with openings at both ends. The wider end was thrust into the water over the prey, and the fisherperson reached through the smaller opening, still above water level, to take out the catch.

Frogs were hunted within their holes by using two metal implements, one to widen the hole and another to impale its inhabitants. Fish were taken in deeper rivers, canals, or lakes by means of fishing lines with baited hooks or, more commonly, by nets that were cast from or pulled by small boats. Peasants also dredged the bottoms of rivers and lakes for snails and other mollusks. Coastal and deep-sea fishing was mainly practiced by professionals. Many coastal villages devoted themselves almost entirely to fishing and related activities, using their catches to purchase agricultural and other goods. Well-organized fishing brotherhoods took multiple-mast sailing ships to sea for weeks on end pursuing desirable species, netting and salting the catch before returning to shore to sell the proceeds.

Fish was eaten fresh, dried, or salted. If eaten fresh, it was fried, boiled, grilled, or added to soups. A Ha-noi specialty called *cha ca*, for example, featured grilled chunks of catfish (*ca bong lau*) served on a hot plate in sizzling fat. The fish morsels were plucked from the plate by individual diners, garnished with mint, coriander, scallions, ground peanuts, chili peppers, and *nuoc mam*, and eaten. In the absence of refrigeration, drying in the sun was often used as a method of preserving fish for later consumption; smoking of

Fishmongers at a periodic urban market, Ho Chi Minh City, southern Vietnam

fish, by contrast, was rare. Larger fish were gutted before drying, but smaller species were dried and eaten in their entirety.

Crustaceans, mollusks, and other related animals were prepared and eaten in a like manner. Fresh crabs and shrimp, for example, were steamed, boiled, grilled, fried, or prepared in soups. A specialty of Ha-noi joined tiny crabs and asparagus into a soup called *mang Tay nau cua* (literally, "Western bamboo shoots cooked with crab"). Drying was likewise commonly used to preserve shrimp and squid, although it was considered inappropriate for crabs. Sun-dried squid (*muc kho*), for example, was a favorite snack (*do nhau*) to accompany alcoholic beverages.

In addition to serving fish and crustaceans directly in soups, main dishes, and salads, pre-colonial Viet also processed them with salt and other ingredients to produce condiments and sauces, including crab paste (*mam cua*), shrimp paste (*mam tom*), and fish sauce (*nuoc mam*). Among these, the most widely used sauce was *nuoc mam*, which was considered indispensable in the daily meals of pre-colonial Viet; it remains so today. Although many different kinds of fish were used in making *nuoc mam*, and many peasant households simply used whatever kinds were available, the preferred variety—and the one used in commercial production—was a tiny anchovy called *ca com*. In high-quality commercial production, anchovies are heavily salted and left in a large barrel to ferment. After about three months, the liquefied portion of the mixture is drawn off from the bottom and reinserted on top of the remaining fish solids. Three months later, the dark-brown liquid portion is skimmed off the top; the solid remains of the fish, having settled to the bottom, are removed and may be used as fertilizer.

Alternatively, water may be added to the solid remains, which can then be pressed to produce more batches of sauce, but the additional pressings yield a lighter-colored, weaker-tasting product. The best quality *nuoc mam*, called *thuong hang*, is deep amber in color with a pungent, salty taste. It was used as a flavoring in cooking and added directly to food as salt would be at a Western meal. A popular dipping sauce (*nuoc cham*) was made by mixing *nuoc mam* with water, lime juice, chopped chilies, pressed garlic, chopped scallions, and sugar; it was used extensively to add spice to many different dishes and salads. Even today, no Vietnamese meal, except for a vegetarian one, is complete without *nuoc mam* or *nuoc cham*.

Unable to consume adequate quantities of meat, fish, or batrachians on a continual basis, many pre-colonial and colonial-era families had diets that were lacking in protein. Additional sources of animal protein were sought in the insect world. Southern peasants, for example, searched coconut trees for palm grubs (*con duong*), which were rolled in flour and fried. Northerners, for their part, captured and ate grasshoppers (*con chau chau*), and boiled grasshoppers were commonly sold in rural markets of the North. However, while palm grubs as a snack food were appreciated by all classes, grasshoppers were considered a "poor person's food" and were disdained by elite consumers. Farming families still seek to augment their diets by hunting for these and other traditional hedges against hunger, but the increased use of chemical fertilizers and pesticides in rice farming has dramatically reduced the number and variety of fauna in the deltas.

DRINKS AND DESSERTS

The main beverage during pre-colonial times was tea, of which there were many varieties and methods of preparation. Farming families used Vietnamese green tea, called *che tuoi* or *che xanh* (*che* and *tra* are the general terms for teas), which was grown in household gardens and picked right before use. The untreated leaves were boiled in an earthen pot, from which large bowls of the strong, hot liquid were poured as desired. Given the warm climate and heavy workloads of the peasants, copious amounts of green tea were consumed daily for refreshment and for the mildly euphoric state that the leaves produced. According to custom, anyone calling upon family or friends for help in fieldwork or construction was expected to provide lots of hot green tea to keep up the workers' energy and spirits. Other varieties of Vietnamese teas included dried tea (*che kho*), grilled tea (*che man*), and tea made from seeds instead of leaves (*che hat*); in addition to these domestic varieties, which provided the bulk of daily consumption, Chinese teas of all sorts (generally called *che Tau*) were imported for elite consumers.

The Viet elite did not generally participate in an elaborate tea ceremony comparable to that of the Japanese. Nor did Viet connoisseurs place the same emphasis on the myriad varieties of luxury teas, as did their counterparts in China. However, the pre-colonial Viet elite did develop an institutionalized practice of tea consumption. As noted earlier, beverages, including teas, were not served during meals; generally speaking, tea and other nonalcoholic beverages were served after meals, and alcoholic beverages before, either alone or with snack foods such as palm grubs. Thus, a special table called *tra ky* with three places was set up against a wall and reserved for tea drinking. Hot brewed tea was poured from a teapot into a large bowl called the *chen tuong*, or "general's bowl," and placed on the tea table. The three connoisseurs then served themselves in tiny "soldiers' cups" (*chen quan*), held with the thumb and forefinger and perhaps the middle finger (but never the ring or little fingers). The use of the "general's bowl" ensured that the tea in the "soldiers' cups" was of uniform strength, which would not have been the case if they had been filled successively from the teapot. The drinking cup was never to be completely emptied, because undissolved particles of leaves collected on the bottom.

Teas of all kinds, Vietnamese as well as Chinese, are still widely consumed in the S.R.V. today, and hot green tea remains the Vietnamese peasant's drink of choice. However, teas are being eclipsed by imported or foreign-inspired beers, soft drinks, and coffees among urbanites who can afford them.

Alcoholic beverages were an important feature of life in pre-colonial Vietnam, used by all classes for ritual, medicinal, and recreational purposes. By far the most commonly consumed variety of alcoholic drink was *ruou nep*, a liquor (*ruou*) distilled from glutinous rice (*nep*) and resembling Japanese *sake* in taste and color. There were numerous variations: rice liquor made with red glutinous rice was called *ruou cam*; lotus flowers added flavor and aroma to *ruou sen*; and goat's blood was mixed with rice liquor to produce *ruou tiet de*, prized as a tonic. Most of the alcoholic beverages consumed by pre-colonial Vietnamese were domestically produced, but some were imported from China, particular a sorghum liquor called *ruou cao luong*.

Rice liquor, being a distilled and therefore purified product, was one of the traditional offerings to deities and ancestors. According to the proverb *Vo tuu bat thanh le* ("Without alcohol, rituals lose their character"), offerings omitting alcohol were meaningless.[3] (This did not apply to Buddhist offerings, however, since Buddhism advocates self-mastery and forbids intoxicants.) Rice alcohol was also used therapeutically in Vietnamese and Sino-Vietnamese traditional medicine, either alone or mixed with the blood of animals such as goats or snakes. *Ruou nep* was consumed during the Fifth Month Festival because it was thought to kill worms in the body. The most common use for alcohol, however, from pre-colonial times to the present, was for relaxation and entertainment, usually in a social context, with groups of males drinking together. Glasses of liquor, in contrast to those of tea, were drained completely. Intoxication was permitted as long as disorderly behavior did not result. However, this relatively tolerant view of alcoholic consumption was extended to males only; drinking was considered immodest and improper for women, no matter what the conduct.

While rice-based liquors are still consumed in Vietnam today, Western or Western-inspired alcoholic drinks, especially beers (called *ruou bia*, or simply *bia*), well suited to Vietnam's tropical climate and spicy cuisine, have been gaining in popularity since colonial times. In addition to the many imported brands available, of which Singapore's Tiger Beer is the most prized, many kinds of beers are brewed in the S.R.V., either in cooperation with foreign firms (Huda Beer, for example, is a Danish-licensed product brewed in Vietnam's Hue City) or independently (Vietnam's "33" Beer). Bars, restaurants, and cafes routinely offer an assortment of domestic and imported beers. While the prices of imported brands remain too steep for the budgets of most working families, many working men regularly consume copious quantities of inexpensive local draft beers (*bia hoi*), which at about 2,000 *dong* per liter, cost no more than a pot of tea. Some urban professional women have begun to use alcoholic beverages in recent decades, although traditional taboos retain much of their potency.

Coffee is another rising star among Vietnamese beverages. Introduced by Western traders and popularized by French colonists, who founded coffee plantations in Vietnam's highlands, coffee is now avidly consumed by all but the poorest Vietnamese. The European and particularly French origins of Vietnamese coffee drinking, as adapted to the local climate and taste, are still evident in the way that the beverage is prepared and served. Vietnamese usually put domestically grown, freshly ground beans in a small metal filter (called *phin* after the French *filtre*), which is placed on top of a clear drinking glass. Boiling water is poured into the filter, giving a small amount of strong, black coffee similar to European-style expresso. According to preference, it may be served black (*ca-phe den*) or with sweetened condensed milk (*ca-phe sua*), either of which may be served hot (*nong*) or over ice (*da*). Condensed milk is used instead of fresh as it is easier to preserve and is more pleasing aesthetically to Vietnamese, who, lacking a dairy tradition, generally find fresh cow's milk disgusting and indigestible. A recent innovation is a Vietnamese version of the Starbucks-style coffee shop chain called *Trung Nguyen* ("Highlands"). These shops can be found in most of the S.R.V.'s major cities, serving a variety of luxury coffees by the cup or ground to be consumed at home.

Pre-colonial Viet enjoyed a wide variety of cakes, candies, and puddings. *Banh Trung-thu,* the cakes that were served during the Mid-Autumn Festival, had a glutinous rice crust that was oval-shaped, and they were stuffed with sweet sesame paste and decorated with auspicious dragon images. Another delicacy, this one associated with the New Year's Festival, was the *banh chung*, a square-sided cake made of glutinous rice and stuffed with meat and beans. The log-shaped cakes were wrapped in banana leaves, boiled, and allowed to cool. Before serving, the banana leaves were stripped away, and the portions, sliced off as needed, were seasoned with pepper and other spices and served cold or grilled. Candies called *mut* were made from papayas, coconuts, lemons, and other fruits. Often sold by ambulatory vendors, they contributed to the gaiety of Tet and were enjoyed year-round as well. Pre-colonial Viet also used fruits, vegetables, and legumes to fabricate sweet puddings called *che*, which were consumed as desserts or with ice as refreshing late afternoon snacks. *Che chuoi*, or "banana pudding," for example, blended bananas, coconut, and tapioca; *che bap*, or "corn pudding," utilized coconut and tapioca but replaced bananas with corn as the main ingredient.

Whereas most contemporary Vietnamese confine themselves, by taste or budget, to the sweets described above, a number of Western, particularly French, desserts have been gaining in popularity among well-to-do consumers since the colonial era. Western-style frosted cakes using wheat flour (called *banh ngot*, literally "sweet cakes"), for example, may be ordered by elite families for special occasions such as birthdays or graduations. Flan, or French-style custard, is considered a delicacy, and ice cream (*kem*) is a favorite among upper-class youths, as the mushrooming of *ca-phe kem* or "ice cream cafes" in urban centers testifies.

Areca Nuts, Tobacco, and Opium

Though neither food nor drink, several other plant-based products consumed by pre-colonial and colonial-era Vietnamese deserve mention: areca nuts, tobacco, and opium.

The areca nut chaw included nuts from the areca palm (*Areca catechu; cay cau*), betel vine leaves (*Piper betle; la giau* or *la trau*), and lime. The smallish areca nuts were sliced, mixed with slaked lime, and wrapped in the betel vine leaf. Although the ingredients were nearly universal, the quality of instruments for preparing and serving them varied widely according to social level, with ornate instruments being used by the well-do-do and basic utensils by the poor. Chewing the resulting chaw (*mieng giau* or *mieng trau*) produces a euphoric state, which some users enhanced by adding Vietnamese tobacco (*thuoc lao*) to the mix.

Betel chaws were regularly enjoyed by all classes and played an important role in enhancing social interactions. Guests were offered a chaw to welcome them, with the household children often being asked to prepare chaws for guests. Also, since the betel vine and areca palm so often appear together in nature, they came to represent marital fidelity and happiness. The leaves and nuts, along with instruments for their preparation and consumption, were exchanged in celebration of betrothal and marriage.

The practice of chewing betel contributed to the custom of blackening the teeth with lacquer. Betel chewing stained the teeth unevenly in a way that was considered unattractive; the solution to the problem was to blacken them entirely by lacquering, which came to be considered attractive, especially in women, to the point that one could describe (as the writer Le Qui Don did) a beautiful woman in eighteenth-century Vietnam as having "rosy cheeks and black teeth" (*ma hong rang den*).

Under Western influence, the new standard, first felt in the cities in the early decades of the twentieth century, called for white teeth, and both betel chewing and teeth blackening gradually went out of practice. Today neither is widely seen, although elderly peasant women, particularly northerners, still chew betel, which is, along with its accompanying paraphernalia, still given as betrothal and wedding gifts.

As stated above, Vietnamese tobacco, or *thuoc lao*, was sometimes inserted into a betal chaw to enhance its effects, but *thuoc lao* was also used independently, usually by smoking in a long-stemmed water pipe. Increased contact with Western products and practices during the colonial period brought Western-style tobacco (called *thuoc la*—literally, "medicine leaf") smoked in cigarettes into prominence, particularly among urban males. Cigarettes have recently extended their range into the countryside as well, and it is probable that most Vietnamese men are now smokers, which means that Vietnam must expect significant increases in cardiopulmonary disease and cancers among males within the next ten to twenty years. So far, Vietnamese women have been more reluctant to take up the habit, probably because public smoking by women still connotes loose morals. Vietnamese tobacco, how-

Young man smoking *thuoc lao* (Vietnamese to-bacco) at makeshift café, Ha-noi, northern Vietnam

ever, still has its adherents, particularly in the North, who consider it more intrinsically Vietnamese than the varieties introduced from the West. Its hold on users is described in a folk song: "I have never missed anyone the way I miss *thuoc lao*. Every time I bury the pipe, I have to dig it up again."[4]

Opium was also smoked by a minority of Vietnamese during the colonial era, when the French government encouraged its use by granting monopolies on its sale to private firms in return for a share of the profits. It has been estimated that approximately 2 percent of the overall Vietnamese population and 20 percent of the Vietnamese officials working under the French administration were addicts. Although old-style opium smoking has largely been stamped out under the S.R.V., increasing numbers of young urbanites are again using opiates, including heroin, usually through injections. While their numbers remain small by Western standards, the phenomenon is alarming to Party and state officials, who fear increased incidences of anti-social behavior and infectious diseases such as AIDS among users.

DAILY FARE IN THE S.R.V.

The typical daily fare of urban and rural families living in the S.R.V. today is similar to that of pre-colonial times. Urbanites generally eat three meals a day: a light breakfast (*bua diem tam* or *bua an sang*), followed by a more substantial lunch (*bua an trua*) and then dinner (*bua an chieu*). Snacks (*do an choi*) such as pudding (*che*) may be eaten throughout the day as desired. Country people tend to have a heavier breakfast to fortify them for the demands of agricultural work. Although the practice in pre-colonial times was to drink alcoholic beverages before meals, if desired, and tea afterward, the modern trend—at least among those urban families who can afford to do so—is to have beverages available throughout the meal, including soft drinks, beer, and iced coffee.

According to custom, breakfast is usually eaten in the home with the entire family present before family members depart for their daily routines of work, study, or shopping. However, given the system of regular workdays and hours (often six days a week and more than ten hours a day) and the faster pace of life as Vietnam industrializes, breakfast may now be eaten on the way to work or school, often at makeshift roadside stalls (*com bui*, or "dust cuisine," as Ha-noi residents call them) or at tiny *quan an binh dan*, "popular" (i.e., affordable) restaurants. For urbanites, breakfast commonly consists of rice gruel (*chao*) with meat or fish added. *Chao long*, a rice gruel with pig's intestines, or *chao huyet*, rice gruel with curdled pig's blood, are common variants of this. Another common breakfast option is soup, such as *pho Bac* ("northern-style" soup also called *pho Ha-noi*, or "Ha-noi-style"). Boiling-hot beef stock, flavored with dried shrimp, *nuoc mam*, and ginger, is poured over thinly sliced pieces of raw beef and rice noodles in a bowl. The boiling stock quickly cooks the meat, and fresh bean sprouts, coriander, mint, onions, lemon juice (or slices of lemon), and chili peppers are added by the individual diners. (*Pho* is not just a breakfast food, though; it may also be eaten for lunch, dinner, and as a snack.) Another breakfast option is *xoi*, steamed glutinous rice wrapped in a lotus leaf and larded with, for instance, shredded coconut meat and sugar. In middle-class families, Western influences are more evident. *Ca-phe sua da*, or iced coffee with sweetened condensed milk, is likely to accompany an adult's breakfast, whereas children might eat buttered French-style bread or *banh mi thit nguoi*, French-style bread with cold cuts.[5]

Farming families stick closer to pre-colonial breakfast fare for reasons of taste and economy; the *xoi*, soups, and breads of the urbanites are not for them. Farming families will more likely consume copious servings of rice dishes, perhaps fried rice (*com chien*) or rice gruel made from the previous day's leftovers. If rice is not available, they may substitute a potato or corn gruel (*chao khoai, chao ngo*), flavored with shrimp paste (*mam tom*) or salted eggplant (*ca muoi*).

Although many working urbanites return home to have lunch with their families, it is increasingly common for office workers, civil servants, students, and the like to pack a lunch of leftovers from home or to patronize roadside stalls or "popular" restaurants. An inexpensive restaurant meal might include *banh cuon* (steamed ravioli) dipped in *nuoc cham; hu tieu* (Sai-gon–style chicken and noodle soup); or *com dia*, a dish (*dia*) of rice (*com*) topped with barbecued beef or pork and pickled vegetables, washed down with sweetened *sua dau nanh* (soy bean milk) or iced coffee. Lunch at home with the family might include a bowl of rice, a fish or meat dish, and a clear vegetable soup. Whether eaten at home, at work, or in a restaurant, lunch is usually followed by a dessert (*do trang mieng*, literally "something to wash the mouth") of fresh fruit—for example, sliced mango (*xoai*) or jackfruit (*mit*), depending on the season—or sweets such as corn pudding (*che bap*), and then a siesta.

In the countryside, lunches tend to resemble breakfasts, consisting of rice or rice gruel or a rice substitute, flavored with shrimp paste or salted eggplant; only rarely will pieces of meat or fish be included. Farmworkers whose fields are close enough to their homes walk or bike home to eat with their families; those who work at greater distances have a family member bring their lunch to them or bring their meal with them in the morning—most likely, the leftovers from breakfast or some cold, compressed rice. Dessert, if any, consists of a hand of bananas or a draught of green tea. Lunch is usually followed by a nap in a shady spot.

Dinner is usually the most elaborate meal, as it typically reunites the family after the day's work is done, with everyone sitting on grass mats (*chieu*) or on a low table (*phan*). (The Western-style high table with chairs is increasingly common in cities.) Urban dining at home usually includes one or more fish, fowl, meat, or boiled vegetable dishes and rice. Because of the expense, dinner in a restaurant is reserved for special occasions, at which time family members might enjoy a southern delicacy such as *chao tom*. Shrimp meat is wrapped around sugar cane and barbecued; individual diners then peel off a morsel of shrimp, garnish it with fresh herbs and bean sprouts, wrap the bundle in lettuce leaves or rice paper, and dunk the packet into *nuoc cham* before eating it. Dinner at a restaurant includes soft drinks, iced coffee, or beer; at home it includes iced coffee, black tea, flower-blossom tea, or soy milk. As with lunch, dinner might be followed by fruits and pudding, or perhaps a Western-style cake to mark a special occasion.

In the countryside, dinner is usually eaten at home after the family members have returned from their work and gathered in the main (or only) room of the house on a mat. Rice remains the basic ingredient for dinners in the countryside, mixed with or replaced by corn or potatoes as necessary, enlivened by shrimp paste or salted eggplant, and washed down with a clear vegetable broth. Dessert, if any, usually consists of green tea, fruit, or perhaps some locally made candy.

NOTES

1. Cited in Nguyen Huu Tan, *La vie quotidienne dans le Viet-Nam d'autrefois* (Paris: Thanh-long, 1983), 50.

2. It is interesting to note that, because of the Buddhist prohibition against the taking of animal life, there was a considerable onus attached to the butcher's profession. According to popular visions of Buddhist hells, torments awaited butchers on the Mountain of Swords, where their own flesh was to be torn from their bodies by sharp knives and swords for seemingly endless eons until they had atoned for their sins and could be reincarnated.

3. Cited in Thai Van Kiem, "Curiosités gastronomiques vietnamiennes," *Bulletin de la societé des études indochinoises* 36, no. 4 (1961): 21.

4. Cited in Toan Anh, *Phong tuc Viet Nam: Tu ban than den gia-dinh* (Lancaster, Pa.: Xuan Thu, 1979), 70.

5. "French-style" here refers to the baguette loaf, still baked daily by Vietnamese bakers, who have been producing it according to French recipes since colonial times. Bakeries in France itself are increasingly resorting to frozen prepared dough, and some French tourists have noted that "French" bread now tastes better in Vietnam, where the old methods of preparation are still used, than in France itself.

7

Family, Gender, and Youth Culture

THE FAMILY IN VIETNAM nowadays seemingly straddles multiple worlds: tradition and modernity; capitalism and socialism. From North to South, from countryside to cities, the changes that resulted from decades of war, the return of peace in 1975, and the opening of the country under *doi moi* (Renovation) have affected the very foundation of Vietnamese society, the family (*gia dinh*). What the family is nowadays is a reflection of the past with its deeply held values that encompassed thousands of years of existence, and yet concurrently the Vietnamese family of the twenty-first century has been shaped by profoundly different conditions that have influenced the society for the last fifty years.

THE VIETNAMESE FAMILY IN PRE-COLONIAL TIMES

In pre-colonial times, the Viet were defined first and foremost by their families, which were fundamentally patrilineal and patriarchal in character. The "clan" (*toc*), which included a number of families related to each other through a common male ancestor (*thuy to*), formed the basis of society. Each clan was identified by a specific lineage name (*ho*), or surname, of which there are approximately 300, the most common being "Nguyen," followed by "Tran," "Pham," and "Le." To the clan leader (*truong toc*)—the eldest male in the oldest branch directly descended from the founding ancestor— fell a number of duties: for instance, keeping and preserving the genealogical register (*gia pha*), which records the names, births, and deaths of members. Well-kept registers would list the land or other properties used for the maintenance of the ancestral cult. The *truong toc*, who resided in the ancestral home and presided over the family council, was the one to whom related families or members within each familial unit would turn to resolve disputes; he made decisions related to lineage matters; and he served as the protector of widows and minors as well as the moral anchor for all within the clan.

Within this larger body of the *toc*, there was the family (*gia dinh*): traditionally multigenerational (grandparents, parents, and children, uncles and aunts, and sometimes great-grandparents); it revolved around its central figure, the family head (*gia truong*), who could be the grandfather or the father (*bo* or *thay*). All owed obedience to him. The family head ruled over all family members in all matters, including property rights, education, marriage, and profession, and he spoke on their behalf in dealings with the outside world. He had the power to reward or to chastise; to him were incumbent the duties of protection, of feeding, and of education, both morally and academically, vis-à-vis everyone in the family.

In practice, such absolute patriarchal power was tempered by a tradition stemming from Vietnam's distant past as a Southeast Asian matrilineal culture, which gave women some rights and protection along with a stronger voice in the family's decision making. Thus, although the patrilineal character was given precedence, the maternal lineage was not neglected. On the contrary, pre-colonial Viet identified themselves by reference to two lineages (*ho*): the internal one of the father (*ben noi*) and the external one of the mother (*ben ngoai*). Duties and obligations were owed to each, with the paternal lineage given primacy. A complex kinship terminology existed that allowed for the distinction in terms of reference between uncles, aunts, and cousins on the father's side and these on the mother's side.

The Vietnamese family was shaped by three fundamental values and customs embedded in the Vietnamese ethos: filial piety (*hieu*), moral debt or gratitude (*on*), and merit (*duc*). Filial piety, the most heavily stressed value, encompassed the duties and obligations of children toward their parents. It bound the son or daughter in an unbreakable parental relationship because of the moral debt or gratitude that he or she owed and that could never be fully repaid. Vietnamese were taught from birth—through the telling of innumerable folktales and songs, popular sayings, and mythological and family stories—about the sacrifices that parents had to endure in order to raise the child, who learned that what he or she is today results from what the parents and ancestors had accomplished in the past, stretching over many generations. He or she was admonished to always remember "those who had planted the tree that gave the fruits that he is enjoying" and "the spring whence the water came that quenched his thirst."

The child also learned that the prosperity, wealth, and happiness that he or she currently enjoyed was the result of the merit accumulated by ancestors through successive generations of ethical observance and good deeds. Such merit was considered to be an inheritance as solid and worthy as land or a house, and the adult child was expected in turn to contribute to the amassing of such merit to be bestowed on those that would follow. Conversely, one's poverty, misery, and unhappiness were considered to be the result of some past evil deeds committed in previous lives or by some ancestors, and thus it was one's duty to make amends to prevent one's own child from experiencing suffering and misery in the future. Filial piety, moral debt or gratitude, merit accumulation, and their obligations were projected beyond the parents and ancestors to one's relatives, friends, superiors, village, ruler, state, and people. Hence pre-colonial Viet paid enormous attention to such values as loyalty, respect, and gratitude toward all these entities.

The internalizing of these three values obligated the sons to ensure the continuity of the male line through procreation, which explains the centrality of the institution of marriage and its obligatory and arranged character. Marriage as early as fifteen for the boy and twelve to fourteen for the girl, the "normal age" being sixteen for the latter and eighteen for the former, brought numerous children as insurance against the ending of the line, whereas celibacy, a proof of filial impiety (*bat hieu*), was unacceptable, particularly for males. The marriage match was arranged by a go-between (*nguoi lam moi*), usually an elderly woman known for her cleverness and knowledge of the prospects, or in the case of prominent families, a learned and high-ranking man of good repute, who was to ascertain the honorability and social prominence of the prospective family as well as the virtuousness and accomplished domesticity of the girl (if the investigation were initiated by the boy's family). Extreme importance was accorded to the social concordance of the families, as reflected in the saying "Houses equal in standing, comparable in income" (*Mon dang ho doi*).

The process went through three stages: the preliminary discussions (*cham mat*), the betrothal (*le hoi*), and the wedding itself (*le cuoi*), each stage being preceded by offerings of betel leaves and areca nuts. When a match had been found, interminable sessions of betel chewing ensued during which all details were probed, bargained about, and agreed upon. The girl's horoscope had to concord with the boy's to ensure that the combination of the elements and the signs would lead to a harmonious and fertile marriage. The agreement for the match was to be sealed by a formal marriage proposal by the suitor's parents. The two families discussed the formalities for the betrothal ceremony—in particular, the amount of betel and areca and tea that the suitor's family was to bring on the day of the ceremony. The more prominent the betrothed's family, the larger the amount, which was to be distributed to relatives, friends, and acquaintances as a form of announcement. The betrothal ceremony would take place on an auspicious day, with the two sets of parents meeting to discuss the wedding day, as well as the presents that the boy's family must offer: money, jewelry, furniture, silk bolts, and so forth. Poorer families made simpler offerings of tea, rice, bananas, and extra betel and areca.

Several years might elapse between the betrothal and the wedding ceremonies, especially if the prospective bride was very young, but the prospective groom had to visit and bring presents to his betrothed's family to mark important occasions, such as the New Year and the Mid-Autumn Festivals. On the wedding day, at the fixed hour, the groom—accompanied by his father, brothers and sisters, relatives, and friends—formed a procession heading toward the bride's house in a ceremony known as the "bringing of the bride" (*le ruoc dau*) to her husband's house. Upon their arrival, all were invited to sit and were served tea; meanwhile, the bride's father (or the eldest representative) invoked the souls of the departed at the ancestral altar to inform them of the marriage; the groom, followed by the bride, lit incense at the altar and bowed down three times to his wife's ancestors to announce his taking the bride home. Both groom and bride performed obeisance to the bride's parents, who acknowledged them in turn by presenting the couple with their gift (in cash or kind) and their wishes for long life and numerous (male) progeny. The same ceremony was performed upon the bride's entering into her husband's home, which then became hers as well.

Marriage was patrilocal; that is, a couple lived with the husband's father, mother, and unmarried siblings. It was expected that the eldest son would care for his parents in their old age. Privacy was not highly valued, and aunts, nieces, grandparents, and grandchildren could be found sharing the same room. Seldom did the son move away to a distant land outside the confines of the ancestral home, defined and attached as he was by his birthplace, land, and village, which had been those of his ancestors. Were this to happen, he would become that most unfortunate, rootless person, "without a hearth, without a tomb to call his own."

The patrilineal, patrilocal character of marriage was further affirmed by the fact that, once she was married, the new bride became part of her husband's family and only saw her own family on occasional visits. Thus, in pre-colonial families, the raising of daughters was considered a "waste" of resources, for they were "children of others" and could not be relied upon for succor in old age. The new bride was incorporated not only into her husband's family but also into his ancestral line, which became her own. She then began that fearful apprenticeship known as *lam dau*, "to serve as a daughter-in-law" to her mother-in-law. This was part of the second stage of the "three subserviences" (*tam tong*) of a woman—to her father before her marriage, to her husband upon becoming his wife, and to her son when she became widowed. A mother-in-law had full authority over her daughter-in-law; she could work her to the bone from dawn to dusk, starve her to death, or beat her black and blue, and few would find that reprehensible. A rich folklore illustrates this aspect of the Vietnamese family: "Mother and daughter-in-law are like mistress and servant; there is no love lost between them" is a representative expression.

Within the marital relationship, the husband had the right to chastise his wife physically as well as verbally and to repudiate her if she was found guilty of lacking respect toward her in-laws, of not producing a male heir, or of committing adultery. Nevertheless, the husband was not totally free to do as he pleased with his wife, as his parents, relatives, neighbors, and even village elders could intervene. Divorce existed but was rare, as it brought opprobrium to the divorced woman and a taint of scandal to the family. Men were permitted to take several wives (although the first one was considered the wife of first rank), especially if the first wife did not provide a male heir. In fact, the first wife often participated in the selection of secondary wives to ensure that the latter would "merge" harmoniously with the family. Secondary wives were obligated to obey the first wife in all things, and their children were regarded as her own. When widowed, a woman was to remain chaste and faithful to her husband's memory. It was incumbent upon her to raise the children and, while her son was still a minor, to perpetuate the cult of the ancestors, aided by her husband's relatives. If it happened that the family had no male heirs, the eldest daughter inherited the eldest son's privileges as well as duties, the most important being the perpetuation of the cult of the ancestors. If the couple was childless, adoption was an acceptable practice. Whenever possible, the adopted child (*con nuoi*) was sought within the extended family, leaving behind the family of origin to be an integral and permanent part of the adopted family.

The patriarchal character of the Vietnamese family was further reflected in the fact that it was the eldest male child in the family who had the duty to perpetuate the practice of ancestor worship (*tho cung ong ba*). Ancestral spirits are believed to inhabit this world, witnessing their progeny's every thought and action, helping their every move, appearing in dreams to warn them of imminent disasters and dangers. Thus, prominently placed in every pre-colonial home was the ubiquitous altar with its bronze incense burner, candleholders, flowers and fruits, and the tablets bearing the names of the ancestors and deceased family members. Every year upon the anniversary (*ngay gio*) of a death, it was incumbent upon the eldest son to organize a celebration, the importance and elaborateness of which increased in proportion to the recentness of the death and the rank within the family. A vast array of dishes would be presented to the ancestors; incense would be burned, and the whole family, beginning with the eldest male (and his wife), would do their obeisance, calling on their ancestors to partake of the feast. Relatives and other guests would follow their example in lighting the incense. Only after a decent interval could all share in the feast (their seating being determined by their rank within the family hierarchy), renewing familial bonds as well as sharing the latest gossips about weddings, births, and deaths.

Within this prevalently patriarchal tradition, there were a few customs that corrected this imbalance. One of them was the inheritance custom, which stipulated equality between sons and daughters in the division of the patrimony, except for the provision that a specific body of land, the "incense and fire" (*huong hoa*) parcel, be given to the eldest male sibling to provide resources for the maintenance of the ancestral cult. Along with that practice, the elder male sibling in the family, in the event of the death, absence, or incapacity of the father, was also expected to be responsible for his mother and his younger siblings, seeing to their education and marriage.

Vietnamese children of both sexes were usually doted upon by their parents, who lavished them with love and care. A mother would sing her babies to sleep with age-old lullabies and would breast-feed them until they were three. Fathers were often indulgent, giving rise to the saying "If the children are spoiled, it is because of their father." Out of fear that their children would be taken away or rendered mortally ill by evil spirits, parents gave them coarse nicknames such as "pig, "dog," or "stupid," which were supposed to make them undesirable in the eyes of the spirits. All parents' ultimate dream was that the male child would grow up to become a laureate to bring honor to his family. During their tender years, children were allowed to roam in bands through fields and ponds and to play games (e.g., cricket fights, kite flying), watched over by their older brothers and sisters. As they grew older, these children were given tasks, such as herding water buffalo or ducks, baby-sitting the younger siblings, whom they would carry wherever they went, and cooking in the absence of the mother.

Throughout childhood, Vietnamese children were taught the moral lessons of filial piety, obedience, and proper social behavior through songs, sayings, and stories. Upon reaching his sixth birthday (Vietnamese children are considered one year old at birth), a bright boy might go to the village school to acquire an education that was the first step in the preparation for the civil service examinations. A girl, however, stayed home to help her mother in all the domestic chores and to begin her training as a future bride, for her destiny was to get married. "A girl who is slow to marry makes her parents weary," says an ancient proverb.

Within such a patriarchal world, male and female assumed different, and not necessarily equal, roles and worth. Although women in Vietnam—unlike their counterparts in China, for instance—shared more equally in an inheritance and had more rights because of an ancient Southeast Asian tradition of matrilineal descent, they nevertheless were not considered as standing on an equal footing with the men. Bound as they were by a set of firmly entrenched values (chastity, obedience, fidelity, self-sacrifice) aimed at regimenting their behavior so as to ensure the perpetuation of the male-dominated family, women from birth to death were expected to give precedence to males—be they the father, husband, or brother—in most matters that counted (e.g., inheritance, marriage, education).

Despite these constraints, throughout the centuries Vietnamese women had forged a tradition that gave them supremacy within the family in terms of familial economics. Thus, popular sayings referred to the housewife as *noi tuong* (the "general within"), as it was she who managed the income brought by her husband and often supplemented it through secondary economic activities such as weaving, animal husbandry, and cultivation of fruits and vegetables to be sold in the village market. Within the pre-colonial legal system, Vietnamese women had the right to jointly own their family properties with their husbands, and although they were led by them, they "co-officiated" with their husbands in ancestor worship. Overall, Vietnamese women had never been perceived or portrayed in folktales and popular sayings as weak, subservient, and docile. On the contrary, many folktales and songs perpetuated the image of a strong-willed, resilient woman, sharp of tongue, quick of wit, and swift in her revenge on an unfaithful husband.

THE FAMILY IN TIMES OF WAR

During the French colonial era, on the surface, few of the traits that characterized a pre-colonial family changed. Still, some undercurrents began to manifest themselves in the 1920s and 1930s, especially among the educated upper class, which had more opportunities to be in contact with Western civilization. Western values began to seep into Vietnamese society, starting from the top down. Once unleashed, the forces of change affected everyone, men and women—in immeasurable ways in the case of the latter.

The wars that started in 1946 and went on for thirty years (with a brief and incomplete interruption from 1954 to 1960) shook the foundations of Vietnamese society and in particular the family. Families that had been bound together for generations and who had never left the confines of their villages now found themselves disintegrating under the pressures of military service, enforced migrations, separation, and, all too often, death and disability. Fathers, husbands, brothers, and sons left to fight a war that was to become a seemingly endless one, scattering some of them from North to South, not to see each other again for decades, if ever. In such circumstances, all the patriarchal characteristics of the traditional Vietnamese family could not remain intact, since their main actors and tradition holders were no longer there to enforce them. Women were called upon to fulfill roles that were by tradition male, and they would both benefit and suffer from these exceptional circumstances.

Under the R.V.N. in the South, to keep the social fabric intact the government saw to it that the Confucian values for family life were reinforced by the law. Theoretically, it emphasized the moral duty of all of its members and, in particular, of the woman. Yet paradoxically, by necessity women were pushed to the forefront as their men were taken away by the draft. Some of the impetus was provided by Madame Ngo Dinh Nhu, the sister-in-law of the president of the R.V.N., Ngo Dinh Diem. A headstrong woman who did not hesitate to speak her mind (as when she blamed the existence of the atomic bomb on male domination) or to grab the limelight, Madame Nhu launched her own women's emancipation campaign, which was behind such spectacular decisions as the creation of a female militia and her public condemnation of polygyny (polygamy for men). Madame Nhu was instrumental in the passing of the 1958 Family Law, which attempted to suppress the traditionally sanctioned polygyny that had led to so much dissension within the family and to eradicate the forced character of arranged marriages. Yet while theoretically affirming the right of women to choose their marriage partners, the 1958 law nevertheless reaffirmed the sanctity of marriage by interdicting divorce, denying the legitimacy of children born out of wedlock, and reaffirming the assumption that the family was to be a woman's sole goal in life and the focus of her social obligations. Feeble attempts were made to enroll women in organizations like the Vietnamese Women's Solidarity Movement, but these were short-lived and narrowly based, as they spoke only to the urban elites. Women of the countryside were barely affected by the 1958 Family Law. Lukewarm efforts were also made to recruit young people into the Republican Youth organization, both in cities and in the countryside, in part to stem the phenomenon of rising juvenile delinquency and, above all, the potential appeal of the enemy. Overall, most of these family-, women-, and youth-oriented efforts led to insignificant results, so vast were the problems of a rapidly militarizing society.

In the North, under the D.R.V., the situation was different because of the combined pressure of the government's effort to mobilize the entire society for the war while trying to enforce a socialist revolution in which both men and women would be equal in rights and in duties, and in which women's emancipation was part and parcel of the class struggle. A year after its counterpart had done so in the South, the D.R.V passed the Law on Marriage and the Family in 1959, which contained provisions similar to the southern 1958 law—with, however, fundamental differences. Arranged marriages and polygyny were abolished by the Marriage and Family Law, which also declared the equality of the sexes and affirmed women and children's rights (e.g., freedom from abuse). Literacy campaigns aimed especially at women were launched with the contribution of the Vietnam Women's Union in order to give women better access to jobs and a stronger role in the decision-making process in the government and the Communist Party. Improved health care and child care were among the benefits enjoyed by women in the D.R.V during the war decades.

Nevertheless, as the war intensified, women unavoidably became a larger force in the daily activities of the D.R.V. Sixty percent of the "laboring peasants" and 33 percent of the labor force in state enterprises were women. However, while positively contributing to the war effort and making gains in the emancipation campaign, women were still expected to shoulder the burden of housework and child care during a time of war-induced shortages. By 1965, the "three assumptions of duty" policy (production, family, and military work) meant that women's capacities were stretched to the limit of endurance, and often beyond.

It was during the war, paradoxically, that Vietnam (or rather, the D.R.V.) was among the Third World nations with the highest birthrates. Aware of the potential negative impact of large population increases, the government began to launch birth control campaigns in 1962 that advocated the use of the IUD (Intrauterine Device) and legalized abortion in cases of unwanted pregnancy. Positive incentives (work promotion, maternity and nursery care, allocation of living space) and negative incentives (suppression of the above advantages) were also applied to persuade the woman to use birth control. Over the long term, the family planning policy as enforced in the D.R.V. was partly successful, but women (and their men) also showed an often determined resistance to the two-child policy and to the use of the IUD and other birth control methods.

FAMILY LIFE IN THE S.R.V.

Decades of war, the opening of the country, the demands of a fast-paced market economy, and the ever increasing intrusion of globalization have affected the Vietnamese family greatly, stretching its traditional fabric to the limit while leaving some core values intact.

The multigenerational and patriarchal aspects of the traditional Vietnamese family are less prevalent nowadays, particularly in the cities. The nuclear, two-generation family (parents and children), though not a new phenomenon, has been increasingly prevalent since 1975. A number of factors account for such increase: migration from rural areas to cities, from the overpopulated Red River Delta to the southern highlands and provinces in the Mekong Delta, urbanization and industrialization, with the concomitant rise of the job-providing service sector and factories, and the desire of a generation to live apart from its parents, in a freer and less constraining environment. It also stems from the government's family planning policy, which encourages the ideals of the nuclear family with two children as part of a national effort to stem the demographic explosion. It has encountered strong resistance as the result of the traditional patriarchal influence (the need to have a male heir) as well as the desire by young couples to perpetuate their own images and achieve their ambitions through their children.

Consequently, the customs and values that once defined the Vietnamese family—such as ancestor worship, filial piety, obedience, loyalty, the primacy of the ancestral home, and the extended patrilineal and patrilocal family—have suffered from the intrusion of the modern industrial world. The ties that used to bind all the participants of this entity together have become somewhat looser, with the priority given to the more immediate members (husband and wife, parents and children, and grandparents) while ancestors recede further into the past in terms of familial memory. Although parental authority remains strong, it is expressed less in decrees than in discussions with the children, and this is reflected in many areas that used to define the Vietnamese ethos—for instance, filial piety and marriage. Concern for the care of aging parents as well as the related notion of family honor remain at the core of the Vietnamese value system, but the crystal clarity of their past definitions has become murkier, and expectations have diminished. Although still somewhat obligatory (in particular for the sole male heir), marriage, another pillar of the Vietnamese family, has somewhat lost its "arranged" character, allowing for "chance" to play a greater part. It does not, however, prevent parents, relatives, and friends from attempting to match the parties, with parents choosing criteria based on the social standing of the counterpart

Rural women going to market in Co Loa, northern Vietnam; sign reads: "A stable population means a prosperous society and a happy family. Each married couple should have only one or two children."

family, whereas friends look for psychological affinities between the two potential partners.

The marriage ceremony in the present Vietnamese family often combines West and East, the past with its various traditions and the future with its adoption of Western dress (suit and tie for the groom; white, crinoline dress with bridal veil and gloves for the bride) and other customs. Although it is less complicated and elaborate in terms of organization, the ceremony stripped to its essentials still retains a few outward observations of the traditional rituals, such as the offering of areca and betel by the groom's family to the bride's; the greeting of the bride (*le ruoc dau*) by the groom's party; and the ceremony of obeisance performed by groom and bride to parents and ancestors. However, the cost of weddings—which even in the past drove families to ruination because of home-cooked, sumptuous feasts held to accommodate entire villages and extended relatives—is ever on the rise. Modern brides and grooms greet guests at the door of the restaurant where the wedding banquet is to take place. A live band is a must among the young people, and the felicitous event has to be recorded on video at steep prices. Thankfully, the onerous tradition of *lam dau*, which caused so much suffering and led to a rich folklore about the misfortunes of the daughter-in-law and the wickedness of the mother-in-law, is no longer tolerated. The young bride does not feel obligated to live with her in-laws, and even when she does live with them she no longer submits to the will and whims of her mother-in-law.

The Vietnamese family today tends to be assimilated to the legal concept of a household. Each household is provided with a family registry (*ho khau*), a booklet in which the members are numbered and identified in terms of their relationships with the household head. The registry provides the residency proof for the household members and makes it possible to obtain essentials such as land-use rights for cultivation (but not ownership) in the rural areas as well as housing allocation in the cities; the size and quality of the latter depend on the number of members, widows and other elderly people, and on military service and war veterans' status.

The proportion of families with gender equality—in terms of domestic chores as well familial decision making—is higher in the cities, in particular among the educated milieu. In the rural areas women still bear a larger burden of both domestic and occupational obligations. This is particularly true in the less urbanized North, where the different phases of agricultural production are carried out largely (60 percent) by women, and domestic chores solely by them. The tradition of women earning secondary incomes (in addition to the husband's principal one) through outside economic activities is stronger than ever, with increasing numbers of women setting up their own small-scale businesses at home or at the market. Along with these changes, the reports of domestic violence have also been on the rise, with physical abuse often resulting from drunkenness or a refusal to allow the wife to adopt contraceptive measures (out of a desire to have more children, especially if there is no male heir).

In a population where females are a majority (53.6 percent, 1989 census), the percentage of married women is higher than that of married men because polygyny is still a prevalent social phenomenon. Concurrently, the number of widows, divorcees, and separated wives is also much larger than the number of widowed, divorced, and separated men. It has always been easier for men to remarry several times, whereas social constraints and the legacy of tradition make it hard for women to do so. Studies have shown that the incidence of husband-absent families is quite common, usually because the husband has perished in war, has left his family behind to find a job in a city or abroad, or has begun another family without officially divorcing his first wife. Women having children out of wedlock is also a common phenomenon, as more and more single women in distant rural areas migrate to cities to find work. The responsibility of raising children in or out of wedlock weighs heavily on women, who work long hours in physically demanding jobs, rice fields, plantations, road repair teams, and factories. Patriarchal influence lingers, especially in northern rural areas, where it has been understood and accepted that a man's place ought not to be in the kitchen and that domestic chores are women's "natural duty."

With a population that is now more than 80,000,000, more than half of which (53 percent) is under the age of twenty-five, Vietnam is a country composed primarily of females and the young. With the opening of the domestic market to the outside world, it has been presumed that women would have better opportunities and that, in the eyes of the law, men and women are equal. Nevertheless, in reality, as shown by a number of studies by the Center for Research on Female Labor of the Ministry of Labor, Invalids, and Social Affairs, the gap between men and women has widened; so has that between rich and poor. For instance, although there are more employment opportunities for English-speaking, educated women in the private sector (in foreign-owned companies, for instance), who are now forming a newly emerging middle class, their sisters in the countryside, which contains 90 percent of Vietnam's poor, fare much worse. Not only do they carry most of the burden of agricultural and domestic work, they also encounter obstacles in finding capital for start-up enterprises or loans because they lack collateral (which is usually in the man's name). They also lack educational opportunities. All of these factors explain why a large percentage of the low-skilled, low-paid workforce in labor-intensive industries like food processing and garment making is female (mostly young and single).

Notwithstanding the difficulties, there are examples that bode well for the future of Vietnamese women, such as the success story of the two sisters, Nguyen Thi Anh Hoa and Anh Hong, who are the owners and managers of Citimart and Maximark, among the largest supermarkets in Ho Chi Minh City and Ha-noi, or the story of Mai Kieu Lien, the general director of Vinamilk, the leading dairy products corporation in Vietnam. Women who head corporations and small businesses can be found in greater numbers in the South than in the North. It is not surprising that the first Women's Business Luncheon—organized to allow businesswomen, both Vietnamese and foreign, private and governmental, to meet, network, and exchange experience—was formed in the South.

GENERATION 2000

The VCP—concerned by the rapid and pervasive corrosion of its image as society's guiding light, and "the embodiment of virtue" (in the words of

Youngsters hawking newspapers near the Perfume River, Hue City, central Vietnam

journalist Huu Tho, the head of the Central Committee on Ideology and Culture)—has been careful in nurturing the post-1975 generations in the "right direction" through a number of its youth-oriented organizations. The Vanguard Youth (*Thanh Nien Xung Phong*), for example, sends young men and women (mostly orphaned or from low-income families) to settle in the highlands or mangrove-covered, swampy coastal regions. The VCP sponsors a school curriculum that insists on core values such as patriotism, heroism, self-sacrifice, respect for elders, frugality, and hard work and it attempts to control the flow of information that floods the country, particularly through the internet.

However, the Party's efforts have not been able to slow Vietnamese youth in its race to embrace the outside world with all of its positive as well as negative traits. Young people have absorbed Western ideas about self as an individual rather than as an appendage of a larger entity; about love, marriage (at a much later age), and sex; and about the latest fads in fashion and music.

Generation 2000, young men and women (in their twenties) born in a time of peace, have aspirations and tastes that are similar to those of youth the world over, starkly different from those of their parents' generation, a generation of war. Yet, with their roots deep in the past, they are nevertheless steeped in that pride of the ancestral land that made Vietnamese nationalism such a force in the nation's history, albeit tinted with uncertainty and cynicism. Their first concern is job-related; this is expressed in terms of global market awareness, which guides their choices of career—computer-related and English-based—whether in business administration, economics, law, or medicine. They fret about their future and place in society, worry about an education that may be inadequate in terms of preparation for the ferocious competition for job openings, refuse to follow their parents' path of wartime self-sacrifice and hardship, seek that most elusive attainment of *hanh phuc* ("happiness") through friendship and love, and above all, value the rapid accumulation of material wealth manifested in the acquisition of consumer goods: refrigerator, washing machine, big-screen television, house or apartment, and a sleek motorbike from Japan, Taiwan, Korea, or China.

In the domain of music and fashion, one can see most clearly the influence of the West through the adoption of musical styles (from rap to hard rock) imported from the United States, Hong Kong, or Japan, with the formation of rock and rap bands and the popularity of chart-listed singers playing to capacity audiences (see chapter 9). Vietnamese rap, for instance, though having integrated the rhythms and fashions of its American model, still shies away from its counterpart's glorification of violence and reliance on obscenities in its lyrics, choosing instead to talk about love and heartbreaks and youthful angst, or adopting a comical style that makes light of the foibles of scorned swains and shallow, vain belles. Overall, the music that Vietnamese youth (and their elders) listen to morning and night, blasted out in karaoke bars and cafés, is the Vietnamese equivalent of pop music in the form of perennial, saccharine love songs accompanied by a synthesized orchestra. Rather surprisingly, the public has shown an inordinate fondness for Western music of the 1960s and 1970s, embodied by such hits as the Eagles' "Hotel California" (in the original, or in Vietnamese translation!) or "Aline" by the French singer Christophe, played endlessly over the radio in shopping centers and cafes.

Whether young or old, male or female, Vietnamese now mostly prefer to wear Western-style clothes—professional men wear dress shirts and ties; women wear dresses or, more frequently, pantsuits. These are the mores of city people; the farther South, the more vivid and fashionable. Fashionwise, urban Vietnamese youth have totally and wholeheartedly adopted Western-style fashion, becoming a brand-conscious, jeans-clad generation that would

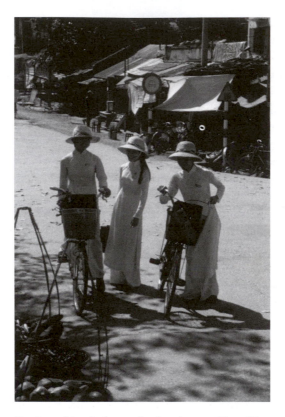

Students bicycle home for lunch near Hue City, central Vietnam; the white *ao dai* is required for female high school students.

never want to be seen cruising on their Honda motorbikes in downtown Sai-gon or Ha-noi wearing anything other than Calvin Klein T-shirts, Levi's jeans (pressed and starched stiff), or Armani-logo sunglasses, shod with Nike sport shoes (made in Vietnam) and sporting the perennial baseball cap. No one seems to mind that the brand names and logos are not authentic but are rather copies mass-produced in Vietnam, Thailand, or China. The more affluent tout cell phones in the latest models, using them in bars, on terraces of cafes, or in the smoke-filled rooms of trendy eateries.

The youth in rural areas (at least those whose parents cannot afford to send them to the cities for their education) are less flashy and brand-conscious, as a Western-style suit can cost two or three times a worker's or peasant's yearly income. The farther from the cities one travels, the more "conservative" or "proper" is the manner in fashion and in social mores, as the fear of social, neighborly, and parental disapproval is much stronger and more dissuasive than any desire to imitate their urban brethren. It is mainly in the countryside, for example, that the *non la*, or conical "leaf hat," is still commonly worn, primarily by elderly men and women. Many young men have taken up the Western baseball cap, which offers less protection from the rain and sun but symbolizes greater sophistication.

The one symbol of the past that has weathered the passing of fashion is the *ao dai*, the form-fitting tunic of the Vietnamese woman, slit up the sides but worn over white trousers. Considered by many to be the Vietnamese women's "traditional" attire, it was actually designed in the 1930s. Whether in the countryside or in cities, the wearing of *ao dai* has become fashionable once again. Scorned a few years ago, it has made a comeback in the guise of a bold, color-blocked, patterned dress, trimmed in contrasting ribbons and lined with rich material. Fashion designers like Minh Hanh, for instance, have their creations presented by Vietnamese models at local festivals and international fashion competitions, splashed across calendars, and worn by fashion-conscious, affluent women at soirees, weddings, and beauty pageants. For their weddings, Vietnamese women wear immaculately white wedding gowns for the ceremony itself, but they also appear on that day wearing the *ao dai* in glorious red and gold brocades, in patterns of apricot blossoms and bamboo trees, and coifed with the tall turban headdress of yore. The *ao dai*'s more demure, everyday version, a white tunic worn over white pants, in simple cotton or synthetic fabric, is still the school uniform *de rigueur* for females at middle and high schools, whereas their male counterparts wear a white shirt and blue pants as a school uniform.

8

Festivals and Leisure Activities

INTRODUCTION

THE PRIMARY FESTIVALS celebrated by pre-colonial Vietnamese were *Tet Nguyen-dan* (New Year's Festival), *Le Han-thuc* (Cold Foods Festival), *Le Thanh-minh* (Pure Brightness Festival), *Le Doan-ngo* (High Noon or Double-Five Festival), *Tet Trung-thu* (Mid-Autumn Festival), and *Le Tao-quan* (Household Gods' Ritual).

These festivals derive from the amalgamation of religious beliefs discussed in chapter 3. Like the beliefs on which they were based, the festivals were observed by most Vietnamese rather than being the exclusive property of a particular faith, although regional preferences and variations were marked. Given the extensive contact with Western powers and the tragic events that have marked recent Vietnamese history, many of these festivals are no longer celebrated or have been reduced to abbreviated or localized observance. The major exception is the *Tet Nguyen-dan*, or New Year's Day Festival, which is still widely celebrated in Vietnam and has assumed the character of a national holiday. It is also popular among overseas Vietnamese. To a lesser degree, the same may be said of the *Tet Trung-thu*, or Mid-Autumn Festival.

THE LUNAR CALENDAR

The celebration of festivals in pre-colonial Vietnam was regulated by a lunar calendar. Like the Chinese lunar calendar, from which it is derived, the Vietnamese calendar begins with a date equivalent to 2637 B.C.E. in the

Gregorian calendar. It features a 355-day year, divided into twelve months of twenty-nine or thirty days each. To bring the twelve-month cycle of 355 days into accord with the 365-day solar year, an intercalary month (*thang nhuan*) is periodically inserted between the third and fourth months, an adjustment necessary every three or four years. In practice, the Vietnamese year begins in spring, but the precise day varies by as much as several months in comparison with the Gregorian calendar.

The important unit in the traditional calendar is a sixty-year cycle, termed *van-nien luc-giap* and based on repetitions of ten- and twelve-year cycles, called *thap-can* and *thap-nhi-chi*, respectively. The ten-year *thap-can* cycle, based on a doubling of the five elements (*ngu hanh*), runs as follows:

1. *Giap* (Water in Nature)
2. *At* (Water in Usage)
3. *Binh* (Fire)
4. *Dinh* (Latent Fire)
5. *Mau* (Wood in General)
6. *Ky* (Wood Set to Burn)
7. *Canh* (Metal in General)
8. *Tan* (Wrought Metal)
9. *Nham* (Uncultivated Land)
10. *Quy* (Cultivated Land)

The twelve-year *thap-nhi-chi*, based on zodiac animals, runs as follows:

1. *Ty* (Rat)
2. *Suu* (Buffalo)
3. *Dan* (Tiger)
4. *Mao* (Cat)
5. *Thin* (Dragon)
6. *Ty* (Snake)
7. *Ngo* (Horse)
8. *Mui* (Goat)
9. *Than* (Monkey)
10. *Dau* (Rooster)

11. *Tuat* (Dog)

12. *Hoi* (Pig)

Years are not designated by numbers but by combinations of the symbols from the ten- and twelve-year cycles: a pairing is made of the first symbol of the ten-year cycle with the first symbol of the twelve-year cycle, followed by a pairing of the second symbol from each cycle, and so on. Once the ten-year cycle has been repeated six times and the twelve-year cycle has been repeated five times, the full sixty-year cycle is completed and a new one begins. No named year is repeated within a single sixty-year cycle, giving each year a distinct appellation composed of the two elements. In popular speech, though, only the second of the two, the animal names, are used: Year of the Rat, Dragon, Tiger, and so forth.

Requiring periodic adjustment, Vietnam's lunar calendar was regulated by the ruling dynasties, which considered fixing the date of New Year's Day to be an imperial prerogative. In Nguyen times, the lunar calendar was drawn up by the Hue court's Imperial Observatory. When Bao-dai abdicated in 1945, the observatory ceased to function. The D.R.V. government, which accepted the Gregorian calendar and made it the basis for official functions, refused to take up the relay. Since traditional festivals, marketing, and rice-planting cycles still followed the lunar cycle, private publishers began issuing their own lunar calendars, but their results did not always agree, and confusion reigned. Finally, in 1967, the D.R.V. solved the problem by issuing a lunar calendar alongside the Gregorian calendar which remained in force for official business.

FESTIVALS

Tet Nguyen-dan, the New Year's Day Festival, was and remains the most important and longest lasting of all Vietnamese festivals. Its celebration formally began on the first day of the New Year, but preparations often started at least one month in advance and continued for another month or more after New Year's Day. The coming of a new year was regarded as an important transition from one time-cycle to another. The word *Tet* comes from *Tiet*, meaning "section" or "period"; by extension, *Tet* refers to the passing from one season or year to another. Given the importance of the transition, pre-colonial Vietnamese made every effort to settle outstanding affairs before New Year's Day: for example, to pay off debts or to collect them. Selection of clothing to be worn on New Year's Day and preparation of foods with

Buddhist nuns preparing candies for the Tet holidays, Ho Chi Minh City, southern Vietnam

which to celebrate it also began well in advance. Each household planted before its door a *cay neu*, a bamboo "tree" decorated with leaves, gold- and silver-colored paper, and wind chimes; its bounty was intended to attract benevolent spirits, its noise to repel malevolent ones. A fish image was also hung from the "*Tet* tree": at the appropriate time, it would sprout wings and fly the household gods to heaven, where they would report to the Jade Emperor, as will be explained below. Stocks of firecrackers were laid in. Considered efficacious in frightening away wicked spirits but harmless to beneficent ones, they would be set off to initiate *Le Tao-quan* (Household Gods' Ritual) and the New Year's Festival. Branches of abricot or peach blossoms were purchased to decorate the house, which was usually cleaned, painted, and adorned with banners written in Chinese or Vietnamese *nom* characters.

One week before the New Year was to begin, each household celebrated *Le Tao-quan*, a ritual honoring the household gods. According to a Vietnamese tradition (there are many variations), in ancient times there lived a husband and wife named, respectively, Trong Cao and Thi Nhi, who were devoted to one another but childless. The Vietnamese view a childless marriage as tragic, and the couple began to quarrel. Trong Cao struck his wife in a fit of rage. Thi Nhi, chafing at this unfair action, left the household and wandered until, exhausted, she sat down at the roadside to rest. She was seen by Pham Lang, who invited her to his home. Meanwhile, Trong Cao, consumed by remorse, swore that he would find his wife and make amends, no matter how long it took. After searching for years in vain, he stumbled upon Pham Lang's house, where the latter and Thi Nhi now lived as husband and wife. Seeing her former husband at the door, Thi Nhi invited him in and offered him food and drink. Hearing Pham Lang returning from the fields, she told Trong Cao to hide in a haystack near the house. Unaware of Trong Cao's presence, Pham Lang set fire to the hay to use the ashes as fertilizer. Fearing for Trong Cao's life, Thi Nhi rushed to the burning haystack; finding him dead of asphyxiation, she hurled herself into the flames to atone for causing his death. Pham Lang, seeing his wife aflame, rushed into the fire to save her but met the same fate.

The Jade Emperor, impressed by such devotion, transformed all three members of this "love triangle" into deities and assigned them the task of recording Vietnamese households' merits and demerits and reporting to him on an annual basis. (They are symbolized by the three blocks that support cauldrons in traditional kitchens.) *Le Tao-quan* involved the propitiation of the household gods just before they were to ascend to heaven to report to the Jade Emperor, who rewarded or punished the household's members accordingly in the year to come. Sometimes, for convenience, the three gods are conflated into one, known as *Tao-quan*; hence the ritual's name. On the twenty-third day of the last month before the new year, family members presented the household gods with gifts, typically live carp, intended to facilitate their flight to heaven, in the hopes of winning their favor and influencing their report to the Jade Emperor. The carp, thought to sprout wings to fly the gods to heaven, were released after the ceremony. The paper carp hung from the *cay neu* was thought to accomplish the same mission. The household gods' absence was believed to last for seven days, ending on the last day of the year. The ritual thus symbolized nature's death during the winter and rebirth with the advent of spring.

The most important spiritual event of the New Year's Festival proper was the *le ruoc ong ba*, the "ancestor-welcoming ritual," carried out on the last day of the twelfth month. Family members invoked their ancestors and invited them to take part in the *Tet* festivities, as they had done when they were alive. The ancestral spirits were expected to stay in the household for the first three days of the year, to share food offerings with their living descendants, and to help the latter begin the year auspiciously. To make the ancestors feel welcome, houses were perfumed with incense, and firecrackers were set off to deter invasive evil spirits from consuming the ancestral offerings. Once the offerings had been made to the ancestral spirits, the food and drink were consumed by the living descendants in a spirit of reverent gratitude to the ancestors but also of joyful celebration of the coming of spring and the New Year. Young as well as older Vietnamese enjoyed the feasting during the New Year's Festival, and delicacies such as candied fruits were especially appreciated and characteristic of *Tet*. After three days' visitation, the ancestral spirits were presented with gifts of paper money to cover their needs upon their return to the spirit world for another year.

New Year's Day itself required careful planning, for events on that day were thought to presage those of the entire year. Of particular importance was the need to ensure that the first visitor to enter the house in the new year would be someone blessed with good fortune, or *phuc*. After inviting an auspicious person to pay the first visit, some families sealed their windows and doors to prevent a less felicitous visitor from entering while the family was off its guard. Similarly, care was taken not to perform any onerous or inauspicious task on New Year's Day (for example, sewing or sweeping), and above all not to curse or quarrel, for the atmosphere established on that day would extend to the whole year. Among the activities of New Year's Day, the most important was the New Year's greetings and good wishes that a household's younger members owed to its eldest. Prostration and recitation of formulas expressing the three traditional blessings of *Phuc, Loc, Tho* (Good Fortune, Wealth, and Longevity) were customary. In return, the senior members would distribute, in red envelopes, much anticipated gifts of money called *tien mung tuoi* ("age-celebrating money"). Feasting and merrymaking usually continued throughout the first week of the year, by which time most households had completed their ritual obligations, exhausted their budgets, and returned to their working routines. Well-to-do families might continue to celebrate for the rest of the month.

The *Le Han-thuc*, or Cold Foods Festival, was celebrated on the third day of the third month. The primary ritual was the preparation, ceremonial offering, and consumption of rice cakes called *banh chay* ("burnt cake") and *banh troi* ("submerged cake"). According to Chinese tradition, in the year equivalent to 654 B.C.E., a Chinese monarch was overthrown and forced to flee his kingdom. In exile, he met a general (known to Vietnamese as Gioi Tu Thoi) who marshaled the necessary forces to put the ex-monarch back on his throne. Once the campaign had been concluded, the king rewarded everyone involved except Gioi Tu Thoi. Angered by the king's ingratitude, Gioi Tu Thoi fled into a forest to hide. When the king learned of his oversight and the offense it had caused to his savior, he tried to find Gioi Tu Thoi to make amends, but the latter, deeply hurt, would not leave his hideaway. Wanting to force Gioi Tu Thoi to show himself, the king ordered the forest burned down, but the stubborn Gioi Tu Thoi refused to yield. He remained in the forest, climbing its highest tree to avoid the flames. His flight was in vain, and he was burned alive. Throughout Sinitic Asia, including Vietnam, the loyal general's memory was honored and his spirit was appeased with offerings of rice cakes placed on altars dedicated to him. Once the offerings were completed, participants consumed the cakes themselves in a festive atmosphere. However, in order not to remind Gioi Tu Thoi of his fiery death, no cooking was done on the day itself; the cakes were prepared the night before, allowed to cool overnight, and eaten as cold food. Beyond this main event, Vietnamese celebrated the Cold Foods Festival with other practices as well. For example, in rural areas, young men and women gathered on opposite banks of rivers and released flowers on the water; if the flowers sent by a boy and a girl met each other, it was considered a sign that destiny favored their marriage.

The *Le Thanh-minh*, or Pure Brightness Festival, was celebrated during the third lunar month, fifteen days after the spring equinox and likely to be a clear, sunny day; *thanh* means "pure" and *minh* "bright." It was devoted to enjoying the beauty of spring by hiking, gathering flowers, and similar activities. This festival, with its emphasis on the renewal and beauty of nature, reminded Vietnamese of their ancestors and encouraged them to fulfill their filial duties. One of its main activities was the cleaning of ancestral gravesites, before which offerings of incense, food, flowers, and votive objects were made.

The Pure Brightness Festival is observed today throughout Vietnam. In order to preserve arable land for farming, burial now more commonly takes place in established graveyards rather than in isolated plots selected in accordance with geomancy, as in former times, and many municipalities organize bus trips to allow residents to travel to their ancestors' graves to "tidy them up" and make offerings.

The *Le Doan-ngo*, or Double-Five Festival occurred on the fifth day of the fifth lunar month in recognition of the summer solstice. In a largely rural country with a tropical climate, disease was more prevalent in the summer, and the Double Five Festival was part of a number of observances intended to protect people from disease as they "entered summer" (*vao he*). The consumption of raw fruits and vegetables, of herbal infusions made with wild leaves, and of rice alcohol (*ruou nep*), which was intended to kill disease-causing parasites, was one way of protecting oneself. Another was to appease the gods controlling sickness by praying and burning gold- and silver-colored paper offerings. Human-shaped paper images called *hinh nhan* were also burned to fool the death gods into thinking that their intended human targets had already been killed. Warding off the spirits by wearing amulets was also popular. Although many of these practices are currently discouraged by the Communist Party as wasteful and superstitious, they are still carried on in various ways throughout Vietnam. For example, inhabitants of Nha-trang city still bathe in the sea to mark the solstice's arrival in the belief that parasites will be killed in this way.

Vietnamese practices during *Le Doan-ngo* are also influenced by a legend borrowed from the Chinese tradition. A third-century B.C.E. Chinese mandarin (known to Vietnamese as Khuat Binh) warned his monarch against taking a seaborne journey that Khuat Binh considered dangerous. When the monarch departed anyway, Khuat Binh committed suicide by throwing himself into a river. Learning of Khuat Binh's suicide, the monarch ordered a bundle of food to be ceremoniously dropped into the sea as an offering. When fish devoured the package, the monarch ordered another one to be prepared, this one to be wrapped in banana leaves and covered with brightly colored paper to frighten sea creatures. In honor of this loyal mandarin, many Vietnamese still float offerings on rivers, wrapping the packages with brightly colored paper in order to protect them.

Next to the *Tet Nguyen-dan*, the *Tet Trung-thu*, or Mid-Autumn Festival (often called the "Moon Festival" by Westerners), was the most important and widely celebrated festival in pre-colonial Vietnam. Like the New Year's Festival, the Mid-Autumn Festival is still widely observed in contemporary Vietnam and in diaspora communities. It is held on the fifteenth day of the eighth lunar month. According to tradition, an emperor of China's Tang Dynasty, known to the Vietnamese as Duong Minh-hoang, was strolling about the palace grounds on the full-moon night of the eighth month when he was approached by a Taoist saint who proposed to transport him to the moon. When the emperor accepted, the saint erected a heavenly bridge, and Duong Minh-hoang spent a blissful night on the lunar surface, dancing with beautiful fairies and listening to unearthly music. After returning to earth, he longed to re-create the experience and organized annual festivals on the fifteenth day of the eighth month that featured processions with multicolored lanterns, unicorn dances, and feasting on seasonal delicacies, including special moon-shaped cakes.

Vietnam's Mid-Autumn Festival is above all a time of excitement and merrymaking for children, who parade about at night with colored lanterns, dancing the "unicorn" or "lion" dances. Since the moon in Vietnamese tradition is the abode of Nguyet-Lao, the "Old Man in the Moon" who arranges conjugal unions by binding couples with a silk thread, the Mid-Autumn festivities permit much flirtatious behavior among marriage-age young men and women, including "alternate-verse singing," in which couples engage in poetic teasing. Adults, for their part, enjoy a relaxing evening with friends and family, gazing at the moon, sipping tea, and eating *Banh Trung-thu* as well as other delicacies, such as boiled snails and seasonal fruits.

GROUP-SPECIFIC OBSERVANCES

In addition to celebrating most of the above festivals, Vietnamese Catholics observed their own, uniquely Christian ones, the most important of which were Christmas and Easter, celebrated according to the Gregorian calendar. In contemporary Vietnam, Western-style Christmas, called *Le Giang Sinh* (Festival of the One Sent to Be Born) or simply *No-en* (Noel), is celebrated as a day of feasting and gift-giving by many urban Vietnamese of all faiths, including Christians, for whom it retains a sacred significance. Easter, or *Le Phuc Sinh* (Festival of Restored Life), by contrast, is observed almost exclusively by Christians.

Vietnamese Buddhists, in addition to partaking in the festivals common to most pre-colonial Vietnamese, also celebrated and still observe many events and festivals specific to their religion. Sakyamuni Buddha's birthday is celebrated on the fifteenth day of the fourth month of the lunar calendar, as is the date of his enlightenment, the eighth day of the twelfth month. On the fifteenth day of the seventh month, Buddhists observe *Le Vu-lan*, similar to Christianity's All Souls' Day, on which the spirits of the dead were released from their torments in hell (*dia nguc*) and allowed to return to the earth. Rather than visiting ancestral graves on this day, however, Vietnamese Buddhists usually decorate their ancestral altars and invite the ancestral spirits to partake of offerings in the home. For those unfortunate spirits who do not have living descendants or who died far from their homes, believers leave offerings of rice in banyan leaf containers at roadside altars. Hopefully, these lost souls (*vong hon*) will be appeased and refrain from venting their frustrations on the living.

Finally, the VCP has added a number of celebrations commemorating turning points in its march to power as well as its reference points in the international workers' movement. Among these holidays, marked according to the Gregorian calendar, the most important are the anniversary of the founding of the Communist Party in 1930, which falls on February 3; National Day, which falls on September 2 and commemorates the founding of the D.R.V. by Ho Chi Minh in 1945; Ho Chi Minh's birthday, May 19;

Liberation Day, April 30, which celebrates the ending of the Second Indo-china War with the "liberation" of Sai-gon, the capital of the former R.V.N., in 1975; and International Workers' Day, May 1. Party and state offices at all levels organize parades, speeches, and musical and dramatic performances in celebration of these events. Their commemoration is considered to play a crucial role in bolstering the Party's legitimacy by reminding the people of its past victories against foreign domination.

LEISURE ACTIVITIES

Aside from the rituals and celebrations associated with the festivals dis-cussed above, pre-colonial Vietnamese engaged in a number of activities and games for relaxation and amusement, usually as members of associations organized for that purpose.

Pre-colonial villages housed a variety of organizational forms that brought villagers together to pursue shared interests. Some focused on mutual pro-tection, as in the case of funeral societies, which helped members to afford dignified burials despite their limited finances. Many associations were rec-reational in nature and permitted their members to enjoy leisure activities together or with their families. For example, New Year's Associations allowed members to pool resources and invest them to produce funds for celebrating the *Tet* holidays. Participants made monthly contributions during the first five months of the year. With the proceeds, the association made short-term, interest-bearing loans; the returned capital with interest was used to buy grain during the tenth-month harvest, when prices were lowest; the grain was then sold at year's end, when prices were at at their height. If all went well, the association would buy meat, cakes, fabric, and ritual items with which to ensure members a festive holiday season. A complete list of such organizations would be endless, but a typical village might house organizations of members of the same hamlet or the same professions (e.g., officials, soldiers, mer-chants), of hobbyists (kite flyers, songbird breeders, cockfighting enthusiasts), of students of the same teacher, or even of people born in the same year. Each of these had its own rules and schedule of meetings and celebrations, as well as its patron deity or deities, which were often spirits associated with the particular activity pursued by the association or that of its founder.

As the variety of associations indicates, villagers had a world of activities from which to choose, within or without organized groups. Many activities involved simple materials such as a shuttlecock, which was kicked back and forth or tossed through a goal of bamboo rods. Solid bamboo poles were also made into platforms for swinging games or for suspending a tightrope above the ground and across an open space on which a person would walk. A more flexible variety of bamboo was the main material (along with locally made paper) used in fabricating kites, the flying of which was passionately pursued by people of all ages. The kites came in many varieties, often bearing names indicating the object, animal, or person that had inspired their design: swallows, butterflies, the moon. Many kites were fitted with hand-carved wooden whistles, designed to produce a variety of sounds, mainly for the amusement of human listeners; some whistling kites, however, were intended to distract the malevolent spirits responsible for epidemic disease.

Given the rural context of village life, many amusements involved competition between animals, fish, or birds. For example, large male thrushes were raised for fighting in special decorated cages. The prized birds dined on a protein-rich diet of millet and egg yolks, augmented with ginseng to fortify them as an important competition approached. On the day of the contest, the birds were transferred to special fighting cages that allowed the owners to place the cages face to face, show the male fighters a female to excite their competitiveness, and then, by withdrawing the fronts of each cage, create a common fighting chamber. Bets were placed on one or the other of the contestants. As the birds proceeded to strike each other with their feet and beaks, points representing portions of the wagered sums were awarded in response to the blows landed by the chosen animal. The birds were so valuable that fights were usually interrupted whenever one of them was wounded or ceased resistance. Other competitions, such as those between fighting fishes in southern Vietnam, continued until the death of one of the animals.

Competitions in which villagers would match their strength or fighting skills were also popular, with awards of money or other prizes adding to the interest. On village festival days, for example, a prize would be announced, and a wrestler claiming to be the village's strongest man would claim it. If no challenger contested the claim within three days, the prize would go to the self-proclaimed champion. If a challenger or challengers appeared, however, a match or matches would take place to decide the matter. The contestants, wearing only a loincloth and with their heads shaven (wrestlers were called *chui vat*, "shaven-headed fighters"), would first pray to the village spirit, showing it the prize for which they were competing. Then, accompanied by drum rolls, the wrestlers would try to pin each other back to the ground, with the match continuing all day or for several days until one of them had succeeded. Sometimes similar contests were arranged between groups of wrestlers from different villages, with each group representing the village of its origin.

Less taxing physically were gambling games. Card games, particularly one called *to tom*, or "shrimps' nest" (a modernized version is known in the West as mah-jongg) were extremely popular, especially during the New Year's holidays. Board games such as chess, which originated in India and has been known throughout Asia since ancient times, were also avidly played in traditional Vietnam. In addition to the usual variety of chess played on a board, Vietnamese played "human chess" (*co nguoi*), in which people wearing the insignia of the various pieces moved about a giant outdoor board under the direction of the primary players. Another variety of game existed in which players would attempt to toss coins or chopsticks into a small opening. In one popular version called *dao dia*, or "hitting the dish," a small bowl was placed on a bamboo table located several feet from the players or, ideally, in the middle of a stream while players gathered at its banks. Contestants took turns trying to toss their coins into the bowl. The prize, usually some object of value suspended above the bowl, would go to the best "shot," while the person who had organized the game would keep the coins that fell wide of the mark or bounced off the bowl. Gambling per se was generally not considered improper unless indulged in to excess, when high losses or unsavory connections could threaten the stability of the gambler's family. As the proverb expresses it, "If the husband gambles and the wife plays cards, then the husband must have two or three wives, and the wife several husbands."[1]

SPORTS AND LEISURE IN CONTEMPORARY VIETNAM

In contemporary Vietnam, the busier pace of life and the generally dim view that the Party and state take of unofficial organizational allegiances and gambling (except for state-sponsored lotteries) have reduced the above-described activities to the margins of life. Taking up the relay and replacing the traditional leisure activities are a variety of sports as well as amusements associated with Western pop culture.

Early in the colonial era, a limited number of elite and middle-class youths took up Western sports such as tennis, soccer, weight lifting, and bicycle racing. During the 1930s and 1940s, such sports and physical fitness generally came to be associated with nationalism because a connection was made, as elsewhere in Asia, between a people's physical fitness and its ability to regain or defend its independence. Given this connection, and despite limited means and the imperatives of war, the D.R.V. supported physical education for the masses and national competitions for the more athletically gifted during the 1950s, 1960s, and 1970s.

After the Renovation movement began in the late 1980s and reducing the state's role in the economy became the order of the day, the state reduced its support for athletic activities at all levels. The 1980s and early 1990s were a "dark decade" for sports and physical fitness in the S.R.V.: facilities declined, personnel were released, and funds for athletes' training and travel were reduced. As the middle of the 1990s approached, however, the government began responding to popular demands for Vietnamese participation in the international sports world, which was by this time avidly followed by Vietnamese of all ages (including Party and S.R.V. officials). In 1994 and 1995, the portion of the government's budget allocated to physical fitness and sports increased dramatically, with several major stadiums being erected or planned and National Sports Festivals organized for national competitions among schoolchildren. Since that time, the S.R.V. has given priority to less expensive sports, such as martial arts (including the Vietnamese style, called *Vo Viet Nam*), soccer, volleyball, table tennis, and chess, which require little equipment and few training facilities. Private sponsorship of sporting activities, long frowned upon by the authorities, began to emerge as an alternative source of funding. International corporations—including producers of soft drinks, cigarettes, and alcoholic beverages—began sponsoring Vietnamese national competitions in soccer, bicycle racing, and other sports, and private Vietnamese firms have also begun to sponsor competitions, albeit on a more modest scale. The higher-level athletic competitions, whether officially or privately organized, are avidly followed by Vietnamese fans, whose interest is stoked by ample television coverage for national and international events. The Vietnamese national soccer team's success in the lower levels of the Tiger Cup games in 2000, played in Songkla, Thailand, for example, provoked flag-waving pandemonium in Vietnamese cities. Likewise, homegrown sports heroes are treated like celebrities by Vietnamese magazines and newspapers, which feature athletes' images on covers and print long articles and interviews on their lives and achievements. For example, Tran Hieu Ngan, a twenty-six-year-old martial artist from central Vietnam, was hailed as "the pride of the country" after winning a silver medal in Taekwondo (women's fifty-seven kilogram weight class) at the Sydney Olympic Games in 2000.

Besides the higher-level and organized competitions, many Vietnamese are participating ever more actively in informal physical fitness and sporting activities, despite a shortage of available urban space. In major cities, early risers will observe groups of older people out in the street doing group calisthenics or performing tai chi movements in unison; others may be seen playing badminton in temple yards or bouncing tennis balls against walls. Young men are particularly fond of soccer and play pickup games at every opportunity in vacant lots, quiet streets, and even in deserted war memorials. Western-style body building and weight lifting are also gaining in popularity, with private gyms popping up seemingly on every block in the larger cities. People fortunate enough to have access to Vietnam's lovely beaches (Nha Trang and Vung Tau are the most popular) can enjoy swimming. The paucity of well-maintained swimming pools and the widespread pollution of lakes and rivers puts the safe practice of this activity beyond the reach of most Vietnamese, however.

For the less athletically inclined, modern Vietnam's cities offer a variety of entertainment. Affluent urban Vietnamese visit Western-style bars and nightclubs or socialize at coffeehouses and *café kem*, which specialize in ice cream, popular since French times (the Vietnamese term for ice cream, *kem*, comes from the French *crème glacée*). Movie houses are frequented by urban Vietnamese, although the limited funding available to the national film industry and its tendency to produce political films of waning interest to the population mean that the most popular films are now foreign ones, including American blockbusters and Hong Kong martial arts adventures dubbed in Vietnamese. Discos usually charge an entrance fee, which entitles clients to an evening of dancing and listening to recorded music or local groups playing Western or Vietnamese songs. Although it is too early to speak of a "car culture" among affluent Vietnamese youth, a "motor-scooter culture" is developing. (The recently coined Vietnamese word *hon-da*, derived from the name of the Japanese manufacturer, means motorcycles in general, given the popularity of Honda motor scooters and motorcycles, which dominate the Vietnamese market despite increasing competition from Chinese, Taiwanese, and Korean brands.) Urban youths with some means like to "cruise" the main streets of their cities on their *hon-da*, two or more people to a vehicle, socializing with their friends and escaping temporarily the constraints imposed by the government, schools, and family. Young well-to-do urbanites have taken to the Internet with enthusiasm. Since few Vietnamese can afford personal computers, they rely on Internet service centers. They pay by the minute for computer use, spending hours in "chat-rooms" and e-mailing their friends and relatives in Vietnam and throughout the world. They also enjoy roller skating at urban pleasure gardens or attending concerts by Vietnamese pop stars, such as singer My Linh, as well as the rare Vietnam appearances of Western performers. Some urban Vietnamese have begun to enjoy Western-style tourism, usually within Vietnam itself, visiting locales famous for their beauty or historical interest: for example, Ha-long Bay in the North; Hue City in central Vietnam; or Vung Tau, the southern beach resort. "Pilgrimage tourism"—that is, visits to famous pagodas or temples (the Heavenly Lady Pagoda in Hue is one popular destination)—that com-

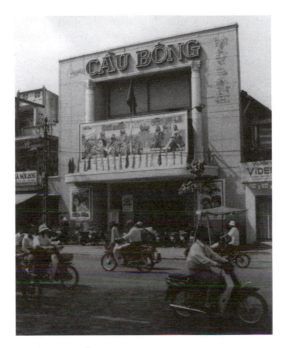

Motor-scooter culture in Ho Chi Minh City, southern Vietnam

bine entertainment and piety (and, increasingly, photography), are likewise attractive outings for those who can afford them. The Vietnamese tourist industry, however, is still oriented overwhelmingly to providing services to Western and foreign Asian tourists (including some *Viet Kieu*, or "overseas Vietnamese") since insignificant numbers of Vietnamese citizens can afford such activities.

Indeed, most of the activities described above are beyond the modest means of working urbanites and nearly all rural people, who must content themselves with less expensive fare. In the poorer neighborhoods of the cities and in most villages, enterprising local residents have set up karaoke, compact disk, and video bars, where clients sit at tables as at an ordinary cafe but are entertained with CD music, video, and sing-along programs shown on a television screen; the entertainment is free on the condition that one purchases coffee or other drinks. In such bars or at private homes, rural people and the urban poor pass their leisure time playing games such as *to tom* or chess; watching television (in this medium also, the most popular programs are Western shows or movies, usually reruns, dubbed in Vietnamese); drinking tea, beer, or coffee; and talking with friends and family members long into the night.

NOTE

1. Cited in Nguyen Huu Tan, *La Vie quotidienne dans le Viet-Nam d'autrefois* (Paris: Thanh-Long, 1983), 114.

9

Performing Arts

THE PERFORMING ARTS of Vietnam (i.e., music, theater, and dance) are alive and well in today's scene. Whether in their pre-colonial forms or in their most contemporary expressions, the performing arts are richly varied from North to South, keeping the traditions alive through teaching and performances while welcoming and adapting outside influences. New beats and trends are quickly adopted in cities still resonant with melodies of decades ago. Whatever forms they may take, the performing arts are beloved by the Vietnamese, young and old.

MUSIC AND DANCE

Music is at the heart of the Vietnamese soul. In whatever form, sung or instrumentally performed, it is intrinsic to Vietnam's national character and a mirror to its history. Its various forms are expressions of the external influences that have shaped its development as well as of its regional roots—initially in the North, the cradle of the Vietnamese civilization, and later in the Center and the South. Vietnamese music can be divided into traditional and modern music, and within the traditional forms, court, folkloric, chamber, and liturgical music. Almost indistinguishable from Vietnamese music are its traditional theatrical forms, both folk and classical.

Vietnamese music is pentatonic (five tones) in scale, closely adhering to the tonal inflections of the spoken language, and in a society in which amateur and professional singing (*ca hat*) are highly appreciated in festive gatherings, it stresses the voice rather than the instrument. The musical notation as well as some of the instruments (strings, wind, and percussion) were derived from both China and India—by way of Champa for the latter. During French colonial rule, Western instruments like the guitar, piano, and violin were introduced, and it was not until the eve of World War I that the traditional musical notation written in Chinese characters was finally replaced by Western notation. Some percussion instruments (e.g., *trong com*, a long, two-membrane drum) are similar to the Indian ones (the Mridangam drum of South India). String instruments such as the four-stringed, pear-shaped lute (*dan ty ba*), the short- and long-necked, moon-shaped lutes, or the *dan tranh*, also known as *dan thap luc*, the sixteen-stringed zither, come from China. Vietnam also has its own instruments uniquely suited to its culture: the monochord (*dan doc huyen*), a single-stringed zither; the two-stringed, moon-shaped plucked lute (*dan nguyet*); the *sinh tien*, a coin clapper, composed of two wooden pieces hinged together, the top one fitted with copper coins; and the *song lang*, foot clapper. The materials used for all the instruments include silk, bamboo, stone, bronze, shells, and cow or buffalo skins.

Within traditional music, one can distinguish, on the one hand, the peasantry's folk music as manifested in a rich and complex lore of songs reflective of their geographical and village origins and of the annual agricultural cycle. These are called *dan ca* (folk songs). The music performed for the entertainment of the elite, mandarins, scholars, and nobility, by contrast, had to be performed according to prescribed rules. However, following the *hoa la* ("flowers and leaves") principle, which encouraged embellishments upon established musical themes, both forms do allow for, and even invite, improvisations, which are considered a measure of the artist's talent. The Vietnamese musical repertory is divided into two modes or scales (*dieu*): *dieu bac* ("northern mode/scale"), pentatonic, of whole tones, conveying a happy or ceremonious mood; and *dieu nam* ("southern mode/scale"), which carries a greater sadness in its pentatonic, half-tone scale.

Vietnamese court music, influenced by China and Champa, was performed in rituals like the Sacrifice to Heaven and Earth, during which *giao nhac* was played at the Esplanade of Heaven in Hue, during imperial audiences (e.g., *thuong trieu nhac* music for ordinary audiences; and *dai trieu nhac* for formal audiences) and banquets, during solar and lunar eclipses, and for the court's entertainment. Viet kings from the Ly (twelfth and thirteenth centuries) period onwards were fascinated by Cham music and dance, ordering musical pieces based on the music of Champa. As the Viet made further inroads into Champa, leading to the kingdom's extinction, Vietnamese music, court as well as folk, absorbed the sadness of this lost land, which now permeates the plaintive melody of the Vietnamese southern mode (*dieu nam*). The Hue court had also inherited a tradition of imperial dance ensembles that used to sing and dance "civilian" dances (*van vu*), such as the Flower Dance created under the Tran Dynasty, "military" dances (*vo vu*), and dances that re-created mythical animals like the phoenix or the unicorn.

The folk songs of Vietnam carry an imagery that reflects its agricultural roots, evoking the songs of birds or insects, the blossoming of flowers, the flowing of rivers, and the rising of the sun or the moon as symbols of faithfulness, purity, the fickleness of love, or a mother's love for her child. These folk songs can also be inspired by famous poems and composed by classically learned scholars. *Dan ca* comprises different forms: lullabies called in the North *hat ru*, in the Center *ru em*, and in the South *au o*; and the work, love, and festival songs called *ho* and *ly*. Lullabies, though meant to put children to sleep, also narrate the activities of the mother or sister and how hard she works, planting rice, catching fish, or spinning silk in order to feed the child: "Sleep, child, sleep, sleep soundly. / Your mother went planting in the deep rice field and has not come back yet. / Sleep, child, sleep. / She will catch a catfish and bring it back for you to eat." Lullabies from central Vietnam, often poignantly sad, speak of the homesickness of a new wife, away from her mother and father, and her worry that there will be no one to care for her aging parents: "Sleep, child, sleep. / Come afternoon, I stand in the backyard, Looking toward my mother's land. / And my heart grieves and grieves." In the South, almost all lullabies begin with the word *vi dau* ("imagine") as in "Imagine walking on a wooden bridge held together with nails. / On a bamboo bridge creaking and cracking, / How difficult and perilous!"

The work songs belong to the category called *ho*, issuing from the word *ho*, "to call out." These are songs meant to galvanize teams of laborers inland or by the water, pushing carts, pulling wood along the river, scooping water out of a rice field, rowing a boat, calling to each other (call-and-response) in cadence, and responding to the call in turn with nonsensical syllables like *ho do ta* or *hu la khoan*. There are countless *ho* that describe activities like wood pulling (*ho keo go*), rice pounding (*ho gia gao*), lime crushing (*ho gia voi*), or spinning and thread cutting (*ho dut chi*), as well as rest and festivities. A wood-pulling *ho*, for example, sounds as follows: "Let's pull wood, Do! / Pull wood to build the communal house, Do! / Assembly house of how many tiles? Do! / I love you, love you very much! Do!".

While the rhythmic chant is meant to provide encouragement and cadence to the workers, it also speaks of men's and women's eternal quest for the one and only. During a break, these same workers could launch themselves into dual love songs, called *ly*, with men and women alternating, re-creating a chance encounter under the full moon by the lotus pond during harvest time, or lamenting that the loved one had married and crossed a river never to return. Some of the best-known *ly* are *Ly Con Sao* ("Song of the Myna Bird"), *Ly Ngua O* ("Song of the Black Horse"), *Ly Vong Phu* ("Song of the Soldier's Wife"), *Ly Co La* ("The Crane Glides Away"), and *Ly Chim Quyen* ("Song of the Nightingale"). *Ly Co La*, for example, sung in the northern "voice," a solo with an accompanying chorus, evokes the crane as it soars away, comparing it to a departed loved one.

Each region has its particular form of *ho* and *ly*, rich in local connotations and history, performed during festivals at temples, on riverbanks, or in the fields. In the north, during the festival season (e.g., New Year, Mid-Autumn), song contests were traditionally organized in villages, some of which—in particular, the forty-nine villages of Bac Ninh province—are famed for their long tradition of *hat quan ho*. Others, for example, those from Hai Phong (*hat dum*) or Phu Tho (*hat co la*) provinces are famous for other variants of call-and-response songs. In *hat quan ho*, groups of young men and women, dressed in colorful fineries, would gather to sing in a call-and-response or antiphonal style, based on poems that they had prepared in advance. One group of girls would sing a song that had to be responded to by the group of boys, who would take up the themes and elaborate on them, weaving their own improvised verses into the song. The contest, requiring a good knowledge of folklore, would last for several days, allowing friendships to form between members of the different teams, which would tease each other with jests and challenges as to their abilities in versification and vocalization.

In central and southern Vietnam, *dan ca* is as rich as in the north—perhaps richest in the central provinces of Quang Nam, Quang Tri, and Thua Thien—but each has its particular regional "voice," singing style, and melodies. For instance, *Ly Con Sao* ("Song of the Myna Bird"), when sung in the Hue voice is inimitable because of certain gliding tones that northerners and southerners cannot reproduce. The reverse is true for the other regions. In the South, where the *ho*, or call songs, are mostly related to aquatic activities, there is a slower, more languid, almost dreamy rhythm that conveys feelings of calm and patience but also of joy and often humor: "Early morning, I went to market. / And bought some fabric. / First Wife cut, Second Wife sewed, Third Wife overcasted, Fourth Wife bordered, Fifth Wife stitched the buttons, Sixth Wife made the buttonholes. / I put the shirt on. / But Seventh Wife held on to me. / And Eighth Wife pulled me back. / Oh, Ninth Wife, Why don't you do something?" Folk songs in the South, both *ho* and *ly*, as they issued from a region of more recent settlement, also integrate modern activities like playing the lottery (*ho lo to*). In recent decades, Vietnamese folk songs have been undergoing a sort of "renaissance" thanks to the efforts of musicologists like Luu Nhat Vu and Le Giang. With state support, many songs have been "modernized" (thus the term *dan ca moi* or "new folk songs") to adapt them to the taste of the urban younger generation, integrating Western-style instruments and harmony. While this practice has made the younger generation familiar with an important aspect of its heritage, it also deprives the songs of their social functions and messages while stylizing them in a certain way.

Unlike *dan ca*, a popular form that used to be performed by villagers and enjoyed by all during festivities, *hat a dao, ca Hue*, and *nhac tai tu*—forms of chamber music specific to northern, central, and southern Vietnam respectively—were traditionally executed by a small instrumental (string and percussion) ensemble in performances for an elite audience of connoisseurs. *Hat a dao*, or "the singing of songstresses," rooted in the traditional society of the North, evolved from ceremonial music to a music of entertainment. It puts to song classical poems chosen for their beauty or specially written by the listeners and performed by talented songstresses accompanying themselves with percussion instruments. Listeners beat specific cadences with a drum, *trong chau*, each cadence signifying their appreciation of the singer's talent or the poem's beauty, the beginning or end of the session, or the speed at which the musicians or songstress should perform. Concurrently, in central Vietnam, *ca Hue* ("music of Hue"), emerged under the Nguyen Dynasty's patronage as a specific repertory music of the region. More instrumental than vocal, it stressed melody above lyrics, although it does include long songs and adapted folk songs sung by professional songstresses. *Ca Hue* originated from the tradition under the Nguyen Dynasty of organizing imperial orchestras to play court music. The musicians played for the court but also taught music to members of the imperial family, their retinues, and the mandarins. Hue music was carried South with the settlers who moved to the Mekong Delta, and adapted to the southern mood, becoming *nhac tai tu*, or "music of talented persons," also called "amateur music." *Nhac tai tu* used to be played by aficionados, from intellectual and musical milieus mostly, who performed for friends and family. These "amateurs," while retaining traditional string instruments like the sixteen-stringed zither, integrated Western instruments like the guitar, the cello, or the violin. It was this music that nourished the framework for the reformed theater or *hat cai luong*, to be discussed later in this chapter.

Finally, there is a form of poetic singing (*ngam tho*) that is not truly singing but is halfway between declamation and chanting without a fixed rhythm.

Its subject matter is poems like the masterpieces *Kim Van Kieu* or *Luc Van Tien*, which tell stories and legends and speak of heroic feats. One such example is the famous *Chinh Phu Ngam Khuc* ("Complaint of a Warrior's Wife"), an eighteenth-century poem that evokes the sorrow of a wife whose husband was called to the front.

Nhac Phat Giao and *hat chau van* form the body of ritual and religious music. Of long historical tradition, Buddhist music, or *nhac Phat Giao* can be divided into two types: one meant strictly for prayers, worship, or meditation, called *tung*, in which the monk, accompanying himself on a slit drum called the *mo gia tri*, recites the sutras; and the other, *tan*, a form of melismatic chant, involves a string and percussion ensemble which plays during funerals and wakes. Percussion instruments commonly used in liturgical music include, for instance, the big drum (*trong bat nha*) and bell (*dai hong chung*). Buddhist musical liturgy, like its counterparts, varies according to the regions. However, one of the most recurrent and impressive ceremonies is the seventh lunar month soul-salvation *Chan Te* ("Distribution") ceremony, which can last a whole week and involve an entire ritual orchestra going through most of the musical styles.

Hat chau van is a form of religious music performed to induce trances in a medium and to bring him or her into contact with the spirits through songs sung by the high priest of the cult. It was also performed during seances of exorcism to chase away evil spirits that had possessed an ailing person.

Nhac le (liturgical music) also exists in the other religions (Catholicism, Caodaism). For example, the priest-composer, Doan Quang Dat, had written numerous musical pieces, such as "Celebrating the Birth of Jesus at Midnight," which combine the tradition of Vietnamese music with Catholic liturgy, making it easier for Vietnamese Catholics to sing at mass.

Tan nhac, or "modern music," a Westernized popular music, emerged in the 1930s with the adoption of Western rhythms, to fulfill the needs of a Vietnamese youth eager for change and whose hearts were overflowing with idealism and romanticism. During the times that led to the August Revolution of 1945 and the war against French rule, a multitude of songs blossomed that galvanized the combatants (*nhac chien dau*, or struggle music), taking them to the battlefield singing, while others (*nhac tinh cam*, or sentimental or romantic music) spoke of hopeless love in golden autumns of fallen leaves. Of the struggle music, one may note composers like Van Cao, Luu Huu Phuoc, Hoang Viet, Van Chung, or Tran Hoan with songs about separation from loved ones, about Viet Minh soldiers departing for the North in 1954, or about the battle of Bach Dang against the Mongol invasion. Of the romantic music, there was an abundance of memorable songs that were remarkable because of the lyricism of the text and the originality of the melody: for instance, Le Thuong with his song "The Sound of Music in the Dark of Night," Dang The Phong's acclaimed "Autumnal Night," or La Hoi with his famous "Spring and Youth." Many of these, composed in the 1930s to 1950s, have survived decades of wars to be performed and appreciated again in the late 1990s, albeit with a new orchestration. During the 1960s and 1970s, a form of antiwar music began to appear in the South with songs by composers like Truong Thin, Ton That Lap, La Huu Vang, Trinh Cong Son, and Pham Duy that spoke of murderous battlefields, charred houses and fields, madness and suffering (e.g., "What Did We See in the Night" by Trinh Cong Son), and the tears of mothers who had lost their sons to the war (e.g., "The Rain on the Leaves" by Pham Duy).

In the post-1975 period, Vietnamese modern music went through a period of limbo, producing mediocre melodies and lackluster and weakly attended performances. Beginning in the late 1980s, as Vietnam opened to the outside world, modern Vietnamese—that is, Western-influenced—music has been on the upsurge, with more professional-standard performances and a distinctively greater Western influence. This music has been drawing large, young audiences that buy Vietnamese-produced CDs and throng to festivals and solo performances of their preferred artists. The current *tan nhac* scene is very lively: festivals and individual performances are staged every week and strongly attended. Young performers like My Linh, Phuong Thanh, Tran Thu Ha, Hong Nhung, or bands like Little Wings, Guys by Chance, or the 3A, are experimenting with rhythm and blues, hip-hop, alternative rock, and even American-style country music, although most sing songs, predominantly romantic ones, that have been around for years or even decades. Hence the need for young composers like Vu Quang Trang, Viet Anh, Xuan Phuong, or Ngoc Chau, who can create music adapted to the tastes of the younger generation, albeit on eternal themes like love and loss.

In this diverse pop scene, jazz per se has a devoted but minuscule and geographically limited appeal, to be found solely in Ha-noi and Ho Chi Minh City, and only in a few cafes like the Jazz Club in Ha-noi, where bandleader and saxophonist Quyen Van Minh plays regularly. Jazz influences, however, permeate much of the new pop music, as My Linh's hugely successful album *Toc ngan* ("Short Hair") demonstrates.

Western classical music is of a rather recent emergence in Vietnam and has evolved in rarefied circles with a stronger tradition in the North, as the result of the influence of the former Soviet Union and former German Democratic Republic, than in the South. Vietnam boasts several classical performing artists, such as Dang Thai Son (piano) or Ai Van (vocal), who have won prestigious awards at international festivals and competitions (Chopin Competition of 1980 for the former and the Dresden Festival of 1981 for the latter). One should also mention in this context the symphonic composer Nguyen Manh Cuong, whose *Phuong Vu* ("Dance of the Phoenixes") received a composition prize at the 1984 Asia-Pacific Festival in New Zealand.

Besides the music composed, performed, and appreciated by Viet, there is the music of the minorities of the mountains of the North, of the Vietnamese Cordillera, and of the Central Highlands as well of the former Champa kingdom and of Cambodia. Musical instruments used by the highlanders include the ancient lithophone, bronze gongs, bamboo mouth organs (or *khen*), and xylophone (or *ding but*). The latter instrument, known to the Bahnar and Sedan peoples of the Central Highlands, consists of ten hollow bamboo pipes strung together and set on the ground; the performer claps hands near the mouths of the pipes, producing musical notes. Ethnic minorities of the mountains and highlands of Vietnam, the Cham of central Vietnam, and the Khmers living in the Mekong Delta have a vast lore of folk songs consisting of work, love, festival, and funeral songs, narrative songs that recount a lost past. For example, one song tells the story of King Che Man, who foolishly exchanged the two districts of O and Ly of the then Champa for the hand of the beautiful Viet princess, Huyen Tran. There is also the theater form as, for instance, the *tuong gia hai* of the Tay of northern Vietnam or the *du ke* theater of the Khmers of the Mekong Delta, inspired by the Indian epic of *Ramayana* or *Mahabharata*.

TRADITIONAL (MUSICAL) THEATER

Traditional Vietnamese theater encompassed all the artistic expressions of song, dance, mime, and declamation, in which the performers act alone, without the support of a single stage prop or scenery, and are surrounded by the spectators (adults and children). Springing from the common source of ancient Viet folk songs and dances, *hat cheo* and *hat tuong* (also called *hat boi*) are the two ends of the traditional theatrical spectrum, the former is considered as popular theater and the latter as classical, but both are performed in open air at temples where religious festivals usually take place, as well as in courtyards of art patrons.

Folk theater (*hat cheo*), rooted in rural life, is found mostly in the North and is played by actors and actresses garbed in the peasant style—women in the *ao tu than* ("four-piece tunic") of contrasting colors and men in the mostly brown peasant dress, with only one character, the buffoon, wearing heavy makeup. Originally, *hat cheo* was a form of peasant entertainment acted by farmers. Thus, its plots carry a markedly social and sometimes political emphasis, with realistic characters assuming roles close to those of everyday life within a rural setting.

Meant to entertain, *hat cheo* also carries moral lessons, chastising the corrupt and extolling the virtuous. To the accompaniment of a small ensemble, *hat cheo* opens with the jester singing the prologue and dancing with his torch to clear the stage. An actress then sings the play's introduction, summarizing and commenting on it as she walks around, clicking and opening her fan. One of the most popular plays is *Quan Am Thi Kinh*, which tells the story of a devout young Buddhist woman named Thi Kinh who disguises herself as a man to enter a monastery. In her monk disguise, she is pursued by a young peasant woman named Thi Mau, who, upon being rejected by the "monk," becomes pregnant by a local peasant but falsely accuses "him" of fathering her child. Unwilling to reveal her identity lest she be expelled from the monastery, Thi Kinh accepts the beatings meted out by the local authorities and raises the child herself. As a result of the positive karma generated by her sacrifices, Thi Kinh is transformed after her death into a bodhisattva.

Hat cheo plays used to be unscripted, and both singing and speaking (in a melodic form) are used along with dancing. All three expressions are stylized but allow more spontaneity than *hat cheo*'s classical counterpart, *hat boi*. *Cheo* focuses on women, with lead characters played by women, who show their steadfastness, vivaciousness, sadness, or cruelty by comparing themselves to animals like the catfish, spider, or dragonfly. Like the other forms of theater and music, *cheo* did not remain static, and in order to survive it attempted to adopt new styles and urban-related themes. Nowadays, *cheo* has been revived in its more rural forms to be performed mostly in yearly festivals by professional troupes in the North.

Hat tuong, or *hat boi*, was staged for the entertainment of the court from Tran times in the thirteenth century until the Nguyen era in the nineteenth century by court-appointed groups, which the emperor would occasionally join for a part in a favored play. Thereafter, *hat boi* was performed by small theater groups that would tour the countryside to present well-known classical pieces such as *Xuan Nu* ("Young Girl"). The plays were inspired in part by Chinese history and literature and used to be written in Chinese and *nom*, although a number of them (written by librettists like Dao Tan) are derived from Viet mythology and history, often stressing the heroism of figures like the Trung sisters in *Trung Nu Vuong* or *The Trung Queens*.

These plays carry moral lessons and emphasize virtues such as faithfulness, loyalty of subjects toward rulers, sacrifice, valor, and dedication. The hero almost always goes through trying times while keeping faith with king and country to eventually find himself justly rewarded. Certain characters may sing in a falsetto voice to express sadness; others may declaim verse, which is in turn sung in prose to clarify the meaning. Percussion instruments are central to *hat boi* to signal the beginning of a scene or the entrance of characters, to accompany the singers, and to signify the public's pleasure or displeasure with the performance. Inseparable from the singing, acting, and miming, dancing is used to convey and enhance the messages or the plot line of a particular piece. Movements of the eyes and hands, inclinations of the head, caressing of the beard, closing or opening of the fan, and gliding or springing of the step are accentuated by the rolling of the drums, the clanging of the cymbals, and the sad lament of the monochord, which carry as much significance as the voice and the words.

For example, in order to show that he is riding a horse, the actor would use a whip and, through different gestures and steps, indicate the mounting or falling off of a horse, or the leading of a horse through mountainous gorges. The nature of the *hat boi* characters is signaled by the colors used in the heavy makeup worn by actors and actresses: red for virtue, black for honesty, and so forth. Although it has been criticized as a fading, stagnant art of the past that fewer and fewer people can comprehend and appreciate, *hat boi* is still performed throughout Vietnam with regional nuances and adaptations, depending on whether the play is presented in cities or in villages.

During the 1920s, the need arose for a theater that would be less rigid and difficult to understand than *hat boi*, that would integrate music and dance and not be just spoken, as in the French-inspired "talking theater" (*kich noi*), which translated and adapted French plays into Vietnamese. Thus was born in the 1920s in the South *hat cai luong* ("renovated theater"), which fused the southern amateur music (*nhac tai tu*) with the Western-inspired realist modern theater. Central to it is a musical piece, initially a love song, which later became a musical mode called *da co hoai lang* ("listening to the drum sound at night, thinking of the loved one"), finally evolving into *vong co* ("nostalgia of the past"), a melancholic melody aimed at conveying sadness, nostalgia, or the poignancy of betrayed love. The plays were initially Chinese-inspired, but in terms of plot, acting style, and music, the renovated theater soon strayed from the stylized *hat boi*, using a less formal language and adding scenery and lighting. As it evolved, the renovated theater, appealing to a wider, if less cultivated, audience, has focused on plays that have modern, social, or religious themes. These may be derived from the French repertoire (e.g., *Tra Hoa Nu*, or *The Camellia Lady*), Vietnamese novels (e.g., *Hon Buom Mo Tien*, or *Butterfly-Soul Dreaming of a Fairy*), or works written for the theater (e.g., *Tim Hanh Phuc*, or *In Search of Happiness*). Artists famed for their voices and capacity to sing the *vong co* were Nam Chau, Phung Ha, Ut Tra On, Thanh Nga, and Thanh Duoc, who performed in theatrical troupes like Van Hao or Thanh Minh Thanh Nga. Although *hat cai luong* incorporated new, Western-inspired rhythms like cha-cha-cha or rock-and-roll, accompanied by guitar, violin, saxophones, and even synthesizer, it has kept traditional instruments like the two-stringed fiddle *dan nhi*, the transversal flute *sao*, the foot clapper *song lan*, and the monochord, originally used in *nhac tai tu*. Overall, *cai luong* is an eclectic form that allows the inclusion of almost all musical genres and inspirations from East to West and permits almost all mediums from circus acts to documentary segments projected in the background. Unfortunately, in recent decades, the quality of the renovated theater, both in terms of content and performance, has decreased. In cities throughout the country, the audience for the renovated theater has dwindled over the years, losing the battle to Hong Kong kung fu videotapes and Hollywood movies. In the countryside, however, *cai luong* is still the entertainment of choice; it can be heard floating in the air, amplified in the marketplace, and sung by aficionados during family celebrations or public festivities.

Modern theater—that is, the Western-style talking variety (*kich noi*)—was born under French colonial rule, when plays such as Moliere's *The Miser* were translated into Vietnamese and performed for Vietnamese audiences. Like *hat cheo* and, to a certain extent, *hat boi*, *kich noi* is meant to entertain while conveying moral lessons. Although initially influenced by French theater, during the anti-French struggle Vietnamese talking plays often critically examined the negative impacts of French culture on Vietnamese intellectuals and the petite bourgeoisie. For example, a play entitled *The Annamite Frenchman* derided the latter groups by accentuating the ridiculous character of their exaggerated and fawning imitations of French mannerisms. In the 1930s and 1940s, novels like *Nua Chung Xuan* (*Mid-Spring*) or *Doan Tuyet* (*Rupture*), written by members of the socially concerned Self-Reliance Literary Group, were adapted to the modern theater. In the era of the D.R.V. and the S.R.V., modern plays have treated a variety of topical themes. In the early 1980s, for example, *The Red Metallic Stars* celebrated the heroic part played by border minorities during the Chinese invasion of 1979. Likewise, the plot in *In the Name of Justice* centers on a murder committed by the spoiled son of a high-level cadre and his family's failed effort at covering it up. Some plays even venture into the sensitive field of historical revisionism. Nguyen Huy Thiep's *Love Remains*, for example, presents an account of the 1930 uprising organized by the nationalist leader Nguyen Thai Hoc. Nevertheless, the most successful plays carry plots that dissect themes of generational conflicts or passion, love, and betrayal. For example, *The Last Passion* tells the story of the patient love of a forgiving wife whose husband betrays her repeatedly until the last fatal affair.

Generally speaking, in the era of the D.R.V. and the S.R.V., music, dance, and theater have been perceived as political instruments. As such, they have been patronized by the government, which supports efforts at renovating *hat cheo, hat boi, dan ca, hat cai luong*, and *kich noi*, organizing festivals, launching folklore-gathering programs, establishing schools for training artists and performers, and recognizing artists through the conferring of awards, medals, and the creation of categories like "Artist of the People."

WATER PUPPETRY

No discussion of Vietnamese performing arts would be complete without treating an ancient folk art form unique to Vietnam called *mua roi nuoc*, or "water puppetry" (as opposed to "land puppetry," or *mua roi can*). Public performances by village-based artisans manipulating wooden puppets over bodies of water date from at least the tenth century. The practice originated in the villages of the North and is derived from harvest festivals involving dancing, wrestling, boat races, and other popular amusements.

Their impressive skills notwithstanding, puppeteers were not professional entertainers but were farmers or fishermen who had formed a local water-puppetry guild and performed free of charge in their leisure time, mainly at local festivals. The guilds were usually founded by pooling funds for the support of the craft and for mutual aid among members. Some supporters enjoyed the prestige of membership but were not themselves performers or puppet makers. Since participation would bring knowledge of the puppets' manufacture and manipulation, a new member's initiation required unanimous support of existing members and often involved a ritualized drinking of blood and swearing not to reveal the guild's secrets to outsiders. Furthermore, because patrilocal marriage meant that village girls might go to live with their husbands' families in a different village, females were not allowed to join puppetry guilds, and so membership was an exclusively male prerogative.

The Vietnamese term for water puppetry, *mua roi nuoc*, literally means "dancing on water," and the "stages" on which the puppets "danced" were indeed bodies of water, usually natural or artificial lakes. Village-based performance guilds usually owned a lake as well as a pavilion located about twenty feet from the shore. The pavilion faced the shore and contained three chambers, a central "manipulation room" and two lateral chambers. The lateral chambers' floors were above water level and were used for storage and for seating the musicians, chorus, and other performers. The central chamber had a sunken floor, where the puppet masters would stand, waist-deep, and, from behind an opaque bamboo screen, manipulate the puppets on the watery stage between them and the audience on the shore. Modern troupes are usually peripatetic (traveling), and simplified pavilions often have a single elongated chamber, with the front section's floor below the water level, and a raised rear floor; the aquatic "stage" is now more often a portable basin than a lake.

The puppets were made by members of the guild, carved of wood, covered with protective resin, and brightly painted. Rather than being manipulated directly by hand, rod, or strings, water puppets were controlled at considerable distance by submersible rods and sometimes by wires concealed beneath the water. Through their skillful manipulation of the rods and strings, often with ringed stakes placed in the lake's bed, the puppeteers could cause their charges to perform a variety of movements. From submerged invisibility, the puppets could spring upward into the spectators' view and then move forward, backward, or transversally across the water before sinking out of sight. Many of the more complex puppets were fitted with strings and pulleys that allowed rotation of the torso, head, or arms. While the puppeteers manipulated a variety of puppets on the watery stage, other hidden performers in the lateral compartments supplied the character's voices, sang choral accompaniment, or played a variety of percussion instruments—including firecrackers! The water itself heightened the effect of the performance, concealing the attached rods and strings while reflecting the sky and surroundings as well as the puppets' images. The sounds of the chorus and orchestra reverberated from the water's surface, creating an impact on the audience unlike that in any other theatrical tradition.

Rather than presenting a single long and complicated piece that might be taxing for both performer and audience, the traditional water puppet theaters would undertake ten or twenty vignettes of several minutes each and relied mainly on visual impact rather than on the spoken word. The themes derived from three main sources: scenes from the daily lives of ordinary people, including farming, fishing, and hunting; events from Sino-Viet mythology and history, such as Le Loi's victory over the Chinese; and excerpts from *tuong* or *cheo* pieces. All would be known to the audiences in advance and require little elaboration. Modern professional troupes sometimes attempt longer and unitary pieces, but one may question whether these are suitable for water puppetry, given its rural and popular origins.

Given the tumultuous events in Vietnam over the last 150 years, the traditional village-based corporations have all but died out in their birthplace, the villages of the North. However, the governments of the D.R.V. and S.R.V. have encouraged the preservation of this ancient craft by funding urban-based troupes, the most representative example being Ha-noi's Thang-long Water Puppet Theater. These have kept alive the artistry of carving and manipulating water puppets, and the best of these state-supported troupes continue to delight domestic as well as international audiences.

Glossary

Am. In Taoism, the feminine principle of concentration.

An chay. Vegetarianism (for religious reasons).

Binh dan. Popular masses, people of modest means.

Ca Hue. Chamber music, central Vietnamese music of the Hue court.

Cao Dai. The "High Platform," the Cao Dai religion.

Chu Han. Chinese, or Han, characters.

Chu nom. Southern script, or vernacular characters.

Chu quoc ngu. Romanized Vietnamese script.

Chua. Lords, the title taken by political-military leaders.

Chua. A Buddhist pagoda.

Chua Thien Mu. The Heavenly Lady Pagoda in Hue.

Cong. Artisans in the four-class hierarchy.

Cong dien. Public or communal land.

Dai Noi. The "Great Within."

Dai Thua. Mahayana, or "Great Vehicle," Buddhism.

Dan ca. Folk songs, singing.

Dao-giao. Taoism.

Dao-Khong. Confucianism.

Dao Thien Chua. The "Sky Lord Doctrine," Christianity.

Den.   A temple honoring a Taoist or animistic deity.

Dieu bac.   The northern Vietnamese musical mode or scale.

Dieu nam.   The southern musical mode.

Dinh.   The communal house of the traditional village.

Doi dua.   Chopsticks (in pairs).

Doi Moi.   Renovation policies.

Don ganh.   Wooden or bamboo carrying pole.

Duong.   In Taoism, the masculine principle of expansion.

Gia-dinh.   The family.

Gia pha.   Genealogical register.

Gia truong.   Family head.

Gio.   Death anniversary.

Gom.   Pottery.

Hanh phuc.   Happiness.

Hat a dao.   Northern Vietnamese-style chamber music.

Hat cai luong.   Renovated theater, an eclectic popular theater.

Hat cheo.   Popular musical theater.

Hat tuong, Hat boi.   Classical theater.

Hieu.   The virtue of filial piety.

Ho.   Lineage name.

Ho Phap.   "Guardians of the Law" at entrance to pagodas.

Hoang thanh.   The Imperial Citadel.

Hoi lang.   The village council.

Hon-da.   Honda motorcycles, and by extension motorcycles in general.

Huong hoa.   Incense and fire (to honor the dead).

Kich noi.   Western-style talking theater.

Kinh thanh.   The imperial city.

Lang.   Village.

Le Giang Sinh.   Christmas, "Festival of the One Sent to Be Born."

Le Phuc Sinh.   Easter, "Festival of Restored Life."

Le Tao-quan.   Household gods' ritual.

Le Vu-lan.   The Buddhist All Souls' Day.

Luc Bo. The Six Ministries of imperial governments.

Mieng giau, Mieng trau. A betel chaw.

Mua roi nuoc. Water puppetry.

Nam Giao. Royal rituals honoring Heaven and Earth.

Nam tien. The Southward Movement of the Viet.

Nhac le. Liturgical music.

Nhac tai tu. "Music of talented persons," southern chamber music.

Nhan. The Confucian virtue of benevolence.

Ngoc Hoang Thuong De. The Jade Emperor of Taoist tradition.

Nguoi hoa. Ethnic Chinese.

Nguoi kinh. "People of the capital," the Viet or ethnic Vietnamese.

Nguoi thuong. The highland peoples, Highlanders.

Nha. House or home.

Niet Ban. Nirvana, the goal of Buddhist practice.

Noi chien. Civil war.

Noi tuong. Term for housewives, the "generals within" (the home).

Non la. The conical leaf hat.

Nong. Peasants in the four-class hierarchy.

Nuoc cham. Dipping sauce.

Nuoc mam. Fermented fish sauce.

Phat Giao. Buddhism.

Phat giao Hoa Hao. Variety of reformed Buddhism.

Pho. Vietnamese noodle soup.

Quan Am or Quan The Am. The Bodhisattva Avalokitesvara.

Si. Scholars in the four-class hierarchy.

Son mai. Lacquerware.

Ta giao. Heterodox teachings.

Tam giao dong nguyen. Three teachings from one source.

Tam tong. Women's three subserviences (to father, husband, son).

Tan nhac. Modern music, Westernized popular music.

Tay-son. "Western mountain" politico-military movement.

Tet. Festival in general.

Tet Nguyen-dan. New Year, New Year's Festival.

Tet Trung-thu. Mid-Autumn Festival.

Thai Hoa Dien. Hall of Supreme Harmony.

Thanh hoang. The patron deity of Vietnamese villages.

Thay. Father, and by extension teacher or master.

Thien-menh. The "Mandate of Heaven" justifying imperial rule.

Tho cung ong ba. Ancestor worship.

Thuoc Bac. Northern, or Chinese traditional medicine.

Thuoc la. Medicine leaf, or tobacco.

Thuoc lao. Vietnamese tobacco.

Thuoc Nam. Southern, or Vietnamese traditional medicine.

Thuong. Merchants in the four-class hierarchy.

Tieu Thua. Hinayana, or "Small Vehicle," Buddhism.

Toc. Clan or extended family.

Truong toc. Clan head.

Van Mieu. The Temple of Literature in Ha-noi.

Viet Cong. Vietnamese Communist (pejorative term).

Vo Viet Nam. The Vietnamese martial art.

Vong hon. Wandering souls.

Xa. Village.

Xom nghe. Specialized handicraft village.

Selected Bibliography

Arts and Handicrafts of Vietnam. Ha-noi: The Gioi Publishers, 1992.

Bechert, J., and D. Gombrich. *The World of Buddhism*. London: Thames and Hudson, 1991.

Cadière, Leopold. *Religious Beliefs and Practices of the Vietnamese*, translated by Ian W. Mabbett. Clayton, Victoria, Australia: Center of Southeast Asian Studies, 1989.

Duiker, William J. *Historical Dictionary of Vietnam*. Metuchen, N.J.: Scarecrow Press, 1989.

———. *Vietnam: Nation in Revolution*. Boulder, Colo.: Westview Press, 1995.

Durand, Maurice, and Nguyen Tran Huan. *An Introduction to Vietnamese Literature*. New York: Columbia University Press, 1985.

Elliott, David W. P., et al. *Vietnam: Essays on History, Culture, and Society*. New York: Asia Society, 1985.

Hoang Ngoc Thanh. *Vietnam's Social and Political Development as Seen through the Modern Novel*. New York: Peter Lang, 1991.

Huu Ngoc. *Sketches for a Portrait of Vietnamese Culture*. Ha-noi: The Gioi Publishers, 1995.

Huynh Dinh Te. *Introduction to Vietnamese Culture*. San Diego: San Diego State University, 1987.

Huynh Sanh Thong, trans. and ed. *An Anthology of Vietnamese Poems: From the Eleventh through the Twentieth Centuries*. New Haven: Yale University Press, 1996.

Jamieson, Neil. *Understanding Vietnam*. Berkeley: University of California Press, 1993.

Karlin, Wayne, ed. *The Stars, the Earth, the River: Short Fiction by Le Minh Khue*.

Translated by Bac Hoai Tran and Dana Sacks. Willimantic, Conn.: Curbstone Press, 1997.

Kerkvliet, Benedict J. Tria, and Doug J. Porter, eds. *Vietnam's Rural Transformation.* Boulder, Colo.: Westview Press, 1995.

Keyes, Charles F. *The Golden Peninsula: Culture and Adaptation in Mainland Southeast Asia.* New York: Macmillan, 1977.

Lockhart, Greg, and Monique Lockhart, eds. and trans. *The Light of the Capital: Three Modern Vietnamese Classics.* New York: Oxford University Press, 1996.

Marr, David G. *Vietnamese Tradition on Trial, 1920–45.* Berkeley: University of California Press, 1981.

———. *Vietnamese Youth in the 1990s.* Sydney, New South Wales, Australia: Macquarie University School of Economic and Financial Studies, 1996.

McLeod, Mark W. *The Vietnamese Response to French Intervention, 1862–1874.* New York: Praeger, 1991.

Ngo Vinh Long. *Before the Revolution: The Vietnamese Peasants under the French.* New York: Columbia University Press, 1991.

Nguyen Du. *The Tale of Kieu: A Bilingual Edition of Truyen Kieu.* Translated and annotated by Huynh Sanh Thong, with a historical essay by Alexander B. Woodside. New Haven: Yale University Press, 1983.

Nguyen Huu Tan. *La vie quotidienne dans le Viet-Nam d'autrefois.* Paris: Thanh-long, 1983.

Nguyen Thi Dieu. *The Mekong River and the Struggle for Indochina: Water, War, and Peace.* Westport, Conn.: Praeger, 1999.

Nguyen Thuyet Phong, ed. *New Perspectives on Vietnamese Music.* New Haven: Yale Southeast Asian Studies, 1991.

Nguyen Van Huyen. *The Ancient Civilization of Vietnam.* Ha-noi: The Gioi Publishers, 1995.

Pham Duy. *Musics of Vietnam.* Carbondale: Southern Illinois University Press, 1975.

Steinberg, David Joel, ed. *In Search of Southeast Asia: A Modern History.* Honolulu: University of Hawaii Press, 1987.

Taylor, Keith Weller. *The Birth of Vietnam.* Berkeley: University of California Press, 1983.

Truong Buu Lam, ed. *Borrowings and Adaptations in Vietnamese Culture.* Honolulu: Center for Asian and Pacific Studies, University of Hawaii at Manoa, 1987.

Turley, William F., and Mark Selden, eds. *Reinventing Vietnamese Socialism: Doi Moi in Comparative Perspective.* Boulder, Colo.: Westview Press, 1993.

Whitmore, John K. *An Introduction to Indochinese History, Culture, Language and Life—for Persons Involved with the Indochinese Refugee Education and Resettlement Project in the State of Michigan.* Ann Arbor: University of Michigan Center for South and Southeast Asian Studies, 1979.

Index

About the Author

MARK W. McLEOD is Associate Professor of History at the University of Delaware. He is the author of *The Vietnamese Response to French Intervention, 1862–1874* (Praeger, 1991).

NGUYEN THI DIEU, born in Vietnam, is Associate Professor of History at Temple University. She is the author of *The Mekong River and the Struggle for Indochina: Water, War, and Peace* (Praeger, 1999).